PENGUIN BOOKS

THE BONDAGE OF FEAR

Fergal Keane was appointed Southern Africa Correspondent of the BBC in 1990, having covered the region since the early 1980s. He was named as Amnesty International's Human Rights Reporter of the Year in the 1994 Sony Awards and won the Reporter of the Year Award at the New York Festival of Radio in 1994.

Fergal Keane was born in London and educated in Ireland, where he keeps a small cottage on the south-east coast.

Fergal Keane

THE BONDAGE OF FEAR

A JOURNEY THROUGH THE LAST WHITE EMPIRE

PENGUIN BOOKS

PENGUIN BOOKS

Published by the Penguin Group
Penguin Books Ltd, 27 Wrights Lane, London w8 5TZ, England
Penguin Books USA Inc., 375 Hudson Street, New York, New York 10014, USA
Penguin Books Australia Ltd, Ringwood, Victoria, Australia
Penguin Books Canada Ltd, 10 Alcorn Avenue, Toronto, Ontario, Canada M4V 3B2
Penguin Books (NZ) Ltd, 182–190 Wairau Road, Auckland 10, New Zealand

Penguin Books Ltd, Registered Offices: Harmondsworth, Middlesex, England

First published by Viking 1994
Published with additional material in Penguin Books 1995
1 3 5 7 9 10 8 6 4 2

The acknowledgements on p. xi constitute an extension of this copyright page.

Printed in England by Clays Ltd, St Ives plc

For Anne

For it is the dawn that has come, as it has come for a thousand centuries, never failing. But when that dawn will come, of our emancipation, from the fear of bondage and the bondage of fear, why, that is a secret.

Alan Paton, *Cry, The Beloved Country*

Contents

Acknowledgements

There are vast numbers of people who have helped in the writing of this book. I can only ask the forgiveness of those I inadvertently fail to mention. First and foremost, my wife Anne, whose wise and incredible support in trying times created the psychological space for me to write. To Milton Nkosi, who travelled the road with me and kept me out of harm's way, a million thanks. A posthumous thank you to the late John Harrison – a generous colleague and friend who was always willing to offer advice. Producers Peter Burdin and Jenny Baxter helped me to steer a calm and clear-sighted course through the election period and never lost their sense of fun. Martin Seemungal and Mary Anne Bueschkens of the CBC deserve special thanks for their support in trying times in Bophuthatswana. At the BBC in Johannesburg, Andrea Pinder did invaluable research work. Julia Bourhill, the Bureau Manager, made sure I got to the right places at the right times. Tim Sheehy, of the European Commission, was always a source of intelligent comment on Southern African affairs, as was Michael, my guitar-playing friend and the best political analyst in the country. Thanks also to Paulina Mabogale, who kept the Keane household ticking over amid the many dramas of South African life. A debt of gratitude as well to Mike Wooldridge and Dr Tony Humphreys, who lit powerful lamps to show me the way. At the BBC in London, Chris Wyld, my foreign editor and friend, and Jeff Spink, of 'From Our Own Correspondent' – both were wonderful sources of encouragement. My editor Tony Lacey and agent Gill Coleridge nudged me gently along, but they always took the furious demands of my job into account. Thanks also to my colleagues Tom Carver and Corrie Caulfield, who shared the highs and lows; to Eric Ransdell, whose manic humour was an endless tonic; and Malcolm Downing, a generous friend and fellow Celt. Last but not least, my gratitude to my mother, Maura O'Shea, and my late father, Eamon Keane, for teaching me to listen out for the voices of the oppressed.

The publishers would like to thank Juluka Musica/H. R. Music for permission to reproduce extracts from Johnny Clegg's 'The Scatterlings' (copyright © 1986) and Empire Music Limited/Windswept Pacific Limited for permission to reproduce an extract from Lucky Dube's 'Victims'.

Every effort has been made to contact copyright holders. The publishers will be glad to rectify, in future editions, any omissions brought to their notice.

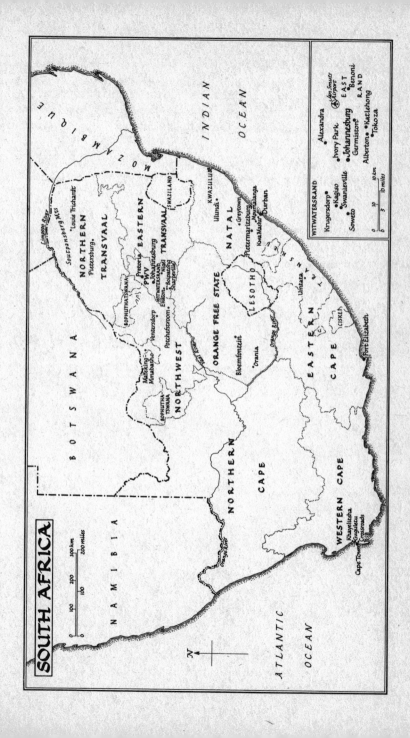

Prologue: The Last White Parliament

CAPE TOWN, DECEMBER 1993

It is Christmas in Cape Town. The mercury is climbing towards ninety degrees and the party is in full swing. The election is three months away, and the children of the white summer have flocked south for one last great spree. With the crowds and the cars and the endless parade of street vendors, it would be murderously stuffy were it not for the wind that periodically gallops in from the Atlantic, sweeping parasols and hats and newspapers into the air. The visitor pushed upwards along Adderley Street by this wind will eventually see before him the immense wall of sandstone that forms the townward face of Table Mountain. On fine summer days it seems to lean protectively over the city, like an old woman peering into the cot of her grandchild. Today, as so often in summer, an avalanche of cloud is pouring over the edge of the mountain, down past the outcrops of the upper ridges, almost sweeping over the pine and gum trees that forest the lower slopes. But before it can reach the trees and the fine houses beyond them, the cloud collides with the hot air that hangs like a great screen across the roof of the city. From this equilibrium is created the impression of a tablecloth of cloud draped precisely over the edge of the mountain.

On this particular day, 22 December 1993, I am watching the natural phenomenon of unfurling cloud from the forecourt of the parliamentary buildings; in a few hours the members will vote on the Constitution of South Africa Bill, which provides for the final dissolution of the white parliament. Around me the members of this most exclusive of

South African clubs are standing in small clusters, waiting for the Speaker's bell and the imminent demise of their world. Some of the most famous names in recent Afrikaner politics are here: the Foreign Affairs Minister, Pik Botha, convincing anyone who will listen that his maiden speech in the House was dedicated to the overthrow of racial discrimination; Adriaan Vlok, the wall-eyed Minister of Prisons, recalling the murder of apartheid's grand architect Hendrik Verwoerd by a deranged messenger on the floor of the House three decades previously, and again, like Mr Botha, assuring whomever he can that he had been against apartheid all along; and, skulking like the bad boys of the class in their own sullen group, are Ferdi Hartzenberg and the members of the Conservative Party, who seem irredeemably lost, the map of their world, with its neat lines of separation, rent from end to end.

They all eventually take their places in the chamber of panelled wood and leather benches, with its scent of polish and ancient certainty. As the mostly male members file in, there is something of the atmosphere of the final day at school before the sixth form empties out into the fraught world of jobs and mortgages and marriages. In direct imitation of the pomp of Westminster the Speaker of the House, Eli Louw, an ageing but loyal party hack, follows the mace-bearing Sergeant-at-Arms into the chamber. Behind them walks the Deputy Speaker. All three men wear the dark formal clothes of the lawyer or the minister of the Dutch Reformed Church: long flowing gown, black waistcoat and starched white collar. Sitting near the Speaker on the government benches is President F.W. de Klerk, heroic saviour to his own backbenchers, traitor to the phalanx of Conservatives who sit opposite.

It has taken forty-six months of negotiations and mass demonstrations to reach the point where the National Party, the party of Verwoerd and Malan and Strijdom, is preparing to vote away its 45-year hold on power in South Africa. The road to this historic juncture has been blighted by the worst political violence in the country's bloody history. Even as the Nationalist MPs and the members of the smaller Democratic Party vote in the constitution by an overwhelming majority, there are threats of a Boer freedom struggle from the Conservatives. As their leader finishes yet another ranting demand for Afrikaner self-determination, the right-wingers leap to their feet and sing a full verse of 'Die Stem', the soon-to-be-abandoned anthem of white South Africa.

Throughout this De Klerk sits stony-faced, waiting for his moment, because, as President, his is always the last word. When he eventually rises to address the ranks of MPs, he urges the South African people, in reality his own mainly white supporters, not to fear the future. 'We are all aware of the dangers ahead, but we are sure of the justice of our cause,' he says, before resuming his seat to the traditional battery of applause from the government benches.

De Klerk is well aware of the magnitude of the moment. He has sat in this chamber since 1972 and served in the Cabinets of John Vorster and P.W. Botha. He grew up in a family steeped in the mythology of Afrikaner supremacy: his father was a National Party politician, and his great-grandfather, grandfather and uncle gave their working lives to the dream of a country ruled in perpetuity by Afrikaans-speaking whites. Now in the final days of 1993 Frederik Willem de Klerk is leading his people into the black-ruled future his entire upbringing had warned him against. He has come to this point less from any altruistic vision of the equality of man than through the realization that the alternative to a negotiated settlement is the eventual destruction of his people's way of life.

As they file out of the building into the blinding white sunshine, the Nationalist MPs give a good impression of cheerfulness, but I am not convinced. There is something forced about their joviality, as if in recognition that their vote was an act without choice, a final forced acceptance of South Africa's unalterable mathematical reality: *Five million over thirty-five million simply will not go*. Many of those leaving the parliamentary buildings are destined not to return. Their benches will be taken over by black faces. Even as the MPs debate the constitution, the lords of the future wander through the building, watching the final hours of the minority-rule legislature. The parliamentary staff have been most helpful, the ANC men say. The new black rulers are sizing-up offices, deciding on which paintings and statues should come down. The building they once swore to storm and reduce to rubble has been taken by persuasion.

That the last act in the deconstruction of the white super-state should take place in Cape Town is supremely fitting. For it was here, three and a half centuries previously, that the first permanent white settlement on the Southern African subcontinent was established in 1652 by Jan van Riebeeck, plenipotentiary of the Dutch East India Company and native of the town of Culemborg in Holland. By the time he left the Cape ten years later, Van Riebeeck had laid the founda-tions of a new African nation: the Afrikaners. Part Dutch, part French and with a hint of German, they evolved into a clan of white Africans whose long shadow was to alter the destiny of great nations and present the world with a concept of racial separation known as *apartheid* – a theory that pro-voked some of the fiercest moral debate of the century. In his diary Van Riebeeck spoke of the native inhabitants of the Cape as 'dull, stupid, lazy, stinking' and recorded the feeling among his subordinates that they 'would rather be hanged than live in this damned country'. Yet, although Van Rie-beeck himself left after ten years, many of his ship's company stayed on in the 'damned country'.

Now, after centuries of conflict, their descendants were preparing to give the land into the hands of those who had once been described in the most pejorative of terms. The ruling caste had tried and failed to impose strict separation of the tribes, and in the end, alone among the whites of Africa, they had decided to negotiate themselves out of power before revolution toppled them. The men who loitered now on the steps of parliament were different from the settlers of Rhodesia and Kenya: there was no mother country to which they could escape when the going got tough. They carried only South African passports, which were of little use when it came to finding refuge in England, America and lately even Australia. In the words of another early governor of the Cape, Simon van der Stel, the Afrikaners, like the black nationalists with whom they now proposed a partnership in power, knew 'no other fatherland'.

What was happening on this glorious summer's day was the logical consequence of Africa's first and only negotiated revolution. For the previous three and a half years the newly enlightened National Party had grappled and sparred and horsetraded with the representatives of the black majority, until they fashioned a constitution to guide the country towards eventual majority rule. It was the product of widely diverging political aspirations and, as such, was far from perfect. Like all power elites the black and white nationalists were, in spite of pious claims to the contrary, vigorously opposed to any diminution of the power of the centre. Thus their opponents were to accuse them of creating a new autocracy, from which those who took a different view were consciously excluded. But the central core of the new constitution was solid, a document that enshrined liberties denied to the majority of the population during the 350 years of white hegemony. The basic principles of freedom of association, freedom of speech and freedom to be *different* were protected by a constitutional court. Given the almost paranoiac attitude of the National Party towards the ANC a few short years before, and the ANC's commitment to a violent revolution, the blend of consensus politics and artful compromise that lay at the root of the new constitution signalled a truly remarkable achievement.

I was present on the sweltering November night in 1993 when the constitution was agreed between the major parties. The leading negotiators from the ANC and the government – men who had crossed great chasms of enmity to find each other – celebrated the event in the small bar at the Johannesburg World Trade Centre, where the talks had taken place. In the early hours of the morning, as the disco music blared and the champagne flowed, I saw the government's chief negotiator Roelf Meyer approach his ANC counterpart, Cyril Ramaphosa. Meyer reached out and grabbed his negotiating partner's hand and shouted, 'Yes, yes, yes.' The other man smiled and said quietly, 'We've done it.' The DJ, who was standing near by, sensed the moment and placed the classic anti-apartheid song 'Give Me Hope' by Eddy Grant on the turntable. The two men were swept into the centre of the crowd and became part of a jiving, twirling mass. The voices of politicians, policemen, journalists and bar workers joined in the chorus:

> Give me Hope Johanna, give me Hope Johanna,
> Give me Hope until the morning comes.

But the story of constitutional negotiation in air-conditioned rooms, the story of parliamentary votes amid the imperial splendour of the House of Representatives, was only half of the equation of transition. The other half was to be seen and heard on the streets, in the vast squatter encampments and the rural villages, on the great swathes of farmland and in the industrial white suburbs. By the time the MPs had left parliament on the day of the vote, there were just enough hours of daylight remaining for me to go and seek the views of those who lived on the other side of Table Mountain, the South African majority who inhabit the endless wilderness of townships and shanties that forms the flip-side of Africa's most beautiful city.

I drove out of Cape Town along the N2 motorway, circling around the foot of the mountain until the road uncurled itself and rolled straight out across the Cape Flats. Before long I reached the first army posts, great watchtowers that gazed over the sullen waste lands of Guguletu, Crossroads and Khayelitsha. There were soldiers on the motorway bridges and crouching by the side of the road. The automatic rifles of the troops were a warning to any youth who might have been tempted to stone the white motorists flocking from the airport to the white sands and wineries of the Cape. The shacks leaned against the roadside fence and formed the outer perimeter of this dusty reservoir of abandoned humanity. Inside Crossroads, in the company of an Irish priest friend who lives among the squatters, I wandered from shack to shack, hearing the same simple refrain: *We want houses and jobs and schools for our children. We want this violence to end.* The parliament building was a million light years away now, the issue of freedom refined to the demands of an impoverished majority who had lived so long with the fear of hunger and violence that the burden of their expectations hung like a sword of Damocles over the future.

Later, as I drove back to Cape Town, I switched on the radio to hear threats of war from the white farmers whose forebears had trekked out of the Cape and into the vastness of the South African interior, and who now sought their own separate white state. The plummy-voiced announcer recited the threats of the far right as if they were words from another planet, detached from the good sense and benevolence of the constitutional settlement. The rightists had few friends left, but they drew some comfort from the fact that the Chief Minister of the Zulu homeland and leader of Inkatha, Chief Mangosuthu Buthelezi, had joined them in an alliance and was echoing their threats of civil war.

On the day the white parliament voted itself out of existence one might have been tempted to believe that the leader of a black nationalist movement would allow himself the liberty of celebration. But the Chief looked on darkly at this event that, with its promise of an election, might all too easily have foreshadowed the end of his days as feudal baron of the Zulu homeland. In the overgrazed, impoverished hills of Zululand, men were being trained in the arts of war. Weapons were flowing in across the border with Mozambique and the fighting between the ANC and Inkatha escalated once again. The forces that apartheid had created through patronage and those it had opposed through repression were beginning their final struggles.

This book is concerned primarily with the human consequences of these life-and-death struggles as witnessed and understood by one reporter. It is not an academic history or a sociological treatise. This is one man's journey through the last years of the white empire. Amid the hyperbole and clichés, the endless wrangling of the politicians and the bloody battles on the streets, I could never forget that what I was ultimately witnessing was a struggle between the most profound human emotions: hope and fear. This was political drama on a grand scale; none the less I have attempted to tell the story through the eyes and words of the ordinary people who were pushed forward by the heave of history. Not all of them were people I liked or even respected, but they inhabited the South African reality; all in their own way struggled with the 'bondage of fear' and thus deserve their places in this book. Although the reporter's craft demands objectivity, I will not pretend that this book is free from the claims of my own emotions. For me the journey too often resembled a form of dazed sleepwalking through the nightmare of violence in which the faces of the dead crowded my dreams on more nights than I can remember. The close presence of senseless death and destruction is a powerful antidote to journalistic detachment. Like so many people who witnessed the transition at first hand, I drifted between periods of calm optimism and profound despair. If that somewhat frustrating polarity of emotions is reflected in the pages that follow, I can only say: that is how *I* remember it, such were the times *I* lived through.

CHAPTER 1

The Scarecrow Man

Blood, no matter how little of it, when it spills,
spills on the brain — on the memory of a nation —
it is as if the sea floods the earth, the lights
go out. Mad hounds howl in the dark; ah now
we've become familiar with horror.

Mongane Wally Serote, 'Time Has Run Out'

About half a mile from Katlehong, Lieutenant Deon Peens reached behind to the back seat and, holding the steering wheel in one hand, removed his service revolver from an attaché case. He did not make any reference to this action but continued to talk about his beloved game of rugby. Lieutenant Peens was a big man, with fair hair and a thin moustache that tried but failed to give him a stern, serious appearance. He had worked as a dog-handler policing riots in the 1980s, but his superiors apparently thought his genial manner more suited to public relations than to the handling of vicious animals. Now he spent his days painstakingly answering the queries of journalists or taking them on guided tours of the most dangerous townships in the country. In the summer heat his car felt like an oven, sucking the air from our lungs as we sat on seats sticky and shiny from the sun. This early sun blazed its white light across the prim Johannesburg suburbs of Alberton and melted the tar so that our wheels made a tisking, sticking sound as the Lieutenant pulled out into the traffic. We passed along avenues where the streets were thick with the purple of newly flowered jacaranda trees. There were

sprinklers hissing in the dead heat of gardens where somnam-
bulant black men moved, clipping and brushing, drifting in
and out of the sacred shade. In one garden the sun painted the
colours of the rainbow on the water as it fanned out across
the rockery. The southern summer had arrived, and Deon
Peens was thinking of the golden beaches of Durban, 600
kilometres to the east. As we left behind the bungalows of
Alberton, their sweating gardeners and suffocating occupants,
the Lieutenant began to regale me with details of a lost drunken
weekend in Durban.

He was determined to make no concession to our changing
environment and the imminent possibility of violence. Outside, the landscape had undergone a transformation. We had
entered the industrial buffer zone, the acres of steel and
machine-tool factories that form an unsubtle Maginot Line
between white Alberton and the black townships of Katlehong and Tokoza. Lieutenant Peens was talking about the
game he had gone to see, the final of the Curry Cup between
his team Transvaal and the home side Natal. The Transvaalers
had won and the Lieutenant and a few other policemen had
gone to the beach and played a long game of touch rugby
before heading into a long, long night moving from pub to
pub, until they all crashed out in the early hours at the hotel.

But Lieutenant Peens and I were now a million miles from
the party atmosphere of Durban or the cheering cauldron of
a rugby stadium, and all the light-hearted banter could not
hide that fact. There were no white people to be seen
walking on these streets and there were very few in cars. An
occasional pick-up truck carrying black workers and driven
by a grim-faced white would pass by in the other direction.
It occurred to me that we were the only whites driving
towards the townships. The Lieutenant sometimes glanced in
the direction of the gun he had placed under the dashboard.
By the time we came over the last bridge that leads into

Tokoza, both the Lieutenant and I had fallen silent. A week previously a white electrician and his black helper had been set upon here and burned alive in their car. After that the police put out a warning that left those with white skins in no doubt as to their probable reception should they risk cruising through the East Rand townships.

I had been through here many times before but always with a streetwise black friend and never with a policeman. Even with the blessing of the ANC and its street committees, entering Tokoza and Katlehong involved a fair measure of risk. Streams of people came against us out of the township. In my nervous state I imagined their curious gazes to be full of hatred. I smiled at a group standing waiting for a minibus taxi, but they did not smile back. There was only a blank expression on each and every face, a sort of collective sullenness as I scanned the group searching for some friendly response.

Just after the bridge Lieutenant Peens turned a sharp left. We bumped down a muddy track for about a quarter of a mile. Then he turned left again into the sandbagged entrance of an army base. Inside the wire I could see soldiers and khaki-clad riot policemen moving around. They were checking weapons and washing armoured vehicles, laughing and joking with one another as they moved through the morning's chores. Once inside the base the Lieutenant relaxed. I could almost feel his body collapse from its state of heightened nervousness into the calm, easy-going vessel it normally was.

We parked, and I followed Deon Peens into the operations room. The building had the spare functional air of a school canteen. Our feet clattered across the tiles until we came to a room at the end of the corridor. Inside, two policemen sat at opposite ends of a long table. Both were talking on the phone. On the walls around them were large aerial photographs of Katlehong and Tokoza. The more dangerous parts of each township had been identified with chalk marks. From the air the images of long rows of houses and the hostels of the migrant workers resembled the grainy photographs of industrial target zones taken by reconnaissance planes in the Second World War.

The smaller of the two policemen, dark brown hair receding on his forehead, placed his hand over the receiver and whispered to us to wait; he would not be a second. He was a lively, energetic character whose eyelids flickered continuously as he talked, the words trotting after one another in rapid sentences. The other man looked oafish and coarse and wore an expression of incurable boredom. I had seen the same face in countless small towns across South Africa, heavy-jowled and pig-eyed, suspicious and prone to sudden outbursts of violence. He mumbled into the telephone as if the conversation, *any* conversation, represented the most supreme of efforts. I do not remember him making any effort to speak to us, although Deon Peens made his usual good-natured attempt to lighten the atmosphere by winking furiously at me.

The smaller man ended his conversation with a swift 'thank you' and in an instant hung up the phone, slid out from behind the desk and bounded across the room to where I was sitting. He thrust out his hand and introduced himself as Major Visagie. He did not offer a first name because, as I was soon to know, his identity was that of the 'Major', purely and simply. 'It's a bit rough out there today. You sure you still want to come?' he asked. I told him I had every faith in his ability to protect me, and he laughed and surged away and out of the door, shouting for us to follow as he disappeared into the throng of young policemen waiting outside.

The Major walked across the yard, summoning different policemen by their surnames. Four of them, two white and two black, followed him to a Casspir armoured vehicle. The

Casspir is a moving mountain of steel from whose sweaty interior the police can fire tear-gas and buckshot into demonstrating crowds, or ride the rutted streets secure from the bullets of snipers. The Major jumped into the driver's seat while his men took positions inside the Casspir.

Once outside the base the radio traffic began to crackle and ricochet around the vehicle. Vehicles prowling near the Zulu hostel had reported coming under fire and there were rumours of bodies lying in the street somewhere close by. The man at base warned the Major to take care. Gunmen had been spotted waiting to attack the patrols as they moved through the township to collect the corpses that appeared in the wake of each skirmish. The light-hearted mood of the Major evaporated as we turned into the main street of Katlehong.

I watched the township slip by, imagining that every sullen face we passed was remembering my face for the day when I would come back alone, without the protection of the police. There were burned-out houses on every side. The lamp-posts and junction boxes bore the colours of the political controllers of the different streets: near the hostel the black, gold, red and white of Inkatha; further away the green, gold and black of the ANC. I had experienced political colour-coding in Belfast and knew its terrible propensity for giving permanence to division.

One of the young white cops stood up and looked out over the township through the open roof of the Casspir. We passed a group of small children and they ran indoors. The older ones stared impassively as we trundled on. WELCOME TO THE WAR ZONE proclaimed the message on the wall near the minibus taxi rank. The young policeman who had been standing up sat down beside me.

He and Deon Peens began a conversation about the phantom rocket launchers that countless searches had failed to turn up. The RPG7 – rocket-propelled grenade – frightened the police more than anything else. A rocket could punch its way through the thick steel skin of the Casspir. Those that didn't die in the scorching heat of the blast would be finished off by the crowd. Deon said there were at least two RPG7s doing the rounds among the young ANC comrades. One rocket had been fired at the hostel but had missed its target; another whizzed past a police car. Nobody in the Casspir would say it aloud but there was no mistaking the subtext of the conversation: *One of these days they'll get lucky and hit us and then the streets will really belong to them.* So far the Major hadn't lost any men and he was determined that it would continue this way. As we crossed a large patch of waste ground, he turned and saw that his men had forgotten to strap on their flak jackets. He barked angrily at them, and stopped the Casspir while they hauled the ceramic plates over their shoulders and into place.

The radio blasted into life again. The man at base was telling the Major about a body. 'Go to the Church of the Nazarene,' he said, 'and turn left. It is lying in the road there.' We found the church easily enough, but there was no sign of any corpse. The Major drove on slowly, his eyes darting furiously from side to side, scanning the ruined houses with their blackened walls and their curtains billowing loose from shattered windows. Apart from these sad flags nothing at all was stirring, until we turned a corner and *they* suddenly appeared, trotting from out of the mouth of darkness to meet us. There were six of them hunched together and moving quickly towards the Casspir. A voice behind me shouted, 'Oh, Jesus Christ . . . oh, Jesus.'

There was the cracking, metallic sound of weapons being cocked. The Major stepped on the brakes and we came crunching to a halt. By now the pack was only a few yards away and in the mouth of the smallest dog I could see a human arm. The other animals seemed to respect the leadership of this small creature, allowing it to trot slightly ahead bearing the arm as a domestic pet might carry a newspaper. I did a double take. *An arm in the mouth of a dog. Dear God, please tell me I am hallucinating. No, let this not be real, please.* This sight did not belong in any frame of reference I might have had: a black man's arm gone slightly pale and eaten away as far as the elbow.

The Major hurled himself out of the Casspir and began shouting at the dogs. The pack leader was stunned and dropped the arm in the grass at the side of the road, fleeing with the others into the shelter of an abandoned house. We piled out on to the road as the Major bellowed instructions to his men. 'Take up positions ... watch those houses for snipers,' he called, striding away from the ravaged limb and following the terrible smell of death that now filled the air around us. I walked after the Major in the direction of a plot of empty ground. As we crunched across the rubble of stones and broken glass, I saw one of the younger men who had gone ahead suddenly double over. He began to retch. Deep heaving sounds erupted from the centre of his body. In the few seconds it took to reach him I too felt waves of nausea flood my head and stomach. The smell was like the smell of the abattoir when the rotting offal is loaded on to trucks for dumping, but that is only a rough approximation because it was worse than anything that might be described by ordinary language.

This foulness was radiating out from what had been until recently the body of a man. But the sight that confronted us was only vaguely reminiscent of the human form. There was a head, swollen and battered with pale blotches like smears of paint where a club or rifle butt had done its work. There were empty sockets in which the eyes had once rested. But below the head there was nothing, only a skeleton that was twisted into an improbable spiral. This we took to be the work of the animals, who must have pulled and pushed as they feasted. There were fragments of charred clothing lying near by. I do not know who he was. I do not know what he did for a living, whether he was married and had children, whether he was a lover of women and nature, whether he was a killer or a peaceful man. I know nothing, only the fact of his debased humanity and my own incapacity to accept that such a thing could happen to a man.

I wanted to give form, to confer identity on the skeleton, and so I called him the scarecrow man. He was the ragged phantom left out to frighten the children, the bogyman we had been warned about as children; he was the creature from the world of nightmares and shadows. I pulled away from the group of policemen that had gathered around the corpse. Tears welled up in my eyes and I wanted to run and run as far as my legs would carry me. There is a loneliness, a hopelessness, that confronts me in dark places. It perhaps comes from long ago, from the shadowlands of childhood when I was powerless and buffeted by marginal circumstances. Now, in the middle of an African township, I felt more lonely and more uncertain of mankind than I had ever thought possible. I had seen many bodies: burned and shot and stabbed, or frozen in rigor mortis, or reduced to ash. But there was something uniquely sad about the scarecrow man. This death by fire and devouring by animals was more than a desecration of a body – it was far worse. This was a humiliation of the human spirit that said: 'You are fit only to lie in the streets unattended by compassion and sympathy, to rot in the sun and be devoured by dogs. Your life is less than the dirt where you lie.'

I was shaken out of my thoughts by the sight of a heavily pregnant mongrel that had appeared from the shadows of an empty house. The bitch growled as it watched the policemen prepare to take its meal away. One of the men ran at the dog and chased it into the derelict houses. He looked as if he wanted to inflict violence.

The Major came towards me, shaking his head. 'Pure savagery. It's just pure bloody savagery,' he said. He wanted to know how it was people could do this to one another. How could they leave bodies lying out like that for the dogs to eat and nobody even call an ambulance? They had no respect for human life. None. That was the problem. He was worried about his young constables. 'It's got to affect them, seeing this day after day,' he went on.

Although the Major did not say it directly, this vision from hell was proof to him of some deep savagery in the heart of black South Africa. It was confirmation of the deepest fears of Afrikaans-speaking whites, people who had grown up on a continent where the blood of innumerable tribal massacres washed across history like a tidal wave. Like almost every other policeman I met, the Major could not see his own tribe's role in any of this. He truly saw himself as a game ranger in a dangerous park where the animals had gone mad and were devouring each other. In Major Visagie's view the blacks had lost all respect for authority once the whites started to let go. The carnage in Katlehong and Tokoza was just one example of this.

We moved away from the corpse towards our vehicle and saw a jumbo jet rise up from the heat haze of Jan Smuts Airport, about five miles away. The aircraft rose steeply and then banked away to the left, turning south in the direction of Cape Town or Bloemfontein with a planeload of passengers who could not even see Katlehong, let alone the group of men who stood around the twisted, stinking corpse of the 900th black South African to be murdered in the township that year.

We had just reached the door of the Casspir when the radio burst into life again, telling of another body. This time the victim had only just been killed. It had happened in a street about a mile away. We left the scarecrow man to the army corpse men whom the Major had called to the scene and drove on in search of the latest victim.

He lay in a pool of blood at the end of a garden watched over by three women and a small girl who cannot have been much older than four. At the end of the street a crowd of several hundred had gathered. They watched silently as the policemen tumbled out of the Casspir and invaded the garden. The blood had now begun to flow into a thin strip of flowerbed upon which the dead man had collapsed. While the policemen were attempting to question the neighbours – *I heard nothing, I saw nothing, I was in the house, honestly* – the child went into the house, emerging a few minutes later with a bucket of water and a baby's bib. These she handed to one of the women, who proceeded to wipe away the blood from the grass and the footpath. Behind her the other women began to cry.

A woman who called herself Pinky came up to me and said she had arrived at the house just after the killing happened. The dead man's first name was Johannes and nobody knew who had killed him. Some gunmen had driven up and fired directly into his head as he stood at the garden gate. Pinky was a small, squat woman with powerful shoulders and a vast bosom. She said she did not trust the police because they did not protect her and in any case she was afraid to be seen talking to them in case the neighbours thought that she was an informer. One of the younger cops walked up to us and asked Pinky if she would give a statement. 'Me, man, I saw nothing at all. I just arrived and didn't even notice the body on the way in. I have nothing to say,' she barked at the policeman. He walked away and began an equally fruitless interrogation of one of the other women in the yard. I made to walk away but Pinky became agitated:

'I am going to be next. They are going to get me next. You just see what happens, they will get me. It's easy for you, you just walk away from here, but me I must stay and be killed. I am afraid, I'm so so afraid, man ... you just don't know.' She left me and walked away in the direction of the curious crowd.

Deon Peens had seen enough for one day and so had I. We left the crowd of people, the crying women and the silent four-year-old and climbed back into our steel protector to begin the journey back to base. I was uncomfortable with the silence so I said something bland about the brutalizing effects of violence on people, and the Major looked back at me but said nothing. The energy had drained out of the man and he drove us back in silence. The sky was growing dark, and I imagined that a summer storm was gathering far above the veld. When we arrived at the base, the men slumped out of the Casspir and walked away, nodding farewell as they went.

I looked up at the sky and noticed that there were no clouds, no sign of the storm waiting to spill its sorrow down on Katlehong and Tokoza. Instead the dullness came from the direction of the sun, around which a circle had formed, a cluster of grey like the haloes of cosmic dust that gather around distant stars. I remarked to Deon Peens that it made the sun look like a spaceship but he was thinking intensely, lost in some distant world, and he did not hear my comment. On the way back in the car Deon turned on the local talk station, Radio 702. People were calling from all over Johannesburg, their voices frantic, describing what was happening to the sun. A scientist called in and appealed for calm. It was a simple phenomenon caused by the reflection of the sun on icy particles of water trapped in the air. The circle was called a Sun Dog because it attached itself to the sun like a loyal animal. But nothing would calm the callers. 'What's happening, for God's sake?' said a woman caller from distant

Randburg. 'It's like the end of the world.' Deon Peens smiled and turned the car into the fast lane, towards the white streets of Alberton.

The scarecrow man was tagged and stored in the refrigerated wall space of Germiston Mortuary, where he joined 300 or so other unidentified bodies. Some of these had been lying there for several months, so badly burned that picking out a distinguishing feature would have been impossible. But people came to the mortuary every day in the hope of reclaiming the dead body of a missing son or daughter, father or brother. Some were township residents, familiar with the ritual of search and identification that had affected so many families in the area. Others were country people who had come hundreds of miles on rattling minibus taxis, crammed with other members of the rural poor. You could always tell the country people from the others who waited patiently at the mortuaries or funeral parlours. They had a lost, panicky look on their faces, awed by the big buildings and the wide roads and the eternal roar of Johannesburg. This was a sound part traffic and part human − the sound of a city that could swallow up a man or woman from the tribal areas without a trace.

Some were fortunate, if that is the word, and managed to find the bodies of their missing relatives. Simon Mabaleka, aged seventy-five, had spent five days travelling from the Transkei because he had been told that his son had disappeared. He went from undertaker to undertaker in an increasingly despairing search for the boy's body. The old man knew nothing of the city and the rituals of anonymous death, how the nameless were stacked up in government buildings awaiting a pauper's burial in a numbered grave. But somebody had told him to try the mortuary in the white town of Germiston near Tokoza, where his son had been living in a squatter camp at the time of his disappearance. There, in what the locals called the 'dormitory of death', Simon Mabaleka found his son lying on a silver mortician's tray, his head shattered by a high-velocity bullet. He had not been set alight or hacked, and this to Mr Mabaleka was a kind of mercy. From the look of things his son had died quickly and suddenly. But now there was the problem of getting the body from the mortuary to a funeral parlour, and from there to the place of his ancestors, where he could be buried. Mr Mabaleka had almost no money left. The journey to Johannesburg had eaten up most of his savings, and he found himself faced with the agony of seeing his son's body but being unable to take it away.

The old man had no relatives in Johannesburg or its satellite townships. He was as lost and alone as a child, but he would not leave without his son. There were no tears in Mr Mabaleka's eyes, and he did not plead for assistance or beg for cash. Instead the look on his face was that of a drowning man who watches the world rush away from him, his only certainty being the knowledge of his powerlessness. He was rescued by the kindly intervention of a local undertaker who had buried hundreds of people for less than the full payment and often for no payment at all. This was regarded by Mr Mabaleka as a form of divine intervention, a kindness that his life had not prepared him for and that now left him weeping the tears he had worked so hard to conceal. But on the scale of tragedies, deprivations and humiliations that characterized black lives in the final years of white rule, Mr Mabaleka's was by no means near the top of the list. In the previous twelve months I had come across scenes where whole families were annihilated, families where only a baby survived because the killers did not see it shivering with terror under a blanket; I had seen scores of shacks demolished by rampaging mobs and train carriages full of the dying and dead after yet another attack by faceless gunmen. For all the endless repetition of the phrase 'a new South Africa' it was as plain as daylight that black lives in places like Katlehong and Tokoza were worse than they had ever been.

The people who lived in these townships did so in the knowledge that their death could come at any time, in the most awful circumstances, and nobody would ever trace their killers. The rate of detection for political murders in the East Rand townships was abysmally low. The dead came from squatter camps, from the little township blockhouses and the long bleak barracks of the migrant workers. They were murdered coming and going from work or the shops, on their way to school or waiting for a train to Johannesburg. There was no real pattern to the story of death. At the height of the battles crowds of several hundred swept backwards and forwards across the disputed territories. Men from the migrant hostels, chanting the fearsome Zulu war cry 'Usuthu', would rampage through areas controlled by the ANC. The ANC might respond by attacking hostel dwellers on their way home from work. Or it would begin with an attack on hostel dwellers gathered at a railway station and spiral into street battles that could rage for weeks. As the fighting continued, Zulus living in township houses were targeted and driven out. It made no difference that these people had no political allegiance to Inkatha or that they had lived in peace with their neighbours for years. I frequently came across families standing outside burning houses, their belongings piled around them, their neighbours watching impassively. There were echoes of ethnic cleansing in this expulsion of the Zulu speakers but the crucial difference was the lack of a history of inter-tribal bitterness. The Zulus who lived outside the hostels had been members of the township communities for decades and were accepted as fellow South Africans by their neighbours. It was a brotherliness that survived the best efforts of the white state to divide and rule on the basis of tribal affiliation. Now, in the heat of the fiercest battles seen in the townships since the unrest erupted in 1990, the stain of suspicion fell on Zulu speakers. Those who were burned out of their homes fled to the hostels, where they found relative safety among their fellow tribespeople.

In the chaos of war humanity was easily forgotten. Men, women and children were butchered while others looked on in celebration or in fear. Most residents shivered indoors during the fighting, listening to the wild chorus of shouting and gunfire that filled the streets. They would hide their children under the bed, turn the radio up loud, weep and pray that the killers would pass by their door. Children were kept from school; parents did not go to work; for much of the time people were too scared to visit the shops or to gather wood for fires. Those that did ran the risk of sudden and senseless death. We would come across their bodies on our morning trawls through the townships. Bodies lying on waste ground, bodies in trenches, or at the entrance to houses. The person with a missing relative faced a difficult choice. To go out and search for the body at the height of the fighting could mean dying oneself. Not to recover the corpse would be to leave it to the dogs. Some people hauled the corpses home and hid them until the fighting died down and it was possible to reach the undertakers. I tried to imagine what it would be like, sitting in a tiny house with the body of a father or brother wrapped in a blanket on the floor – day after day for a week or more looking at what had once been a warm, walking, laughing being, now transformed into a silent bundle.

In July 1993 more than 200 people were killed in Katlehong and Tokoza. They had in common the fact that they were black and had no votes. Whether they came from the hostels or the ANC supporting areas, they were mostly people of no property, people who struggled against the odds to survive in a system that had ordained their economic, political and social impoverishment. One of the most common sights at the height of the fighting was the looting of homes, mostly by hostel dwellers. I watched bands of men roaming through newly abandoned homes, smashing windows and doors, and carrying off television sets, radios, clocks and any remotely valuable item of furniture. This was the dispossessed robbing the dispossessed.

The violence that dominated the transition had its immediate roots in the attempt by Inkatha to spread its political influence from Natal to the ANC-dominated reef townships in the months after Nelson Mandela's release from prison in February 1990. The larger political ambitions of Chief Mangosuthu Buthelezi found expression in an aggressive and sometimes violent campaign to recruit support in townships across the Transvaal. The same political battle that had claimed the lives of 10,000 people in Natal since 1984 now erupted with a vengeance in the Transvaal. In some cases the ANC's supporters refused to countenance the idea of serious political opposition on their turf and intimidated supporters of Inkatha; in other instances they responded to Inkatha's aggression by launching counter-attacks. A pattern developed where Inkatha rallies and marches would frequently be followed by rampages through the townships, with bystanders and householders beaten and murdered. Huge Inkatha war parties, known as *impis* in the Zulu vernacular, became a familiar sight on the weekends. They carried every manner of aggressive weapon – spears, machetes, axes, clubs and AK47s – and were rarely challenged by the police. In fact their right to carry so-called traditional weapons, spears and clubs, was defended by President De Klerk, who enacted a law legalizing the bearing of such deadly implements at cultural gatherings. Thus every political rally was simply described as a Zulu cultural gathering.

It would be impossible to convey the terror felt by township residents at the approach of these war parties, thousands of men jogging and chanting along the streets, hitting out at anybody who dared to venture out and watch them. I recall being surrounded by one group outside Soweto's huge Baragwanath Hospital, where I had gone to interview those wounded in a random attack just before a big Inkatha rally. I was pushed against the car and jostled, and Milton Nkosi, my colleague and translator, was dragged off into the centre of the group. The men around smelled of beer and were clearly drunk, spitting into my face as they railed against me in Zulu. I could pick out only one word, which was repeated over and again: *inja* – the Zulu word for dog and the worst term of abuse in the vernacular. *Injas* were the lowest of the low and those who heard this word directed at them were advised to prepare themselves for the worst.

Milton was pleading frantically now, pulling out his government-issue press card and pointing at the words 'BBC' stamped in bold letters beneath his photograph. The appearance of this official-looking document had a calming effect on the crowd. They immediately demanded to see mine. In a panic I pulled out several press cards, handing over my government accreditation but at the same time dropping my ANC press card on the ground. A fearsome looking character with tribal scar marks chiselled into his cheeks knelt down and grabbed the card. For a few endless seconds I waited, fully expecting a warlike scream and then the inevitable descent of spears and axes. But nothing happened. The fearsome one glanced quizzically at the card and then handed it back. I can only assume he was among the huge percentage of illiterate hostel dwellers. The gang seemed to have been mollified by the sight of our official cards and they moved on, a ragged, chanting scrum in search of trouble. As we got into the car to drive away, I asked Milton what it was they had been saying to each other when they pulled him away. 'Oh that,' he said with an air of forced nonchalance. 'They were arguing about whether to kill us there or to take us to the hostel.'

It was difficult for correspondents to gain access to these hostels. The men inside had a natural suspicion of journalists, a suspicion encouraged by the political commissars of Inkatha, who had in turn been tutored to have an almost paranoiac attitude to the media by their leader Chief Buthelezi. The tales of what happened to people captured by the hostel dwellers and dragged inside those dank barracks were enough to dissuade even the bravest of correspondents from venturing in without having made elaborate arrangements with the residents. Men and women were routinely hauled into the hostels and subjected to torture before being killed. There were legions of scare stories about bodies being chopped up and used for *muti* – a potion with supposedly magical qualities that could deflect the bullets of the enemy. It didn't matter whether these stories were true or simply the product of terrified imaginations. The continuous recovery of mutilated bodies in or near the hostels fed the rumours, until they had achieved the status of incontrovertible fact. Those who emerged alive described horrible tortures in which petrol was forced down the throats of the captured, or in which they were stripped and slowly stabbed until their bodies were a mess of blood and gore. And yet I knew that in not going into the hostels on a reasonably regular basis I was missing a central part of the story; my understanding of the hostel dwellers' case was becoming too dependent on the press releases and slick simplifications of Inkatha central office and the endless round of condemnation from the ANC. The result was that the men who lived inside had attained the stature of ghouls, creatures of darkness from whom all humanity had been drained.

To enter the hostel at Tokoza one did not, as might have been expected, deal with the toughest man in the place, or even with the most venerable of the Zulu *indunas** who lived there. In fact one did not even deal with a Zulu man. The person who controlled media access was a mother of four young children and a member of the Sotho royal house. Her parents had come to the reef from the mountain fastnesses of Lesotho. Now a senior Inkatha official, Gertrude Mzizi enjoyed unrivalled power over the 10,000 or so men crammed into the hostel on Khumalo Street in the centre of Tokoza. She was the wife of a Zulu chief and as such might have been expected to adopt a secondary public role to that of her husband. But even he recognized the striking leadership qualities of this tall, wiry woman with her shock of black hair, her ferocious flashing eyes and lion's courage. As a non-Zulu and a woman, her achievement in rising to the leadership of the hostel dwellers, becoming in the process a modern-day warrior queen, was testament to an inner fire that roused both admiration and fear among her subjects.

I first encountered Gertrude Mzizi on the morning after a night of serious rioting close to the hostel. She stood in a housecoat, shouting at a group of men who were trying to move a burned-out car into the hostel grounds. Her voice seemed to shave the air, harsh and strident, as she urged them on, occasionally delivering a soft kick on the behind to those

---

*A tribal rank approximating to captain but lower in the pecking order than a chief. *Indunas* are responsible for discipline and order in the hostel dormitories.

she thought were slacking. But Mrs Mzizi was hated by the township residents, many of whom had been forced to flee their homes because of the violent activities of the hostel dwellers. The township people regarded her as an Inkatha warlord and made her home the target of numerous assassination attempts. The worst came on a summer's day as she returned from the shops, carrying her two-year-old baby. A group of youths rushed out of a side street and shoved Gertrude to the ground, grabbing the child from her arms and throwing it into the garden of a house. Taunting and spitting, they produced a jerry can of petrol and doused Gertrude from head to toe. They then brought forward a tyre and wrapped it around her waist. She thought that the end, long prepared for, had come and that the next step would be the lighting of the matches and an inferno of fire and melting rubber. But, as she lay waiting for death, she heard voices arguing. Someone had forgotten to bring matches. There was nothing with which to set the 'dog' alight. As the voices grew heated, Gertrude heard the distant rumble of a large vehicle and prayed that it was a Casspir and not a lorry whose driver was carrying cigarettes and matches. The feet that had been standing around her turned and fled. The next thing she saw was the tall shape of a policeman holding her child in one arm and extending the other to pull her up from the ground. Other attacks followed, with bullets smashing into the concrete and through the windows of the house she shared with her husband and four young children. But the bullets could not find Gertrude Mzizi, and her powers of survival enhanced the legend of the warrior queen.

On the day I met her to arrange a visit to the hostel, Gertrude was cooking breakfast for her children in the cramped space that served as kitchen, television den and bedroom. It was hard to associate the woman tenderly stroking the head of her youngest child with the Amazon of popular legend. 'What would you like for breakfast, my darling, some eggs maybe?' she cooed, wrapping her arms around the child and staring into its huge, forever upward-looking eyes.

But in the five or so minutes it took us to walk across Khumalo Street from the house to the hostel Gertrude underwent a dramatic transformation. At the gate a man wielding a machete and wearing a faded red woman's raincoat stepped gingerly to one side as we entered, nodding respectfully as we passed by. Gertrude surged ahead, her shoulders pressed back, her face pushing into the wind like the prow of a mighty warship. Once inside the concrete fence that protects the hostel she began to call men towards us. Her voice was harsh now and she summoned her soldiers in the language of command. Figures emerged from the long barracks buildings and ambled across the waste ground towards where we were standing.

A man who introduced himself as Mthethwa came forward. He was small and broad with a large belly that cascaded over his waistband and flopped as he walked. But Mthethwa had a face whose lurking menace advised against making any jokes about his weight. I tried to catch his eye on several occasions but on each his gaze flickered away in another direction, like that of a lizard. There was a deep scar along the right side of his head and a number of smaller marks that I took to be the dents of old battles. The other men pushed out of the way to make room for him at the front, and he and Gertrude exchanged a few words in Zulu. She told him we had come to see how the hostel dwellers lived. We wanted to get their side of the story. He seemed happy enough with this explanation and in any case the word of Gertrude Mzizi was something even Mthethwa was inclined to obey. Gertrude told us to go ahead and promised to meet us again at the end of the tour.

The hostel compound was a bleak barracks composed of several long dormitories that at the height of the fighting were home to an estimated 10,000 men, women and children. There was a large patch of waste ground that alternately served as rubbish dump, playground and venue for political rallies. A couple of thin, mange-ridden dogs nosed in the huge mounds of rubbish that sat like pyramids outside each dormitory. There were rotting cow and sheep skulls and piles of cloven hoofs bleaching in the sun, the remnants of past feasts. Occasionally the figure of a small child would appear at the door of one of the dormitories before darting into another building or being hauled back inside by a nervous mother. I saw one infant of about three years come into the open and, half tottering, half squatting, leave behind him a trail of diarrhoea. The hostel had become a self-contained slum. Because the facilities of the township were out of bounds, the hostel dwellers had created their own mini-society. There was a barber's shop, a tailor's and shoemaker's, and the inevitable drinking hall, crammed with men who seemed to be lost in some fuddled half-world.

The majority of the ordinary residents were single men like Robert Zindlele. He was fifty-eight years old and had lived in the hostel since 1976. He had a wife and five children in Zululand to whom he returned twice a year and sent regular remittances from the wages he earned as a security guard in Johannesburg. He shared the room with four other men. The air smelled of paraffin and stale sweat, the smell of too many men in too small a place. Although it was around nine o'clock in the morning Robert was already half drunk, his eyes bloodshot and fixed in a dreamy stare. On days off there was nothing to do but sit around and drink. Venturing out into the township alone, or trying to make it into Johannesburg without protection, was asking for death. So he stayed in the hostel with other men who were either on a day off or unemployed, like increasing numbers of the occupants.

When he went to work it was with a large group but even that didn't guarantee safety. Robert showed us into the room next door, where a man lay on a bed nursing a hugely swollen leg. He pulled back the covers to reveal two large dents in the leg both caused by high-velocity rounds fired from an AK47. The man had been with a group of hostel dwellers on their way to work when the enemy opened fire. It was likely that he would never work again.

Next to him an older man was sharpening wooden spears, the rasp of the sandpaper mingling with the tubercular coughing of another inmate who lay hidden beneath a pile of blankets. Robert picked up one of the spears and began to perform a drunken battle dance, full of thrusts and jabs and high kicks. He staggered a few times and then collapsed on to the floor. The man with the wounded leg laughed. 'I am very, very, very . . . so very proud to be a Zulu,' Robert announced to the room at large. 'And you must know,' he went on, 'that I will never, ever accept an ANC government. Never, ever.' The enemy were Communists, surely we realized that. They wanted to kill the Zulus. But the wounded man had other ideas. He had seen enough of fighting. Wasn't his leg proof of that? 'Just let Mandela and Buthelezi get together, man, and work it out,' he said. As he was speaking, Robert drifted out of the door and headed in the direction of the beer hall. Mthethwa reappeared a few seconds later and announced with a smile that the police had arrived.

As we followed him towards the main gate a group of five camouflaged riot policemen emerged from one of the barracks. Mthethwa slowed down and told us to stand and wait while he went forward to negotiate. The sergeant in charge produced five rounds of .28-calibre ammunition that had been discovered under a bed in the barracks. Mthethwa adopted what he must have imagined to be a look of complete innocence. 'I can't imagine how they got there,' he told the sergeant. 'Anyway, the guys who stay there won't be back from work until five o'clock. Maybe you should come back then.' The policeman said he would come back with more men and question the occupants of the building.

As soon as the armoured car had disappeared through the gates, Mthethwa rounded on the group of men who were following us. 'Do you think those bullets grow on trees? We need every bullet we can get and now we have the police taking them from us because you leave them out to be found,' he shouted. The men cringed and looked at the ground. At that moment Gertrude rejoined our group, having finished whatever secret business had taken her to the other side of the hostel. As we spoke, some shooting broke out a few yards away. I jumped and then ran for cover into a shed next to the gate. Gertrude laughed derisively. 'It's only our people,' she explained. 'One of the men was killed by the ANC and they are preparing for the funeral.'

A group of chanting men came around the corner following a white station-wagon in which a coffin had been placed. Sitting in the van were two men and a woman who held a flickering candle over the coffin. The dead man had been caught on his way home from the city and burned alive. Gertrude recited the story in the matter-of-fact way of someone who has grown used to such occurrences. For someone who was at least part politician her attitude to the township war was refreshingly straightforward. 'Yeah, sure, we are willing to kill. I am not ashamed to say it. If someone comes at you with an AK47, are you going to hit back with your hands? Of course not.' She told me that her own death would come violently, that one day her famous luck would run out. This might have been bravado but I doubt it. In a township where people died on the whim of others, Gertrude Mzizi had more enemies than was prudent.

Back in the kitchen, after we had managed to shake off Mthethwa and his dangerous men, Gertrude introduced her eldest daughter, Ntomblyoxolo. The name means 'Child of Peace'. Eight-year-old Ntomblyoxolo spoke the kind of fluent, American-accented English one hears from children who are educated outside the townships. Her mother said that because of the violence she had decided to send the eldest to school in Johannesburg, so that her days at least would be peaceful. But Gertrude knew that if the killers came during the night the whole family would most likely be shot. That was the fashion among the gunmen on both sides. Ntomblyoxolo said she was afraid her mother and father would be killed. 'They must just stop burning the people,' she said. As we spoke, another child entered the kitchen and spun around, making the noisy sound of a police siren. The child was clearly hyperactive, the noises of the streets racing around in her head as she frantically sought our attention. Ntomblyoxolo walked across the kitchen and soothed the younger child into quietness. 'I don't want for my mother to be killed. Just let us have peace here,' she said.

Two days after my visit to the Mzizi family, hostel dwellers kidnapped three men on Khumalo Street. It happened almost directly opposite Gertrude's house. The men, pleading hysterically for their lives, were taken into the hostel and stripped of their clothes. A large group of hostel dwellers set about torturing them with knives, going so far as to chop off the arm of one man. After about one hour of this treatment a man with a pistol put an end to their agony. They were shot with .28-calibre ammunition.

Those of us who observed the marches by hostel dwellers that so often ended in violence were always struck by the reluctance of the police to act against the mobs or to protect the residents of the townships. The same force that had brutally suppressed demonstrations by anti-apartheid organizations in the seventies and eighties now seemed curiously paralysed in the face of these full-scale battles. The increasingly violent nature of demonstrations by Inkatha was mirrored by the establishment of armed self-defence units among township residents with the blessing of the ANC. Before long both sides were involved in a cycle of attack and counter-attack, with the police either unable or unwilling to stop the carnage or in some cases actively involved in the promotion of violence. The massacres that took place on an intermittent basis between 1990 and 1992 were classic examples of police failure to come to terms with the escalating violence:

12 May 1991: Up to 1,000 armed men attacked the Swanieville squatter camp outside Johannesburg. Twenty-nine people were killed and thirty injured. Eight hostel dwellers were arrested. They were found not guilty and acquitted. The judge said it was a 'scandal' that so few people had been brought to trial.

3 April 1992: Unknown attackers, probably ANC supporters, killed twenty-three residents of an Inkatha squatter camp in Katlehong. There were no arrests and no convictions. Eyewitness evidence given to the police was not pursued according to Judge Richard Goldstone's Commission of Inquiry into Public Violence and Intimidation.

17 June 1992: A gang of more than one hundred armed men killed forty-six people in the township of Boipatong, south of Johannesburg. It took police forty-eight hours to search the KwaMadala Hostel from where the attack was launched. Following huge international and domestic pressure, the police eventually arrested seventy-four people. Less than half of those accused were brought to trial, and only seventeen finally convicted of murder.

Why did the police fail to come to grips with the violence? There is no single answer to the question, rather a number of factors, all of them deeply rooted in the history of the apartheid state. The police force had for years been used to crushing the slightest stirrings of revolt by organizations opposed to the government. It was a blatantly party-political machine that owed its allegiance to white rule rather than to any concept of service or responsibility to the community as a whole. Thus, when the battle for turf between the ANC and Inkatha was at its height, the police had little inclination to protect those against whom it had waged war for decades. In some cases policemen simply stood back and refused to intervene when township residents came under attack; in others, such as the Trust Feed Case,* policemen actively involved themselves in the violence. There were notable exceptions to the rule when individual police commanders decided to take action and disarm unruly mobs. I watched one courageous police captain storm a train in Soweto and personally lead the disarming of hundreds of Inkatha supporters, triumphantly brandishing a captured AK47 above his head as he re-emerged on to the platform. The effect of this action was somewhat undermined when, the following day, his superiors took a decision to hand back the confiscated clubs, spears and shields on the basis that they were cultural implements.

*A court in Natal convicted white police captain Brian Mitchell and four black policemen of the murder of eleven people in the settlement of Trust Feed. In his evidence Mitchell said he believed he was doing the state's bidding by taking the side of Inkatha in the war against the ANC. However, Mitchell, who was sentenced to death, had mistakenly killed supporters of Inkatha in the attack on Trust Feed.

The National Party government had for years adopted a strategy of divide and rule among blacks and had no political interest whatsoever in seeing a *rapprochement* between the two major black political groups. It was a truth implicitly recognized by several powerful senior officers in the police and army, who continually warned the government of the need to work against any potential alliance involving the ANC and Inkatha. The only alliance that the security force commanders in Pretoria wished to see developing was one between the National Party and Inkatha; the latter, with its commitment to a free market, opposition to sanctions and history of co-operation with Pretoria, was seen as a far more suitable bedfellow than the ANC. Thus, when the ANC and Inkatha began to devour one another, the partiality of the security forces towards the latter was taken for granted and repeatedly focused on by the government's opponents. The pro-Inkatha tendency at senior levels of government began to change only when it became clear that the ANC alone could deliver a majority of blacks in support of a new constitution and that Inkatha's support was nothing like as large as Chief Buthelezi claimed.

But there were two further factors that greatly inhibited the ability of the police to curb the violence and to effect prosecutions: the woeful lack of training and numbers required to deal with the massive violence that had erupted, and the refusal of most township residents to co-operate with a force they regarded as cruel and illegitimate. In his report on the police handling of the Boipatong Massacre the British criminologist Peter Waddington described a force that was 'woefully inadequate and incompetent' and whose actions suggested a lack of accountability.

I met Waddington during his visit to South Africa and was impressed by his straightforward and pragmatic approach to the investigation. He was no ideologue and understood the difficulties of police work in a politically charged climate like that prevailing in South Africa. 'They're not bad cops, most of them. It's just that for years they've been the apartheid police force and now they're being asked to turn around and be ordinary criminal investigators. It's going to take a hell of a long time to change that,' he told me. Waddington was horrified to discover that the most basic rules of investigation had not been followed in the Boipatong inquiry. There were no case dockets on the murdered people. Crucial forensic evidence had been ignored and the length of time taken to interview the accused enabled the destruction or dispersal of many of the murder weapons. Talking to Waddington, I formed the impression that he believed the police were guilty more of incompetence than of any organized conspiracy to pervert the course of justice. They were for the most part simply not trained or psychologically prepared for the task of treating the murders of black people with anything like the diligence devoted to investigating the violent deaths of whites.

When they did attempt serious investigations, the police were hampered by the refusal of witnesses to come forward. This was partly because of the traditional mistrust of the security forces, but also because of active lobbying and, at times, intimidation by people associated with the ANC. Even when police were investigating attacks on ANC supporters, they often found themselves confronted by a wall of silence. To the ANC and to vast numbers of people in the townships the SAP had enforced the million cruelties of apartheid, had been involved in death squads and, through its security branch, had ruthlessly crushed the black resistance movements. It was the enemy.

The relentless targeting of policemen by criminals and political groups reinforced the siege mentality prevalent among many white officers. In 1993 more than 250 policemen were murdered in the line of duty. Hundreds more were injured or fell victim to post-traumatic-stress syndrome. They were patrolling townships awash with automatic rifles. The very weapons that had been used to destabilize neighbouring Angola and Mozambique were flooding back into the country, being snapped up by small-time arms dealers and resold on to the thriving arms market. Criminal gangs, some of them comprised of out-of-work, disaffected ANC guerrillas, began to stage major robberies up and down the country. Policemen who encountered these gangs and who didn't shoot first could expect no mercy. The job of a policeman in South Africa was closer to that of a deputy sheriff in the badlands of the old West than that of a civil guardian in a society on the threshold of democracy.

The eruption of wars between rival taxi operators over the lucrative routes in and out of townships was a further complicating factor in the grand mess of township violence. The taxi owners – sometimes using hired gunmen from one or the other political organization – staged massacres of passengers travelling on vehicles owned by their enemies. There have been suggestions, thus far unsubstantiated, that these taxi owners may also have been involved in the train violence, intending to frighten the commuters into using minibuses, which, although more expensive, would be safer.

The startling lack of success in investigating the violence, the reluctance of the police to deal firmly with aggression when it came from the ranks of Inkatha and the long history of covert actions against the ANC were, I believe, at the root of the allegations about a Third Force operating from within the ranks of the security forces. The Third Force allegations dominated the political agenda during the first phase of the transition to democracy. The South African press (most notably the *Weekly Mail* and the *Vrye Weekblad*) frequently reported the confessions of hit-squad members or former police and soldiers who admitted to having carried out attacks on trains and buses. Journalists like John Carlin of the *Independent* and Phillip van Niekerk of the *Weekly Mail* doggedly pursued the rumours and frequently exposed examples of security-force complicity in the violence. There were frequent claims from township residents – never proven – that white men with their hands and faces painted black had taken part in the massacres. That many of the allegations made were unprovable was a point lost on the residents, who had suffered grievously at the hands of unknown attackers. People were only too willing to believe that a government that had dispatched hit squads against black activists for decades would now use the same terror tactics against ordinary civilians, on the basis that they lived in ANC-supporting areas. The power of rumour, the willingness to accept hearsay, thrived in townships where ordinary life had become impossible.

The suspicions about a Third Force were given further credence in the public mind by revelations that the government was secretly funding Inkatha, that the army had trained members of a KwaZulu police hit squad, and by the discovery of a secret military intelligence base devoted to anti-ANC operations.* These disclosures confirmed the suspicions of anti-apartheid activists that the state was operating a double agenda: talking peace to the ANC on the one hand while waging war against it on the other.

---

*In November 1992 investigators working for Judge Richard Goldstone's Commission of Inquiry into Public Violence and Intimidation uncovered a military plot to destabilize the ANC and involve its members in criminal activities. Among the chief operatives was Ferdi Barnard, a former member of the notorious Civil Co-operation Bureau that carried out covert actions on behalf of the military, including assassinations. The findings came just weeks after another military plot, 'Operation Echoes', was discovered. This involved an attempt to link the ANC's military wing to the Irish Republican Army.

De Klerk's response in all cases was to let deputy heads roll. Although he fired twenty-three generals in the wake of the military intelligence scandal, the Chief of Intelligence and the head of the army were allowed to stay on; when Inkathagate exploded he demoted but did not fire two senior government ministers, and took no action against Pik Botha, the man most closely linked to the scandal. They were the measures of a man struggling to stay on the right side of his security forces, while at the same time attempting to demonstrate to the world that the bad old days were over. De Klerk believed that a purge of the army's top leadership might precipitate a serious crisis, with the loyalty of the defence force to the reform process being called into question.

Concrete evidence of a large-scale plan to destabilize the country and destroy the ANC did not emerge until shortly before the election, when the Deputy Commissioner of the Police, Basie Sm.., and several other senior officers were suspended on suspicion of having organized a campaign of murder in the Johannesburg townships and Natal. It is hard to believe that high-ranking officers were involved in the manufacture of weapons and the setting up of hit squads without some senior person in the government having been aware. That there was a Third Force and that it involved the very top ranks of the police and military is beyond doubt. What is still unknown is the level of knowledge that the Cabinet possessed.

But any fair assessment of the period must also allow that the government faced serious practical constraints in trying to deal with the township violence. It was simply not in a position to adopt the traditional method of dealing with widespread unrest, the method that had worked so well during the mid-eighties: the state of emergency. The old days when volleys of live rounds were the order of the day in policing public demonstrations had clearly gone for ever. So too were the huge round-ups of activists that typified security-force reaction to violence in the 1980s. Although the police occasionally returned to type and fired into unarmed crowds, they were, generally speaking, no longer able to behave with impunity. Two of the consequences of De Klerk's reforms were a greater demand for accountability on the part of the police and a restraint on government from taking the kind of emergency measures that had brought the previous waves of public disorder in the seventies and eighties to an end. Thus, while pressed by his political opponents to crack down and bring the killings to an end, De Klerk found himself severely limited. Any move to seal off townships, impose widespread curfews and carry out large-scale arrests of activists would have brought down a storm of condemnation from the very people who had demanded action in the first place. De Klerk found himself in the unenviable but entirely inevitable position of a man whose real power had shrunk but who none the less was trapped by the traditional public image of the supremely powerful white president. He had the image of power but much less of the substance.

De Klerk's support among blacks who had initially welcomed his reforms plummeted as the violence escalated. His international image was badly damaged by repeated attacks from Nelson Mandela, who accused the President of caring little for the lives of blacks; in one celebrated comment Mandela claimed that the National Party leader had 'unleashed his dogs of war on innocent people'. Yet the government's response to so-called 'black on black violence' was to behave as if all the responsibility lay with black political organizations. At times De Klerk appeared to have adopted the role of Pontius Pilate, as he lamented the intolerance of the black organizations and spoke solemnly of his party's commitment to peace. Coming from the leader of a party that had used violence as an instrument of repression for decades, the reaction among blacks was predictable. Posters appeared in the townships accusing De Klerk of being a war criminal, a man with blood on his hands. Mandela used every possible opportunity to demonize his main opponent. Witness his speech to the special sitting of the United Nations Security Council in the wake of the Boipatong Massacre: 'It is more than clear to us that the violence is both organized and orchestrated and is especially directed at the democratic movement whose activists, members and supporters make up the overwhelming majority of its victims. It constitutes a cold-blooded strategy for state terrorism . . .' At the root of Mandela's often bitter attacks on an opponent he once described as a 'man of integrity' was an acute sense of personal betrayal. This was something expressed privately and publicly by the ANC President. Put simply, he felt that he had trusted De Klerk to be even-handed, to take serious action to bring the killing to an end, but the opposite had occurred. Mandela was fond of quoting the text of his meetings with De Klerk, in which Mandela made appeals for police action to stop the killing, while the state President and his ministers wrung their hands but in the end did nothing.

With the realization that an election would happen within two or three years, the issues of maiming, destruction and death became political footballs that bounced over the heads of a suffering populace. As the killing continued into 1993, it became clear to me that two of the greatest problems were the willingness of political leaders to use the issue of violence as an electoral weapon and the unwillingness of any side to accept responsibility for the actions of their own supporters. Whatever happened was somebody else's fault. The main players – De Klerk, Mandela, Buthelezi – vied with each other to deliver the most sanctimonious commitments to peace, while in the same breath dumping the responsibility for the killing into the laps of their opponents. Buthelezi was particularly adept at weaving warnings of war and highly emotive phrases like 'ethnic cleansing' into his appeals for peace. The three leaders did sign a peace agreement but even then used the public platform to round upon one another. The one bright light in those dark months was the emergence of a dedicated National Peace Committee, whose workers on the ground did manage to avert several serious confrontations. I watched them hold the line between crowds of angry youths and rows of nervous policemen on several occasions, most notably in the wake of the assassination of the Communist Party leader, Chris Hani, in April 1993. Were it not for their presence, and the televised appeals for calm from Mandela, the assassination might well have led to the worst security crisis since the Soweto Riots of nearly two decades before.

A subtle change in the attitudes of ANC leaders became apparent in the latter half of 1993. It occurred in the wake of the purge of senior military officers and coincided with the gradual coming together of the ANC and the government on crucial constitutional issues. The realization that battle-scarred areas like Katlehong and Tokoza would soon be the responsibility of an ANC-dominated government began to dawn on senior leaders. Local heads of the organization were told to impose discipline on unruly elements; in a number of celebrated cases they even handed over wanted criminals, and those accused of murdering whites, to the police. Although he continued to launch attacks on De Klerk, Mandela now began to give equal prominence to calls for an end to the violence perpetrated by his own supporters. He was no longer the leader of a revolutionary movement urging his troops to the barricades, but a president in waiting, anxious to ensure that his country did not dissolve into an anarchic mess.

It was in Katlehong, on a day thick with the dust of 10,000

stamping feet, that I watched Nelson Mandela deliver the harshest of harsh messages to his supporters, a message that only a man of his remarkable authority could have conveyed. The rally was held in what was rather grandiosely called the Huntersfield Stadium, in reality a bowl of dust around which the municipality had thrown a flimsy wooden stand into which people crammed in the days when football matches were still held in Katlehong. But the 10,000 or so township residents who had marched to Huntersfield that morning were in the mood to fight, not play. Among them were troops of men wrapped in blankets and waving axes and spears. There were members of the Pan-Africanist Congress chanting their ritual slogan 'one settler, one bullet' every time a white journalist approached. And deep in the heart of the crowd there were the gunmen whose weapons were thrust into the air and fired at periodic intervals. Each fusillade of shots produced an ecstatic response from the thousands who waited for Mandela's arrival. When his motorcade eventually swept into the cauldron of sound and dust, the shooting became frenzied. The bodyguards refused to allow the leader to leave his bullet-proof car, and a local ANC leader was dispatched to the platform to plead for quiet. 'We don't know who these gunmen are. They might want to target our leader,' the figure on the stage announced. The warning had the desired effect, silencing the gunmen and settling the crowd. I was sitting a few yards from Mandela and noticed that on the table in front of him somebody had written in chalk: 'Mr Mandela, you talk of peace when we need guns.' The old man must have seen it too, but he was not to be deflected from delivering his most powerful speech since his release from prison. He began with a ritual condemnation of the government, a guaranteed crowd pleaser. But then came the message for his own supporters: 'There are members of the ANC who are killing our people. We must face the truth. Our people are just as involved as other organizations that are committing violence. You want to blame Inkatha only . . . I am not going to do that. We cannot climb to freedom on the corpses of innocent people.' The crowd heard him out respectfully, but I did not have the impression that they were listening. A tall, dignified figure in a place where hatred and humiliation reigned supreme, it was as if his words were tiny arrows that bounced off the rough hide of the crowd's anger. As they made their way home, shots rang out again and some stones were thrown. This crowd was alienated and lost to reason, swept along by the simple desire for retribution. Soon after the speech, trouble began to spread among the ranks of the ANC supporters themselves. The violence that had once been a function of the war with Inkatha now began to infect the ranks of Mandela's supporters. As the country approached its last Christmas under white rule, bitter battles erupted between the leaders of rival factions associated with the ANC in Katlehong and Tokoza. The fight was, as usual, over the control of territory but spurred on and given its true venom by the frighteningly low cost of human life in the area.

And then, two weeks before Christmas, there occurred an event that even by the standards of the East Rand was shockingly callous. It began as a small local row over the behaviour of an ANC self-defence unit (SDU) in Katlehong's Moleleki section, an area of typically run-down township blockhouses intermingled with squatter shacks that had been subjected to months of random attack by hostel dwellers. The SDU had begun to prey on the people it was supposed to serve. There were stories of extortion and of brutal punishments meted out to anybody brave enough to criticize the gunmen. Things finally erupted into open warfare when members of the SDU burned an old woman to death in her shack because she had dared to question their behaviour.

The ANC Youth League moved in and demanded to accompany the SDU on patrol. Another 'moderate' was killed by the SDU and the Youth Leaguers responded by shooting the second-in-command of the SDU. The facts of what happened next are, unusually for South Africa, not disputed by either side. Marching through the Moleleki area, members of the SDU abducted eight members of the Youth League. The abducted youths were all under the age of seventeen. After walking for a kilometre or so, the group of armed men and their young captives came to a patch of open ground known locally as the 'People's Park'. This was an area where political meetings were held but also, the youths knew, a place of execution. They began to beg for their lives. One or two of the younger boys were crying, pleading with the older men to spare them. 'Are we not part of the same struggle?' pleaded Vibbs Matlou, who at sixteen was a veteran of several confrontations with Inkatha and the police. The men from the SDU were hearing none of it. They forced the youths to kneel and bound their hands behind their backs with nylon rope. At this point the executioners stepped forward and fired several volleys of shots into the bodies of the kneeling youths. One boy who must have been the target of particular hatred was decapitated and his head chopped to pieces. The corpses were left lying in the sun as a warning to those who might be tempted to dispute the law of the gun. This, let us not forget, happened among people who were theoretically all on the same side. The killing fields of the East Rand were a prototype of what happened when violence gripped townships and refused to let go. The killing had created its own logic. As always, the roughest and most vicious emerged triumphant and the politics of liberation were reduced to a squalid battle among local warlords.

The SDU frightened the ANC's top leadership almost as much as they frightened Inkatha. They were armed with automatic rifles and many of their members were easily side-tracked into criminal violence. Consider this extract from a BBC interview with one member of a Katlehong SDU on the subject of killing:

> *SDU member*: Well, uh, I'll be honest. I don't think about it. It doesn't trouble me, because the way the situation is . . . whenever you kill a particular person it's like I've killed a chicken because I don't see any reason for him to survive if he doesn't understand what is the will of the people, what we are fighting for.
>
> *Interviewer*: Do you have any idea how many people you have killed?
>
> *SDU member*: No, I don't have an idea because I don't normally count.
>
> *Interviewer*: So when it's happened you don't normally think about it?
>
> *SDU member*: No, I don't normally think about it because what normally happens is that we do it and I forget, because why? It's a process, you know?

The townships of the East Rand may not have been typical of the entire country, but they did represent an area of huge population and they frequently dominated the national political agenda. They were in many respects a prototype of black South Africa's worst-case scenario: a battlezone in which the desperate and the poor destroyed each other without mercy.

There are crowds of people gathering on the street corner next to my office. There are blacks, whites, coloureds and Indians. The entire South African mosaic. It is two minutes away from noon and people are still pouring out of office buildings along the street. They begin to form a line on the kerb, standing in total silence. The quiet is suddenly broken by the ringing of church bells and a blaring chorus of car horns. The buses and cars that pass along the street have switched on their headlights and the drivers are flashing peace signs. A black man in the middle of the line extends his hand to a white woman standing next to him. Soon everybody is holding hands. As I walk along the line with my tape-recorder, I see that there are tears flowing down the faces of many of those who have joined the demonstration for peace. What I am witnessing in this multi-coloured joining of hands is something never seen before in South Africa, a coming-together against the grain of history. It is hard to tell if these are tears of happiness, relief, frustration or the long pain of the years rolling out in one brief moment of togetherness. Everybody I speak to tells me that they want peace, that they are sick and tired of the killing. I believe them, I truly believe them, and for a moment my practised detachment slips and I share in their tears, mourning the dead, the lost and broken who crowd my dreams. After the moment has passed, the people begin to walk back to their offices, led by a group of black women cleaners. They are all singing the peace anthem:

> *South Africa, we love you, oh beautiful land,*
> *let's show the whole world we can bring*
> *peace in our land.*

I want this to last and to spread out from our comfortable suburbs into the nightmare zones of Katlehong and Tokoza. I want it to be heard where it matters, but I do not know that it will be.

CHAPTER 2

Born to be Wild

There lies a boy who died
in the struggle,
Can all these heroes
die in vain
While we slash and kill
our own brothers.

Lucky Dube, 'Victims'

In the townships of the East Rand you drove slowly up to the barricades or you simply didn't arrive at the other side. A car driven fast was a threat to the wild-eyed boys who hung back behind the checkpoints. Only a fool or someone with a death wish would attempt to break through. After the first mound of boulders and trees, there was invariably a second line of defence. This could take the form of a deep trench across the road into which the car would lunge head first, or it could be a group of younger kids armed with outsized rocks to smash through the windscreen or driver's door. Those rocks, even in tiny hands, could make mush of a man's head in a second.

So for a sensible driver there was only one choice: you slowed down and talked your way through. It was rarely a comfortable choice. The youngsters who swarmed around the car were ill-disposed to any strangers. They lived in townships where death travelled by car, ferrying gunmen from one street to another, in a blur of automatic fire and screaming tyres. It was the season of rumour, when each night produced stories of mystery whites roaming the streets and directing bands of assassins. Nobody ever filmed or photographed these terrifying figures, and like demons or goblins they grew more notorious and fearful because they could not be seen or touched. I cannot answer for other white journalists, but I shrank within myself during these barricade encounters. The public show of coolness, the smiles and handshakes, masked an inner trembling. Even with my friend and township veteran Milton Nkosi along-side I felt vulnerable and exposed. The old certainty of a welcome for the press had long since disappeared. The number of attacks on whites in these areas also made it a less than secure prospect to cruise the townships and observe the conflict. Journalists were shot at, beaten and routinely harassed by the supporters of political organizations, or by the gangs of criminals who emerged like vultures to pluck at the remains of the ravaged townships. You did not have to spend any great length of time in these places before grasping a fundamental truth: your life, any life, meant nothing when it gazed down the barrel of some bitter teen-ager's gun. This was the crudest and simplest lesson in the dynamics of power. He had the weapon and all the choices. He could smile and wave you through, he could rob you and take your car, or he could simply increase the finger pressure a fraction and obliterate you from the face of the earth.

When we pulled up to a barricade the crowd would press up against the windows of the car. Those at the front would be pressed against the glass so that their faces distorted, twisted into the grotesquerie of a mask from some primeval African scene. I saw many faces at countless roadblocks, but in memory they have attained the quality of a single malign image. It was the face that did not return the smile but instead looked through you, which pulled away from the window and moved to the corner of the street while never losing sight of you.

This face belonged to the boy with a rolled-up pullover or a greatcoat in whose folds an automatic rifle or pistol were easily concealed. As the other youngsters rolled the stones and barrels out of the way, it was the boy in the coat you kept watching until you were out of range and your stomach disentangled itself once again. I know that those moments left a deep impression on my subconscious because they returned again and again as dreams. In the most frequent dream I would be sitting in the car with Milton as the crowd approached, hurling stones. He would turn the ignition frantically, but the engine could produce only a faint clicking noise. As the mob began to shake the car I would start to scream, blaming Milton for not being able to start the engine. The dream always ended with both of us crying and the car being turned over and set alight. Such was the power of this nightmare that it could induce a deep melancholy throughout the following day.

Once in a while someone in the crowd or a sniper in one of the hostels would open fire and the shooting was louder and closer than anything I had ever experienced. One Saturday morning at the height of the East Rand violence I found myself interviewing a priest who was acting as one of the local peace monitors. We were standing beside a burning house located between the hostel dwellers and the residents. The priest was in the middle of a long explanation about the causes of the violence when several bullets whistled past us. A burst of automatic fire followed and then there was complete silence. We dived on to the ground, gulping down lungfuls of dust. At such moments one feels extraordinarily large, as if the body is growing and growing and with every second presenting a bigger target. In between the spasms of sheer terror, I have often tried to imagine what my prone figure must look like through the cross-hairs of a sniper's gun. On this occasion I had a rare privilege: I actually managed to see the gunman. Peeking up from my position near the kerb, I saw at the other end of the street a boy of no more than fifteen years. He was leaning against a brick wall, an AK47 clutched in his right arm. What really startled me was the expression on his face: a broad smile, which, upon catching my eye, gave way to loud laughter. He laughed so intensely that I began to wonder if he was in the grip of a manic fit. The priest then stood up and dusted himself down, calling out to the gunman that we were simply observers and had nothing to do with the police or army.

The teenager shrugged and turned on his heel, losing himself quickly in the maze of abandoned houses. I do not think that he intended to kill or even wound us. It was perhaps just the result of some desire to see two white men grovel in the dust, experiencing fear at its most raw. But this was not some sudden malfunction in the otherwise dependable psychology of the young comrades. The madness was the poison of an old wound at long last bursting to the surface. It was a three-centuries-old story that had twisted and turned down the years, heaping shame on the young, until the anger of one generation, the children of 1976, ignited a revolution that would alter the course of history.

The children who launched the student protest in June 1976 shook the apartheid state to its foundations, but in doing so they set in motion a cycle of conflict that would claim the lives and futures of many among them. If there can be said to have been one defining moment in recent South African history it came on the morning of the 16th of June in that fateful year. For months before black students had been protesting against the introduction of Afrikaans as a teaching medium in their schools. These were schools where black children were systematically discriminated against; as Verwoerd himself put it, they were not to be educated above what was required for certain forms of labour. Thus, half educated, they were to be fed into the mines and the factories, or to the feudal farms, or if they were lucky to the civilized misery of domestic service. The government spent six times more on the education of a white child than it did on a black; the idea was to keep young blacks off the streets until they could be translated into labour units.

Like all black protest before it, the shouts of anger from the ghetto were ignored. As always the government preferred to believe that a few instigators, Communists, were stirring up an otherwise peaceable mass. But this was a different generation. Many of them looked on their parents as meek and subservient and they no longer saw the white state as omnipotent and immovable. They drew encouragement from the collapse of the Portuguese colonial regimes in Angola and Mozambique in 1975 and had become profoundly influenced by the ideas of Steve Biko's Black Consciousness movement, which preached above all the need for black self-respect. This was a generation that knew it was being groomed for third-class citizenship and was determined to resist.

All that was needed was an issue, and with predictable arrogance the government provided one . . . Afrikaans. Although spoken by millions of non-whites in rural areas, the language was regarded by the majority of township blacks as the tongue of the oppressor, the language of command and cruelty. When the government insisted against all advice that the language would be imposed, the youth in several Soweto schools determined to resist. What happened on the morning of the 16th of June is best described in the words of my friend Milton, who was there.

'That morning was the start of our half-term exams and I remember that we were just sitting there when we heard the

sound of singing in the distance. But nobody paid much
attention because there was always singing and chanting then.
As it got closer we could hear them shouting "Down with
Afrikaans" and "Away with Bantu education", and everybody started standing up and trying to look out the window.
When I got to the window I had a real fright, because outside
we could see the police with dogs and big armoured vans.
The dogs were barking a lot. The teacher told everybody to
get under the desks and she locked the door. By this time you
could hear the singing nearly right outside the school and
there was shooting in the distance somewhere. Then the
police suddenly opened fire with tear-gas and we could hear
screaming and shouting and there were people trying to get
into the school. I thought of my little brother Twoboy who
was in an infants' school across the road and I began to worry
seriously about him because the shooting was coming from
that direction. So I ran out of our school and outside there
was just chaos, complete chaos. The police dogs were attacking people and there were clouds of tear-gas, so I stayed to the
back of the crowd and tried to dodge across the street and
keep away from the police. On the way I met this kid
Mayibuswe whom I knew and he was carrying the body of a
boy and he was crying. I asked him what was going on and
he told me to run away because they were killing people.
The boy he was carrying was called Hector Petersen and
somewhere up the road a photographer took a picture of
Johannes carrying Hector. The photograph became very
famous later because Hector was the first person to be killed
in the riots. When I got to Twoboy's school they told me
that a teacher had taken him home. Now when I got back on
to the street it was hard to see because there were cars on fire
and there was still the tear-gas and a lot of shooting going on.
Somehow I got home, but on the way I saw a white
policeman being pushed into a bin by some kids. I think he

must have been dead because his teeth were on the ground all over the place and he wasn't making any sound at all. That night was really crazy, full of shooting and screaming and cars being stoned. By the time the weekend came my father decided we had to get out, myself and Twoboy, and so he took us to the Swaziland border and sent us to our relatives up there. My cousins were sent to Mozambique but they never came back to live here. I came after about two months when things had quietened down. But this whole thing was like something we had never seen before, taking on the police like that and fighting back. It was bad to see the loss of life but for the first time people of my age felt like the whites were not supermen and that blacks could stand up on their own two feet.'

The sleeping giant of young black anger had been awakened and the growth of a militant youth culture assured. This was not a revolution of well-educated college students but of children who ranged in age from eight to eighteen. It was an uprising characterized by the fierce depth of the anger and the absence of anything remotely resembling a democratic framework within which the feelings of rage could be expressed. An era of street politics was born that was to survive the huge police crackdown. The streets may have seemed quiet in the years that followed, but the bitterness simmered. More importantly, those who had tasted the power of mass protest were not about to abandon hope and sink into despair as previous generations had done. Their protest had drawn world condemnation on the government and had given birth to a new breed of highly politicized youth. In the aftermath of the riots those who had survived the trigger-happy police and who had not fled into exile regrouped and bided their time. The moment of truth eventually came in 1983 when again the government provided the touch-paper.

The Prime Minister, P.W. Botha, had begun tentative

steps towards reforming apartheid by proposing the establishment of a tricameral parliament with separate houses for whites, Indians and coloureds. Blacks, however, were excluded. A coalition of anti-apartheid groups came together under the banner of the United Democratic Front (UDF) and launched a vigorous campaign against the new constitution. The familiar cycle of South African race politics began: huge demonstrations met with tough police crackdowns. However, this new wave of black protestors didn't retreat into sullen silence when they were hit on the head. The demonstrations grew bigger and before long the country was in a state of chaos, with rioting and attacks on municipal buildings and the first appearance of automatic weapons in the townships.

If the events of 1976 were to lay the basis for an enduring militancy, the era that saw the flowering of youth dominance was the eighties. To try and understand the passion that gripped a huge portion of the generation that grew up in the wake of the Soweto Riots, it is important to recall those emergency years. At the time the securocrats in the Cabinet of P.W. Botha had succeeded in their battle with the reformists. To counter the growing success of anti-apartheid organizations in rendering large parts of the country ungovernable, Botha came down hard. He made his move, rather ironically, on the tenth anniversary of the Soweto Riots. Fearing that commemorative marches might lead to a major outbreak of violence directed against state institutions, the Prime Minister declared a state of emergency. Under the terms of the emergency legislation, police could detain anybody they suspected of promoting violence or plotting the overthrow of the state. The move was backed up by sweeping censorship, which banned any reporting of security-force activity. Thus, when the waves of detentions began, the critical voice of the liberal press and the world's television cameras were forbidden to report them.

I was one of a few people fortunate to be able to report what was happening without having to obey these strictures. I flew into South Africa posing as a civil servant; not a total fabrication, as I was at the time working for Ireland's national broadcasting service. The journey involved some hair-raising escapades: lying on the back floor of a car while travelling to visit escaped activists in safe houses; donning an Irish priest's roman collar to enter the townships; interviewing a Cabinet minister who simply assumed my credentials were in order. In retrospect these activities seem almost childishly surreptitious, but in the atmosphere of fear and mistrust that prevailed they represented the only possible means to obtaining and telling the story. In the course of a week I travelled the length and breadth of the country, using Church and underground networks to make contact with those in hiding. I was not a resident correspondent, so there were none of the usual constraints that apply to journalists who must depend on the authorities for work and residence permits.

Even in the midst of the repression it was a strangely exhilarating time. Although the atmosphere was full of fear and I constantly expected to be uncovered and expelled, there was the sense that a profound moment in history had been reached. The state might have been all-powerful, capable of locking up thousands of dissidents, but there was an assuredness among those I spoke to, a belief that the white monolith was at last beginning to crack. The authorities' response to the rising unrest went beyond the declaration of emergency powers and censorship. The police fired at will into protesting crowds, while hit squads targeted and eliminated enemies of the state. With the senior leaders like Mandela, Sisulu and Tambo either in jail or in exile, previously unknown activists sprang up to organize the militant youth and the increasingly powerful black labour movement. Names like Cyril Ramaphosa, Murphy Morobe and Jay Naidoo rose to prominence on a wave of popular emotion and anger. But they were men concerned with the larger political issues, and often the task of mobilizing the mass of people to take part in demonstrations or to participate in boycotts was left to younger and less politically sophisticated individuals – the youth who, having seized the initiative at the start of the rebellion, were destined to be its footsoldiers and enforcers. They were to inflict the greatest damage, forcing the state into increasingly repressive measures and consequently increasing Pretoria's isolation from the community of nations. At the same time, however, they endured untold suffering and, in many townships, began to see themselves as lords and masters of the streets, frequently imposing their will with the use of coercion and brute force. They were encouraged by the exiled ANC leadership to make the townships ungovernable and to stage a people's war, a war that targeted anybody in their communities who could be accused of aiding the state. The category of targets widened as the months progressed: black policemen, state-sponsored local councillors, teachers and workers who refused to obey strike calls. Members of opposing political parties accused of aiding the state or of deviating from the ANC party line were also targeted and hunted down. By the time the government eventually succeeded in crushing the protests some three and a half years later, the political control of the townships had fallen into the hands of a new generation both brutalized and willing to employ brutality itself. In seeking to understand what happened to the youth, and how this directly impacted on the later cataclysm in areas like the East Rand, it is worth recalling an encounter I had on the day the state of emergency was declared.

The previous days had seen unprecedented levels of state violence directed mainly at those among the young and politically active who had evaded arrest. A social worker I had met in Soweto some years previously had heard that I was in town and telephoned to suggest a meeting. 'You must come and see what is happening to the children,' she implored, before suggesting an appointment the following morning. By the time I arrived at the rendezvous – the headquarters of the Council of Churches – the news of the state of emergency had already been broadcast. I remember that it was a bright and cold morning, and that the city had a subdued, almost funereal air. Groups of ten and more policemen walked through the streets clutching sjamboks and batons in a carefully staged show of intimidatory strength. The one visible sign of dissent was a billboard of the *Weekly Mail* newspaper near Johannesburg Railway Station that declared in massive bold type: THE RULE OF THE BIG STICK IS HERE. Inside the newspaper itself were several empty spaces – left thus because the *Weekly Mail*, like all others, was prevented from carrying reports on security-force actions. Among these actions was the detention of thousands of people in overnight raids. Even the vaguest connection with the anti-apartheid struggle was justification for arrest and detention, often in solitary confinement.

The atmosphere inside Khotso House was busy, almost frantic, in marked contrast to the air of paralysis and gloom outside. Church workers bustled from office to office gathering files, telephones rang incessantly, and groups of people, mainly women, arrived in a constant stream from the townships. There were mothers searching for missing children, activists fearing they might be next on the arrest list, some just released and afraid to return home. Once inside I was shown upstairs and told to wait outside the offices of a group helping the victims of state violence. The corridor was packed with people waiting to see the social workers who were working around the clock. The sounds of that morning have remained with me: the low growl of delivery trucks rolling up to the stores that lined the opposite side of the street, the sound of someone shouting or a car horn blaring, black voices raised in argument or salutation on the street.

And then, from a little room at the end of the corridor, there came what I can only describe now as a low keening noise, like that made by an animal that has been badly beaten or that has lost one of its offspring. Hovering just below this sound was the voice of a woman, slow and reassuring. After about ten minutes the keening stopped and there was only the sound of the woman speaking. She was making a phone call and her tone had become businesslike and efficient. When the door opened two boys emerged. Neither was more than fifteen years old. They lurched through the doorway, one holding the other upright and dragging him the few short yards across the corridor to a seat. As they walked, I could see that the wounded boy had a heavily bleeding thigh. Little spots of blood stained the floor where he and his friend had momentarily been standing. The wounded boy's face was puffed and distorted from crying. Now, as he sat among us, the boy seemed overcome by embarrassment, aware that we had heard his crying in the little room. He turned in towards the shoulder of his friend and was silent. The friend caught my eye and made a tentative gesture of smoking with his hand. I produced a packet of twenty and handed them to him. I asked him what had happened to his friend. In a slow, matter-of-fact way he began to recite the story of what had taken place the previous day.

They had been taking part in a march organized by the UDF in a large industrial township, about twenty miles south of Johannesburg. The demonstration had been banned by police, and the two teenagers knew they were taking a chance by joining the ranks of singing and ululating young men and women. As the march rounded a corner near the police station, the crowd was confronted by two lines of policemen standing across the road, blocking the route to the station. The two sides eyed each other warily. A police commander came to the front of the crowd and, lifting a loudspeaker to his lips, gave the demonstrators five minutes to disperse. But they were defiant and sat down in the road, chanting freedom songs. Within minutes the roadway was a storm of tear-gas and rubber bullets. As the crowd turned and began to run away, the police opened fire with shotguns. The two friends jumped over a fence and hid at the rear of a house. But after what seemed like a matter of a few seconds they heard a rough voice calling out to them in Afrikaans to leave the building with their hands up. Neither of them believed the reassurances, but they decided to go and face the danger rather than wait for it to come to them.

But the young policeman was as good as his word. They were not shot but instead were thrown into the back of a Land Rover and taken to a police barracks. Like most police stations in the townships the holding centre was a place black people entered with something approaching a feeling of blank terror. You could die there and nobody would be able to do anything about it. Your obituary would be a five-line statement saying you had tried to escape from custody or had resisted arrest. Scores of detainees had gone to death this way and their killers were still serving officers. The youngsters were pushed into a cell and told to keep quiet.

After a five-minute wait the nightmare began. The older of the two – the one who had asked me for cigarettes – was hauled out by the hair and shoved along the corridor. The policeman laughed and told him he was being taken to the truth room. As he walked along the corridor, he caught a glimpse of a naked handcuffed man sitting over a bowl of bloodied water in a small room. The man caught his eye but looked away quickly when he saw the accompanying police-man. The boy realized that he had seen a large gash across the man's forehead. At the end of the corridor he was pushed from behind into a room where another policeman with rolled-up sleeves sat waiting behind a table. This officer smiled, stood up and extended his hand. Tentatively the boy extended his shaking right hand. The detective grasped it and with a powerful wrenching motion hauled the boy across the desk. What followed he remembered only as a series of unending kicks and blows backed up by a chorus of swear words, among which 'kaffir' was the most often repeated. It stopped with a suddenness that accentuated the terror. If they had finished with the beating, what might follow? In his mind he imagined the electric shocks or, worse, the transfer to John Vorster Square and the possibility of an accidental fall from the tenth floor. The policemen had decided to have a smoke and they told him to stay on the floor and lie flat on his back. He did as he was told, from time to time glancing up at his tormentors as they lit and then smoked their cigarettes. He noticed that the smiling detective had a line of spittle, thick and white, running down the left side of his chin. They finished their cigarettes and then ordered the prisoner to get up. He dragged himself up, aching terribly now and experiencing a fierce thirst. The policemen pulled him out of the room and shoved him back into the cell. They had not asked him a single question.

His friend was next. But he was determined not to go quietly. As the first policeman hauled him out, he began to shout and scream and call for help. This was a foolish move. The policeman was infuriated and started laying into his prisoner there and then in the hallway. The smiling one joined him and in full view of the cells they punched, kicked and spat. Still their victim would not shut up and take his hiding. They wanted him to be an obedient kaffir. They told him this. Exasperated now, the smiling one called out to the station's chief dog-handler: 'Hey, man, where is the bloody dog? I need it here, now now man.' The boy inside the cell realized to his horror what was happening but understood that to protest would be to invite the same treatment for himself. He heard the scratching of paws against the hall door and the deep chesty bark of the dog. The door opened and a fully grown Alsatian bounded into the hallway. The smiling one grabbed the dog by its leash and swung it in the direction of the boy on the ground. His friend inside the cell closed his eyes. What he told me now was the picture composite of the sounds he had heard: wild screaming, the guttural savagery of the dog biting, and worst of all the laughter of two men wearing the uniform of the South African police.

After allowing the dog to savage the boy for a few minutes the policemen seemed to tire of their sport or perhaps became fearful that the death from dog bites of a young prisoner might be hard to explain. The youngster, who was by now a bloodied mess, was dragged back into the cell. He passed out on the floor. Throughout the long night his friend remained awake. He wanted to sleep but there was too much commotion in the cells. Men cried out in the night. But the white voices tormenting them had changed. His own interrogators had presumably finished their shift and gone home to their wives and families. In the morning both of them, bloody and bruised, were set free with a warning from the station commander to stay out of trouble. He did not ask them about their wounds.

Now only hours after their release the older boy told me they were determined to go into exile and return as guerrillas so that they could avenge their treatment at the hands of the security police. It was not a political argument but the simple logic of children to whom a great wrong had been done. They had one aim now and that was to avenge their humiliation. What they had experienced was powerlessness and fear of a kind that would have seriously traumatized any adult.

The boy talking to me had determined that he would return the hurt and the fear one hundredfold when he had the chance.

I do not know what happened to the two boys. My last sight was of them lurching down the hall, the injured one leaning on the shoulder of his friend. They were hoping to make a long journey and join the ANC, perhaps in Tanzania or Angola or Zambia if they could evade the security forces and the legions of informers who infested the underground. However far they travelled, to whatever camp or hide-out, it could never equal the inner distance, the journey from child to scarred victim, that both had made in the cells of the holding centre.

I have thought of these two many times in the intervening years. I have searched them out among the angry crowds on the streets of Sebokeng and Katlehong and other townships. Perhaps they did return, perhaps they never left. They may have grown up into revolutionaries or faded out of the struggle. They might be dead. Their faces have drifted into soft focus with the years, and I can see them clearly now only in the faces of other desperate boys and girls who learned the same simple lesson from the state. It said, embrace the strong arm, the flashing knife, the burning tyre. He who is the strongest and most ruthless will ultimately triumph.

With their leaders in jail or in exile, many youngsters found themselves cast into roles of command for which they had no training or preparation. The vacuum of leadership brought about by the policy of locking up the brightest figures in the movement was being filled by young men and women who at best had limited political consciousness. They knew that they were angry and wronged but, denied their leaders and the stabilizing power of organized and disciplined protest, they could only drift deeper into an anarchic mess. Unable ultimately to bring the government down yet tasting a limited form of power on the streets, many of the youths became oppressors of their own people.

At times the street committees behaved like the special courts of the French Revolution. The merest suspicion of collaboration was enough to send a man or woman to a fiery death. It mattered little that the suspicions may have been planted by somebody with a grudge against the accused, or that the police had deliberately compromised the victim by spreading rumours or constantly visiting his house. In the atmosphere of mistrust and fear that infected the townships not even the loudest voice could triumph over the lost children and their necklaces.

Maki Skhosana, a name lost in history, became one of their earliest victims. Her death in front of the world's television cameras was a stark illustration of the madness that was consuming the young. She lived in the township of Duduza on the East Rand, near the white dormitory town of Nigel. It is a bleak place, bitterly cold and dusty in the winter, suffocatingly hot in the summer. Maki worked as a domestic for a white family in Nigel, but that was not what made her suspect in the eyes of some of Duduza's residents. Her real mistake was to be the girlfriend of a black policeman while at the same time moving in anti-apartheid circles in the township. The atmosphere between police and residents was one of absolute mistrust. In four months of violence involving the police or their local agents twenty residents had been killed. The latest deaths of four UDF activists at the hands of the police had driven the level of suspicion into the fever zone. The mass funeral of the four in Duduza was not a safe place for a policeman's girlfriend to be. But Maki Skhosana knew the deceased and she had a naïve belief that by wearing a UDF T-shirt and joining in the singing of freedom songs she could become part of the funeral crowd and nothing more. A friend of mine, Reuters cameraman Geoff Chilton, recorded what happened. Even now, years later, his voice falters when he describes the death of Maki Skhosana.

'By the time we arrived at the cemetery Archbishop Tutu was already leading the prayers and singing for the dead. We were late so we tried to make our way pretty quickly across to the gates of the cemetery to get a good vantage point to film the coffins and the speeches. In those days the police also tended to shoot at funeral crowds and fire tear-gas so we were keeping a watch-out for any action on the edges of the crowd. That's when we heard this shouting sound, a lot of people shouting, and we looked over to the left of the cemetery and saw this big crowd in a circle. It looked as if they were surrounding someone. Then this man came out of the crowd and he seemed a bit pissed because I could smell the drink on his breath. He said to us, "Come, you must film this, you must film it."

'We didn't really know what was happening so we followed him through and he used his arms to push the crowd back and let us through. I was just looking through the lens and filming as I went along so there was a certain detachment on my part. The sound recordist who was with me was keeping an eye on things. Then all of a sudden we got to the centre of the crowd, the last people got out of the way and we saw her. She was just sitting there and her hair and back were on fire. All she had on was a T-shirt, it was a UDF T-shirt, and her clothes on the bottom half of her body were gone. I will always remember her trying to use her hands to cover up her genitals, even when they were kicking her and battering her head, it was the need to have some dignity that seemed to possess her. She was sitting on her haunches and it seemed like people were taking turns to lay into her. One guy came up and kicked her on the head and she fell to one side, and as she was getting up a woman came in and hit her on the other side of the head. She was on fire all during this.

Other people hit her with a hosepipe and an iron bar. What was strange is that I don't remember her making a single sound through all of this. Like if you or me were on fire and being battered I think we might be screaming, but she was totally quiet.

'The crowd was shouting like crazy, calling her *impimpi*, which means informer. They were full of hatred, I don't think I have ever experienced such hatred in a group of people. But as for her it was like she knew she was finished and had just made up her mind to accept it. As they were closing in on her, the man who had brought us in said we should leave as the crowd might turn on us next. There was nothing we could have done to save her without getting killed ourselves and we wanted to live. When you see that happening to someone you want to live very badly indeed. So we walked slowly out of the crowd trying not to get ourselves noticed and on the way we came across two people carrying a huge boulder between them. They disappeared into the crowd and a few minutes later there was this huge cheer. I think they dropped it on to her head. That night I got really drunk but it didn't get her out of my mind. For months afterwards I had nightmares about her.'

Another eyewitness account reveals that after Geoff had left the scene Maki was draped with a tyre into which a youth poured petrol. He lit a match and completed the task of necklacing. As she lay on the ground, the upper half of her body enveloped in flame, somebody in the crowd produced a bottle and shoved it into her vagina. In this way Maki Skhosana died, surrounded by a crowd that had placed the crushing burden of its rage and suspicion on her innocent shoulders. Eleven people appeared in court in connection with the killing and three were eventually convicted. They were all young, all unemployed and few had any clear political consciousness. They were part of a large angry crowd who lived in a township that had been destabilized and brutalized by months of violence and they needed someone to blame. White policemen were not in the habit of handing themselves over to the township crowds, so the Duduza mob sought a victim from within its own ranks. Maki Skhosana was one of the earliest victims. Thousands have followed in her wake.

Throughout the eighties and nineties local toughs infiltrated the ranks of the comrades using the cloak of political action to rob and murder with impunity. They earned for themselves the sobriquet *comtsotsi*, a blend of 'comrade' and the local word for gangster, *tsotsi*. The rise of the criminal subculture in tandem with the political unrest was inevitable, given the conditions of desperate poverty that existed in most townships. Those who involved themselves in the struggle or who were swept along by it invariably came from miserable circumstances. If they were lucky they lived in two-roomed boxlike houses, crammed in with numerous brothers and sisters and uncles and aunts. The unlucky lived in the tin shacks that spread like a grey smear as far as the horizon in places like Katlehong, Crossroads, Soweto and countless other urban slums. With reality such an unattractive proposition they lived the fantasy of a liberation war, using stones and burning tyres as their weapons. Those who saw the struggle as a meal ticket or the vehicle for personal power revelled in the chaotic atmosphere of the time. There were marches to organize, stay-aways and school boycotts to enforce and for the gangsters rich pickings to be had from those they terrified and intimidated in the name of freedom.

The schools were emptied in a campaign of boycotts, with children mouthing slogans that preached their own disempowerment: 'Liberation before education,' they called out, sweeping aside the restraining hands of their parents. I interviewed one resident of Sebokeng at the time who described how he lived in fear of his son: 'He looks at me with . . . you know, a kind of contempt in his eyes. He thinks me and my generation are weak, that we just let them walk all over us. But you know, I think he will learn too . . . only maybe they won't be as easy with them as they were with us. Maybe they will just kill him.' Other adults found themselves confronted on their way home from work and beaten for disobeying the order to strike, or women would have their shopping emptied and cooking oil forced down their throats because they failed to observe a boycott of white shops. Anybody who condemned such tactics could find him or herself drenched in petrol and staring at a lighted match in the quivering hand of some teenage Robespierre.

The adults I met and interviewed during those years were terrified to take a stand against the mobs. 'It just isn't worth the risk. They wouldn't listen and would probably end up killing you just because you spoke out,' the man from Sebokeng told me. The struggle against the apartheid state demanded, above all, a commitment to the political orthodoxy as defined by the street committees. To diverge or dispute was to betray. For a generation that had witnessed the destruction of free speech and the ruthless demolition of individual liberty by the state, it was the supreme but unrecognized irony: out of the ashes of their struggle was forming an ugly dictatorship of thought and behaviour. The apartheid terror had begun to breed a new regime of fear and violence. It became impossible to escape the conclusion that for many of the youths it had become as easy to kill as it was to allow life to continue. The flaming body writhing on the ground surrounded by laughing teenagers replaced the trigger-happy policeman as the trademark image of South Africa.

Rent boycotts spread from one township to another, and, as they did, the already meagre services dwindled away to nothing. The piles of rubbish grew higher on the streets of many townships. Water and electricity cut-offs became an accepted if infuriating fact of life. The lords of power in Pretoria cracked down even harder, locking up more children and spurning attempts at mediation and negotiations with real black leaders. The statistics from the period are a sad tabulation of official cruelty. At the end of 1985 more than 2,000 children under the age of fifteen were being detained in terms of security legislation. By the middle of the following year the figure had doubled. A study carried out among 131 child detainees details the kind of treatment suffered by the young in police custody. Consider this stark litany: 34 per cent detained in solitary confinement; 72 per cent suffered physical abuse; 25 per cent experienced attempted suffocation; and 14 per cent received electric shocks. How much promise and innocence was destroyed in those lost years we will never know. The drawings of young children made during that era reflect the terrible burden being imposed on youth consciousness. In Alexandra township, north of Johannesburg, 70 per cent of children who were asked to make drawings depicted scenes of army and police violence. From the hands of babes came truths that no political speech could ever convey. The figures in these drawings are the basic, linear shapes drawn by children the world over. There are stick people with unlikely squiggles of hair, square blocks of houses with trails of smoke rising from oversized chimneys. But give these pictures more than a passing glance and you will notice that the figures carry knives and guns. You will see that the smoke from the chimney is really only part of a fire that is consuming the house. Place any selection of these paintings together and you have a mosaic of lost innocence. Children were beaten, shot and abandoned, trapped between the competing pressures of white supremacy and black liberation.

The saddest statistics to emerge from this era of militancy and repression came at the beginning of the new decade, at a time when black leaders like Nelson Mandela were free and the prospect of a non-racial democracy began to take on the character of reality. Instead of a youth population that was being groomed to take over the leadership of Africa's one developed economy, the 1991 matriculation exams revealed an educational tragedy. The pass rates told their own peculiarly South African story: whites, 96 per cent; Indians, 95 per cent; coloureds, 83 per cent; and blacks, 41 per cent. It was even worse at primary level, where only 39 per cent of African children managed to secure a pass grade. I have always mistrusted statistics. They are too sterile, too cold a way of portraying the insanities and cruelties of man. But in South Africa the figures that emerged every year from the painstaking research of the Institute of Race Relations told more about the waste of human spirit and resources under apartheid than any number of angry speeches. Consider the mad mathematics of a system that provided for fourteen different education departments: a department for urban blacks, a department in each of the ten nominally independent homelands, a department each for whites, coloureds and Indians.

Of course to a state that based its existence on the proposition that South Africa was ultimately a white republic with non-white satellites, this kind of duplication made perfect sense. It was also a recipe for monstrous waste and was calculated to protect and promote the white elite at the expense of the black majority. In Nelson Mandela's first year of freedom the state still spent four times more on the education of white children than it did on blacks. There was a belated attempt to inject some justice into the equation. The scrapping of the apartheid education system was announced, more funds were to be diverted to black education and multi-racial schools were to be established as a matter of priority. But black children did not flock to white schools.

73

By the beginning of 1992 only 7,000 black children had been admitted to previously all-white schools. There were still 130,00 empty desks waiting for township children by the end of the year.

For a black boy or girl to enter a white school involved a huge leap of the imagination. To children raised in the highly introspective world of the townships, and who were burdened with deep-rooted feelings of inferiority, entering a school where the overlord class was in the majority was daunting, to say the least. The economic factor was also a major disincentive. Thanks to apartheid most black children lived miles away from the white suburbs where the schools were situated. Getting there and back meant an extra drain on already overstretched household budgets. But even if black children were able or willing to enrol in white schools, the scale of disadvantage, the numbers of illiterate and badly educated children, far outweighed what the state was offering by way of redress. The damage was done. To the 60 per cent of black children who did not pass their matriculation exams, the changes came too late to make any difference.

Township schools were being crucified by a combination of structural discrimination, physical decay and anarchic youth. The physical comparison with the average white school defied belief. A white school had desks in the classrooms, it had functioning toilets, and it was not subject to electricity cut-offs because of rates boycotts. A white school had a swimming pool, a gym and green sportsfield maintained by black gardeners, and not a patch of dusty, glass-strewn ground. A white school had teachers who were qualified and was controlled by a headmaster, not by an ad hoc committee of young toughs. A child could go to a white school and feel sure that he or she would not be robbed, raped or even killed on the way or in the school grounds. This was not a certainty that black children enjoyed.

I had been to scores of township schools, meeting children who would have thrived in better circumstances. Most emerged from homes that were desperately poor, yet somehow managed to wear a clean school uniform every day. Given half a chance these children could have made it through their matriculation examinations. But they had nothing that even resembled half a chance. The township wars raged inside and outside their schools, the older boys organized matters so that most of the time school was closed down for one boycott or another, and there was never any money around to run the school. Without school to attend the children found their benediction in the blind struggle of the streets, or, if they were lucky, their parents found a place in one of the private schools that were springing up in the centre of Johannesburg.

There is no equality of blame when one tries to analyse what happened to the youth in those terrible years. The architects of apartheid who arrogantly clung to the past stand out first and foremost as the guilty parties. At a time when they could have negotiated they chose instead to blunder on, the bullying figure of P.W. Botha wagging his finger at the world when he should have been talking to Nelson Mandela. To compound the errors of the past the government went out of its way to lock up and suppress the leadership of the movements that emerged in the 1980s. These were the only structures that might have channelled the anger of the youth and prevented it from becoming the self-destructive force into which it evolved.

But at least some of the responsibility for what happened to the youth must lie with the political organizations which, once they had caught up with the rebellion, began to encourage the principle of ungovernability. Remember Winnie Mandela clutching a box of matches and telling a cheering crowd that 'together, hand in hand with our sticks and our matches, with our necklaces, we shall liberate this country'. At the time she was probably the most influential internal leader of the liberation movement, a woman whose words were taken seriously and literally. On the crackling distant voice of Radio Freedom, the ANC urged the youth towards ever greater militancy, calling for a struggle that would target all 'puppets of the regime'. The black journalist Noma-vende Mathiane, a resident of Soweto, produced a notable document of the era, *Diary of Troubled Times*. She wrote:

> Political organizations have created monsters they cannot control. In the interests of mobilization they gave the children the power to disrupt life – they used them to enforce boycotts, work stay-aways, etc., etc., and having tasted that power they are not about to give it up ... They were faced with a tough world where the game was always played according to the white man's rules. If the white man had to destroy to survive, to stave off whatever bleak future the black youth seemed to be orchestrating for him, he used violence to try and stop it. And the children learned to retaliate with violence.

The youth were romanticized in popular mythology to a dangerous degree and their angry revolutionary voices were devoured by a media that saw them as the harbingers of a South African apocalypse. The photographic images of a land in flames seemed to foreshadow the imminent collapse of the apartheid order. But the state was not on the verge of collapse. In truth while the youth had shaken the government they had come nowhere near destroying it. The damage done to their own psychology in the service of that struggle was immeasurable. It was the ultimate ironic triumph of apartheid that it forced so many young people into a self-consuming madness. The political scientist Jeremy Seekings, in his book *Heroes or Villains*, offers a clear-sighted analysis of the traumatic changes experienced by the youth population: 'This was a period when there was widespread celebration of violence and machismo . . . the cause of liberation through struggle could be furthered by diverse people in disparate ways, but some of these people and methods repeatedly threatened to turn against the community rather than the state.' In describing what has happened to the youth it is all too easy to lapse into despair, and imagine a future that is entirely circumscribed by ignorance and violence. Certainly the statistical information available suggests a vast body of marginalized people for whom the idea of taking their places as wage-earning, law-abiding citizens of a civil society is impossibly remote. But to despair is to miss the other essential part of the South African equation: the irresistible force for hope even in the midst of supreme desolation. It is a universal truth that even in the great wastelands of defeat and repression there is a voice that whispers the survival of possibility, a voice that cannot be counted on to fade away or to accept the permanence of any misery.

This is a verity apparent to anyone who has traversed the endless squatter camps and townships of South Africa. It can be found any day or night of the week in filthy shacks where mothers scrub and iron school uniforms, in the tired gait of small children who walk for miles to get to schools in the white suburbs, in the faces of domestic workers who devote their nights and part of their tiny salaries to learning English in church and community halls. So often, in the middle of the endless trauma that accompanied the end of white rule, I had reason to celebrate these needlepoints of light that speared holes through the canvas of gloom. Alan Paton called such defiance in the face of gloom the revelation of 'comfort in desolation', and I would be guilty of a gross betrayal if I did not admit to the sustaining power of hope for millions of South Africans. In many cases it was the effort of one or two

77

ordinary people that created the circumstances in which the odds could be challenged.

The story of Peter Kekana and his school made of chicken coops is one triumphant case in point. I found my way to Peter on a morning in midwinter, when the dry sharp wind swept clouds of brown dust along the veld, chafing the skin and covering the clothes of the walking children with a thick grimy film. The sun existed somewhere beyond the clouds of powdered dirt, and would hide there until late in the morning, when the wind subsided and the dust fell at last to ground. The school was situated on the fringes of a major squatter camp, Orange Farm, whose tin shacks were spreading south of Johannesburg into the scrub land that rolls for hundreds of miles south of the city. The traveller on the road to Bloemfontein and other points south would notice Orange Farm as a smear of grey along the hillside, a place remarkable only for the fact that each time he or she passed, the collection of shacks would have seeped even further across the landscape. There were hundreds of thousands of people living here, the overflow from the huge townships of Sebokeng, Evaton and Sharpeville, which between them made up the Vaal triangle. In the more refined language that gained currency among government officials in the post-apartheid years, Orange Farm was known not as a squatter camp but as an informal settlement. But the truth was more prosaic – a tin city like countless others where the dry ground yielded only dust in the winters and a putrid sludge in the stifling highveld summers.

When the settlement first started to grow up in the late 1980s, it suffered the same problems of crime and vandalism that plagued the great townships out of which it had originally sprung. The mass movement of people, with their overloaded vans and their endless sheets of tin and wooden staves, had been accompanied by the transfer of the social diseases that were by now endemic in the so-called formal settlements. But the women of the newly founded camp had different ideas. They began a process of weeding out the criminal elements, subjecting them first to persuasion; and when that failed they employed the traditional methods of fear and violence. When mobsters from Soweto descended on Orange Farm they were abducted and necklaced at the instigation of the women. The killings sent a chilling message along the underworld grapevine: crime in Orange Farm was a lot more trouble than it was worth. In this brutal fashion Orange Farm achieved a measure of stability, though it must be said that outsiders were often regarded with suspicion and hostility. When organizers from the predominantly white and liberal Democratic Party appeared in Orange Farm, they were terror-ized and chased out by youths claiming to represent the ANC and the Pan-Africanist Congress. Yet to those who lived there, the insularity and the sometimes brutal tactics of sections of the community were a small price to pay for peace and quiet.

On the day of my visit the camp seemed to sleep under the haze of dust. The only figures moving in the shadowland of early morning were those of children, children of all ages and sizes whose heads bobbed up and down as they traversed the veld. The car bounced over the gullies formed by the previous summer's rain, and I swerved to avoid the lines of walking youngsters who periodically appeared out of the gloom. In the midst of this waste land I could slowly begin to make out the shape of a building. It appeared small and insignificant at first, but as I approached the structure seemed to spread out on all sides. Eventually I drove into the yard, where several hundred children were playing under the watchful gaze of a young woman teacher. There was an order and discipline to this play-acting that suggested this was a school of a kind quite unlike any other I had previously encountered. Now that I was close I could see that the entire school had been constructed from old chicken runs. The windows were still the narrow slats through which countless birds being fattened for the dinner tables of Johannesburg had seen their first and last slivers of light. But for all the poverty of their construction the walls were clean and free of the ritual graffiti which swallow up the space on the walls of so many township schools. There was not a single VIVA ANC or the now familiar ONE SETTLER, ONE BULLET, nothing except the rough brushstrokes of recently applied white paint.

Inside the former chicken coops children sat with their schoolbooks perched on their knees. The school had not yet managed to raise the money needed to buy desks. It was dependent on the generosity of a local transport company for the supply of ancient bus seats; it was upon these that the children were crowded together. But, as I passed from class to class, there was no mistaking the seriousness of purpose that emanated from within. Here there were no raucous voices, no toughs shouting down the teachers. There was no fear discernible, only a healthy respect. Perhaps most striking of all was the fact that in each and every class there were pupils and teachers. The former chicken-farm school now housed 9,000 pupils and 90 teachers. By any reckoning that made the school one of the biggest in the world.

The man who ran the school, Peter Kekana, joined me half way through the tour, shaking my hand warmly and then quietly recounting his own Pauline conversion to the virtues of self-help and black empowerment. Kekana was a painfully thin man with a drawn, ascetic expression; yet when he spoke it was with a voice full of warmth and laughter. It was a voice that had lived through strange times, experienced hardships and disappointments but which lacked any trace of cynicism. Peter Kekana was a child of 1976 and had seen the revolution from the inside. As a student leader in the year of protest he had 'burned a few schools down' and taken part in the innumerable strikes and boycotts that accelerated the process of black alienation from the Bantu education system. In common with most of the activists of the period, he had been arrested and tortured by the security police. Shortly after his release, and fearing that the security police would eventually kill him, Peter fled to Botswana. He remained abroad until the release of Nelson Mandela brought a flood of political exiles back into South Africa. The man who left as a militant student leader had undergone a radical transformation during his exile years. He had gone to school in Botswana and on to university. By the time it was possible for him to return to South Africa, Peter Kekana was a qualified teacher who believed that by empowering themselves blacks could overcome their crucifying dependency on whites.

And so when he took over the headmaster's position at the chicken-farm school one of his first tasks was to gather the children into task groups to paint and decorate the outbuildings that were to be used as classrooms. 'Basically the children rebuilt these coops and turned them into classrooms and they're damn proud of it,' he told me. What Peter was doing would no doubt have had the wholehearted approval of one of his heroes – Steve Biko, who was done to death by the security police one year after the Soweto Rebellion. It was Biko after all who uttered the immortal phrase 'Black man, hold your head up high.' The message was not lost on Peter or on his young charges. The children were being taught that education was a vital prerequisite to liberation. The old militant slogan of 'liberation before education' was regarded with civilized contempt by Peter. 'I always try and look at it in terms of what I experienced. The school boycotts, the demonstrations, the police raids – all that kind of thing which disrupted normal schooling. I know that I would be a much better person today if it were not for that. It hurt me and I am determined not to allow it to happen to these kids.' For me it was hard to imagine a better kind of person than the one who was giving his mornings, noons and nights to the cause of saving thousands of children from the apartheid wilderness of illiteracy and ignorance. At the chicken-farm school there were no boycotts and no strikes, but there were political debates. There was no corporal punishment but instead a heavy emphasis on mutual respect and the rights of the individual. The preoccupation was with the possibilities of the future and not the wrongs of the past. We wandered from class to class, and each time we interrupted a lesson the children would stand up as a sign of respect before returning to their studies.

The children were not drawn just from Orange Farm. Many came from the larger townships, where violence and boycotts had reduced education to a shambles. For a Soweto child getting to the school on time meant rising at five in the morning, walking several miles to get a bus or a minibus taxi and then trekking across the veld from the highway to the chicken farm. It was a tribute to Peter's staff and the children's determination that the classrooms were packed with young faces eager for knowledge.

The chicken-farm school had large financial problems, and there were discipline problems with some older children, but by and large it represented a model of what education in South Africa could and should be. And so when a child who had no shoes, whose books were ancient and faded, stood up and told me he wanted to be a reporter like me, I was given a gift of humility more valuable than I can describe. His name was Henry and he was twelve years old. Every one of those twelve years had been spent in a shack, living among one of the world's most marginalized communities. But Henry smiled and Henry knew where he wanted to go. With Peter's encouragement the twelve-year-old had at least a fighting chance. As I said goodbye to Peter at the front gate of the school, he shook my hand warmly and in very few words explained his core philosophy: 'Everything we do here is based on the idea that you love the child. We believe that if you do that he will give you love in return. If you teach the kid violence he is going to become violent.'

It was a simple message, blindingly simple but too easily lost in the clamour of battle.

CHAPTER 3

Scatterlings

They are the scatterlings of Africa . . .
with hooded eyes and weary brow . . .
beneath a copper sun.

Johnny Clegg

The air filled with the sharp smell of burning elephant grass and I felt my eyes begin to water. On the horizon the sun withered down and out of sight, a brilliant red clouding into pink through the eternity of smoke and dust. It was the season of endless fog in the squatterland of Ivory Park, and the bright skies of northern Johannesburg were behind me, lost beyond the smoke of a thousand braziers. They flickered like the night fires of a vast army, camped against the city's walls. Around each hissing crackling fire were huddled groups of people. Some had wrapped themselves in blankets; others wore several layers of coats and shirts. Those that had neither pushed closer to the braziers and shivered. It was midwinter on the highveld and the mercury was sinking fast. By nightfall the temperatures would drop to zero and below. When you got closer to the fires it was possible to detect the sour-milk smell of old rubbish, piled and waiting for burning.

Then I heard children's voices and the tinny jangling sound of a tape-recorder. The music was coming in quick bursts and then fading, as the machine was swung to and fro. As the children came nearer, the voice of Bob Marley crooned from the recorder. He was singing, 'Get up, stand up, stand up for your rights.' The children, about twenty of them, came jogging towards me in a cloud of dust. They were stamping their feet and waving bundles of elephant grass above their heads. Each child approached the fire, placed the grass in a mound beside the rubbish, and then jogged away again. The smaller ones appeared to stagger under the weight of the thick bundles and lagged behind the others as they made their way back to the bush and the task of gathering.

I had come here in search of squatters whose homes had been bulldozed out of existence by the Transvaal Provincial Administration (TPA), a white-controlled local authority whose task is to ensure the orderly running of the province. This job has frequently entailed smashing the very disorderly and unsightly tin shacks and plastic huts of the millions of squatters who live on the fringes of Johannesburg. The white people who live in the outer suburbs are frightened of these squatter camps, for they believe them to be dens of thieves. The fear acts as a lever on the white local authority, which in turn moves against the squatters. It goes without saying that the squatters live in constant fear of the bulldozers and the white officials with their pickaxes and crowbars.

Having spent most of the day in Ivory Park, I was preparing to leave, gathering a few last impressions at the fire, when I noticed groups of people breaking away from the warmth and going into the veld with shovels and picks. Each group moved to what appeared to be preordained positions and began striking at the hard earth. The implements clanged against rocks and rasped as they tore away the soil. I watched, mesmerized, while pieces of tin and plastic and wooden staves were raised out of the ground. As more groups began to join the digging, a whole vast encampment rose up where before I had seen only waste ground and clumps of weed. Some people had a roof and walls made of tin. Others took the branches of trees and fashioned them into a wall, over which they placed sheets of plastic. An old woman stood hammering a wooden stave into the ground. Over this she placed a blanket, so that it looked like one of those tents children construct in suburban back gardens on summer afternoons. When she went to sit inside, she brushed against the stave and the tent collapsed. She began all over again, this time driving the stave deeper into the ground. The squatter city was literally growing up out of the dry veld, coaxed into life by people whose shadows worked furiously in the gathering dusk.

I noticed a woman and four young children wrestling with some sheets of plastic that flapped frantically in the breeze. The woman was carrying a baby of about six months, wrapped in a blanket and strapped to her back. My guide was a man named Justin, a community activist who represented the interests of the squatters. He had an acute sense of what attracted the attention of journalists and was so well-liked among the homeless that they invariably welcomed his guests with open hearts. Justin sensed my interest in the woman and her family and suggested that we walk over and talk to her. I followed him and listened to the now ritual explanation of my presence and intentions. 'He is here to help us, sister. Maybe if he can tell your story the bulldozer men won't come back.' The woman was heavy and the exertion with the plastic had caused a stream of perspiration to come coursing down her brow and on to her cheeks. It glistened like tears. I stood directly behind Justin, who continued with his entreaties. After being assured that I wasn't going to give her name to the TPA or the police, the woman agreed to speak. She said that I could call her Cynthia and that she was thirty-two years old. But when I stepped forward to speak the baby began to scream. They were great lung-bursting howls, and the infant began to shake and twist and turn inside the blanket. Shocked, I stepped back behind Justin and walked a few yards in the direction of the fire. The crying stopped as suddenly as it had started. I could hear Cynthia soothing the child, soft warm words that drifted in the air between us. She summoned the oldest of the children, a girl of about ten, and told her to take care of the child for a few moments. Then she told me her story.

'I am sorry, master, the baby she is afraid of the whites. When they came it was in the morning and we were still in the sleep. The dogs was barking so I went out to look, and I see the bulldozers and lots of white men with them. So they started into the shacks, pulling them everywhere. Oh, master, it was too terrible and the baby she saw all this and the white man coming to our shack as well. He was screaming at us to get out and all the children started crying and running away. They were too frightened, I tell you, and the white man called some others and they hacked down our shack with axes and sticks. The bigger children made them run away into the bush but the baby was with me and she saw everything. This baby she is afraid of the whites now, so she went crazy when you come to her.' Cynthia told me that the other children were also suspicious of whites but she had been able to explain to them that I was just a visitor to the camp. She had been squatting in Ivory Park for six months but time was running out for her and the thousand or so people who camped out each night. Soon the TPA would discover their ruse and an earth-mover would come and scoop up the hidden city. She had come to the edges of Johannesburg because she believed that her missing husband might have washed up in one of the city's townships. Cynthia had already travelled to Soweto and Alexandra, two of the biggest townships, but searching for one man in such a wilderness of people proved futile. So she went to Ivory Park because a woman from her home area in the distant drylands of the Northern Transvaal had told her there was space for putting up shacks. Her shack survived five and a half months before the demolition squad came.

As her story unfolded, I became gripped with this image of a woman, a baby and four young children trailing along the endless ribbons of road that wind around the great city. I imagined the warmth she must have felt when, after weeks of wandering, they found the camp at Ivory Park. Here the shacks may not have had water or light, but nor did they have doors that could be slammed in her face. But the few months of security for Cynthia and her children ended in one great roaring sweep across the veld by the demolition squads of the TPA. In the space of a few chaotic hours her home disappeared and her baby learned to fear the sight of a white skin. What disturbed me most was the matter-of-fact way in which she recited this tale of woe, as if poverty and loss had been implicit in her existence from the very beginning.

Leaving the camp, I saw that the dark had begun to swarm all over the veld. Cynthia produced a candle that she lit and placed in the entrance to her plastic hut. I looked back and watched the candle flicker inside the hut and the shadows play against the light. What I saw was the figure of a woman crouched over the small huddled shape of her family on a night without warmth or promise.

About a fortnight later I attended the funeral of ten people from the area who were killed by hostel dwellers. They died in what was apparently a revenge attack for the murder of a gangster who lived in the hostel and paid a percentage of his spoils to the *indunas*. There were perhaps 20,000 people, many of them carrying ANC and PAC banners, stamping their feet in the dust of an overgrown and rubbish-strewn cemetery, so that sections of the crowd were obscured by the murk that billowed upwards. I stood back from the main concentration of people and awaited the arrival of the priests and ministers who were to carry out the funeral service. A figure came towards me dressed in an ancient anorak whose fur-lined hood was tightly fastened in the manner of an eskimo. I could not make out the face until virtually the last minute, when the figure was standing in front of me and extending his hand. 'Hey, my bro ... you remember me, Ivory Park, nah?' he asked. Yes, I remembered him. He had been one of the group of youngsters who trailed in Justin's wake, like loyal courtiers, shy boys who hung upon his every word and nodded vigorously when he delivered his frequent denunciations of the government. He caught hold of my hand, shook it vigorously and asked if I had heard about Justin. I said that I had been hoping to find Justin at the funeral, because I wanted to go back to Ivory Park and spend some more time with Cynthia and her family. 'Oh, you won't be doing that now,' he said. 'Justin, he is dead. He was shot by men a week ago, through the head inside his shack they killed him.' The youngster did not know who had carried out the murder, but there were rumours about criminals who resented his attempts to organize the residents. Most of the youths who followed Justin were on the run, afraid that they would be next on the gunmen's hitlist.

What about Cynthia and her children; were they still there? The young man said that Cynthia had left Ivory Park and gone searching for her husband again, but he did not know where, because she had no forwarding address to leave behind. They had gone just after Justin's murder, for there was talk that the hostel dwellers were going to come and attack. 'It is not good for you to come now, not safe. Bad men there now and they might kill you,' he said. The boy shook my hand and then jogged away in the direction of the main group, quickly losing himself in the mass of heaving, chanting bodies.

★

In the year of liberty approximately one quarter of South Africa's population were living in squatter camps similar to Ivory Park. This meant that at least ten million people lived without a proper roof over their heads, without drinking water, electricity or sanitation. Expressed simply as statistics, these facts are perhaps easy enough to digest; when converted into real lives, lives like those of Cynthia and Justin, they become needlepoints of pain dotting the landscape of transition. The squatter camps that encircled the major cities were the logical consequence of two factors: the stupidity and impracticability of apartheid, which sought to dump people in rural areas where there was neither the agricultural nor the industrial infrastructure to cater for their needs, and the unstoppable trend towards urbanization that had been the dominant feature of social history in late twentieth-century Africa. According to the report of one eminent task force, about 75 per cent of South Africa's population will live in or near the cities by the year 2000. The flood of humanity to the cities has been largely silent. People climb on board buses, or they cram into rusted and dilapidated station-wagons piled high with luggage, to travel hundreds of miles over several days in search of an ultimately illusory place of comfort in the city.

The first-time visitor to the squatter camps will invariably come away asking how people can bear to live in such conditions, convinced that the rural areas cannot have been worse. To such a person I would recommend a journey into the heart of, say, the Transkei, largest and arguably most wretched of the so-called independent states established under Verwoerdian apartheid. I first travelled there in the early eighties and remember a journey through mist and rain along winding treacherous roads, among a population that seemed despondent and sullen. That was a time when it was still relatively safe for whites to drive on the roads of the homeland. By the turn of the decade the situation had changed dramatically. The sullenness had been transformed to outright hostility, with frequent attacks on holidaymakers and business-people who were targeted either for their money or for the colour of their skin.

In 1984, when I drove from the lush sugar plantations and hibiscus-lined roads of Southern Natal into the Transkei, I crossed from a world of relative plenty into a place of hunger. The misted land became a vast tableau of hopelessness, a penumbra out of which barefoot children drifted like ghosts with their hands outstretched. Some offered roots and rough carvings for sale: others simply begged, rubbing their stom-achs in the gesture of hunger. When I stopped at a crossroads to ask directions for Umtata, the crowd of young boys shouted 'isonka, isonka' and pointed at the back seat of my car. I looked behind and saw the remains of a sandwich I had purchased outside Durban several hours earlier. It lay half eaten, curling into dryness underneath a transparent plastic wrapping. The children were hopping up and down now, the bigger ones elbowing the smaller out of the way and demanding the sandwich for themselves. I handed the tiny fragment of food to the forest of hands that pressed through the open window. It disappeared into the hands of the biggest of the boys, who pushed the others out of the way with ease. As I drove away, the others ran after the car, shouting angrily and stooping to pick up stones. Putting my foot down hard on the accelerator, I disappeared into the mist.

Following the road to the capital Umtata, I passed through a land where the hills were shaved bare of arable soil, hills where the combined effects of overgrazing and too many seasons of planting had sucked the goodness out of the ground. The grass on these hills was sparse, like a mangy green fur upon which armies of goats loitered. There were occasional way-stations, garages and small shops, where groups of people sat staring listlessly at the rain as it washed down the hills, carrying away what was left of the good soil in long brown rivers that swept into the ditches by the roadside. And everywhere, at each small stopping point, there were the children and their forever outstretched hands. The Transkei, like most of the other homelands, was a sinkhole of neglect and corruption. By the time the ban on the ANC ended in 1990 the Transkei had rid itself of the puppet ruler installed by Pretoria and acquired a new dictator, General Bantu Holomisa. He owed his allegiance to Mandela rather than to Pretoria, but it made little difference to the thousands who still flocked out of the homeland to the cities. One quarter of the potential workforce was still unemployed; the land was still being overgrazed; the average monthly income of a Transkeian family was R100, about £20; and in the primary schools there were on average seventy-five pupils to each teacher, almost double the national average. Under such circumstances, from the vantage point of some wretched village where nothing could ever improve, it was easy to understand how the distant cities, with their factories and mines, acted like magnets for the rural poor.

The Transkei had been technically independent since 1976, although South Africa was the only country in the world to recognize this bogus state of freedom. Like the other bantustans, it had its own army and police force and rubber-stamp parliament. But in reality the homeland was simply a reservoir for abandoned humanity, the surplus above what was required to serve the factories and the farms of the white state. That this wicked farce was doomed to failure from the beginning could have been seen by anybody with a grain of common sense. In what was probably the single most important document in South African history, the report of Judge Henry Fagan dismissed the notion that Africans could be banished to remote tribal reserves and warned that complete segregation was impossible. The Fagan report was issued in February 1948.

The following May, Daniel François Malan, Minister of the Dutch Reformed Church and Leader of the National Party, was elected Prime Minister. The rest is sad history. The segregation and denial of human rights practised under the out-going Smuts regime was but a mild foretaste of the legislated denial of humanity that Malan and subsequent Nationalist prime ministers enforced. Judge Fagan's report was consigned to the scrapheap and legions of Afrikaner academics set to work to prove that total separation was not only possible but also desirable. But the concentration of wealth and industry in white areas, and the refusal of the white electorate to pay the price necessary to develop the reserves, led to millions of black people voting with their feet and heading for the cities. They faced a battery of laws designed to keep them out of white-designated zones. Policemen swooped on illegals, who were jailed and deported; the task of demolishing squatter settlements was undertaken with brutal vigour by state agencies; and communities that had been settled for generations found themselves uprooted and expelled to the reserves without any right of appeal. It is estimated that three and a half million blacks were forcibly removed. Thus, with a government that refused to recognize the rights of blacks to live in urban areas, that would not even contemplate the reality of urbanization, the townships remained woefully underdeveloped, and the squatter camps began to spread like some pernicious algae that no amount of cleansing could remove.

I always visited these camps with a certain amount of trepidation. They were dangerous places, in which the unemployment rate ranged between 50 and 80 per cent and where crime flourished among people who were at the very bottom of South Africa's scale of have-nots. So when I was approached to spend a night in the Swanieville Camp near the town of Krugersdorp, about an hour's drive from Johannesburg, I at first demurred. But the man who issued the invitation, a local civic leader, was insistent, telling me that it was something I had to experience if I wanted to know how ordinary people lived. After much persuasion I put my fears to one side and agreed to sleep in a shack belonging to the Mayor of the camp. My last visit to Swanieville had taken place in June 1991, after more than twenty residents were massacred by hostel residents from the nearby township of Kagiso. On that occasion I encountered an area that looked as if it had been struck by a hurricane. There were hacked bodies and burning shacks, people wandered about in a daze, some searching frantically for missing relatives, others trying to rescue their belongings from the fires. On the way into the camp I saw a line of refugees walking in single file, dragging bags of clothing and bed linen behind them. Some stuck their hands out and appealed for lifts; most trudged ahead as if in a trance.

Now, nearly two years later, I returned to find the shacks rebuilt and several thousand new inhabitants. Most of them were farmers from the Transkei who had fled the drought and starvation of the homeland and brought their families to Swanieville on the advice of relatives already living there. I was introduced to the Mayor, a man named George, and his wife, Alice, and a host of young children who gazed wide-eyed and astonished at the sight of a white man sitting down to drink tea in their shack. George and his family were among the oldest residents of Swanieville. They had been living in the camp for about four years. He owed his position as Mayor to his willingness to confront the local landowner and demand services like water and sewage in return for the rent that was being paid by the residents.

George explained that as his own shack was overcrowded

he had decided to billet me with a widow named Martha who lived further up the street. When I use the word 'street', I do not refer to a tarred and even thoroughfare, rather to a deeply rutted track through the mud that ran from one end of the camp to the other for a distance of about half a mile. There was the same absence of facilities that characterized almost every squatter camp in the country: no water, no sewage disposal, no electricity, no schools and no clinic. As we walked in the darkness towards Martha's shack, feral dogs lurked along the edge of the track, occasionally advancing in our direction only to be driven back by the curses and stones of George and his children. In the distance I noticed the lights of one of the West Rand goldmines twinkling high above the veld, like the beacons of a huge ship that had become wedged in pack ice. I knew that the seam of gold began somewhere near Swanieville and that far below the surface of the world on that still, starlit night men were hacking away at that fabulous vein through which the wealth of the nation flowed.

Before we reached Martha's home, George insisted that we call and speak to some of the local youth. We followed the sound of booming reggae and after a few minutes arrived at a shack that was a roughly constructed mixture of tin and plastic. The words 'VIVA HAILE SELASSIE' had been painted on the door of the shack, and the clamour of many voices rose above the music. George rapped on the wooden door, which opened immediately. A blast of hot air, in which the odours of *dagga*,* paraffin and sweat blended together, came rushing out. The boy at the door wore dreadlocks and his eyes seemed locked on to some distant vision, but he recognized George and waved us into the crowded room. 'There is

*Marijuana.

about twenty boys here. They used to be in Soweto but that got too dangerous, so they hang around here now,' George explained. Most of those in the room seemed to be between the ages of ten and sixteen. A boy sidled up beside me and asked for ten rands. He wanted it to buy schoolbooks, he said. The others erupted into loud laughter when they heard this. But the youngster persisted. Why would I not give him the money? His friends joined in and began to ask for money as well. A voice in the corner piped up. 'Get that white fucker out of here. Go on, George, take him home,' it said. 'It is wise that we should go now, otherwise there will be trouble. Don't worry about them, let's just get going,' said George.

By the time we reached Martha's place it was already well past midnight. She had divided the shack into two rooms by placing a heavy blanket across the middle of the structure, so that it formed a screen between the sleeping quarters and the living and eating area. Pictures from the pages of magazines had been pasted all over the walls to cover the grim tin. There was a calendar that dated from 1980 and a large, ancient Christmas card, on the cover of which was a single robin sitting on a snow-covered windowsill. The bird gazed forlornly through the window at a family sitting around a roaring log fire. The message said: 'Thinking of you at Christmas.' Martha and her two children were staying elsewhere that night, but before leaving she made elaborate preparations for my breakfast, showing me how to use the Primus stove to boil up water and producing bread and fruit from a plastic bag. She said she was sorry that the place was not more comfortable but assured me that the bed was solid. It had come all the way from her old home in Transkei, and she and the children were always able to sleep soundly. Martha and George and his children said goodnight and disappeared into the darkness outside.

I went behind the curtain and flopped on to the big brass bed. I noticed that it was raised high off the ground and supported by bricks: this was a fetish among many rural and urban blacks, designed to ward off the *tokoloshe*, an evil spirit that was said to lurk under beds. As I lay there, the wind came up and started to rattle the tin roof about two feet above my head; it sent cold air blasting through the gaps in the walls, and quickly turned the bedroom into a fridge. There was no way of keeping this wind out. It found its way through every tiny fissure in the walls and the roof. And so I started to shiver and twist and turn, wrapping the blankets tight around me. I got up again and started to pace around the shack in an effort to keep warm. The dogs were barking again and the reggae music still boomed from the youngsters' shack. Somewhere up the street a baby was crying; its screams rose above the other noises, and went on and on until the exhausted lungs eventually gave up and sank back into silence. A man and woman started arguing in the shack next door. He appeared to be drunk, the words twisting and falling as they came out and collided with her angry shouts. Eventually there was a crashing sound as if somebody had collapsed against a wall. The woman shrieked and a child began to scream. Angry voices in Xhosa erupted from other shacks; I presumed they were telling the fractious couple to shut up. After a few minutes the uproar died down and I could hear only the loud snoring of the man while the woman muttered to herself for several minutes before she too fell quiet.

I lay down again and drifted in and out of sleep until the first grey slivers of light appeared through the gaps in the tin walls. It was then, in the drowsy, freezing dawn, that I heard *the noise* just outside the shack. It began as a low rasping sound and gradually increased in pitch, until I became convinced that somebody was picking the lock of my car, which was parked outside. Forgetting that car thieves happily shoot anybody who disturbs them, I bounded out of bed and hauled open the door of the shack. As I turned the corner towards the car, I shouted 'Hey you!' and sprang upon the offender. To my intense relief it turned out to be a scrawny chicken that had been picking at some seeds lodged in the hub-cap. The alarmed creature fled squawking into the veld, its breakfast ruined. Turning back towards the door of the shack, I heard a male voice laughing uproariously. Across the street a man was washing in the open, splashing his upper body with soapy water, and shaking his head in amusement at the sight of a bleary-eyed white man hurling himself upon a squatter's chicken in the early dawn.

The rise in the size of the black underclass in poverty-stricken camps like Swanieville and Ivory Park was accompanied by a staggering growth in the crime rate. In the three years prior to the elections more than 50,000 people died at the hands of criminals, a figure that exceeded the combined total for the previous seven years and that dwarfed the tally for political killings. In Johannesburg by the end of 1993 an average of twenty-five cars were being hijacked every day – the statistic was more than four times the daily figure for the previous year. Although the gangs targeted black and white alike, the pickings in the white suburbs were generally far richer and it was here that the fear was most acute. The newspapers fed the burgeoning paranoia of the suburbs with headlines that screamed details of each fresh urban slaughter. There were innumerable stories of gruesome deaths: people shot at traffic lights for their cars, others gunned down for the sake of a few pounds, or because they didn't move quickly enough to hand over their wallets or purses, women gang-raped in front of their families and then murdered; in the rural areas elderly couples were picked off on their isolated farms, their screams lost in the vastness of the landscape.

The tales of criminal terror had an unmistakable subtext: *they, them* were on the move; streaming out of the squatter camps and into the suburbs, climbing over walls and into bedrooms with their knives and guns, murder and violation on their lips. At virtually ever dinner party I attended in the first twelve months of my stay in South Africa the talk sooner or later fell to crime and discussions about the best armed-response companies, the strongest burglar bars and almost inevitably, whether it was wise to keep a gun or not. In a white community of less than five million there were three million registered firearms. Many thousands more un-licensed weapons were in circulation. I was sucked into this tunnel of fear and within weeks had erected steel gates in our sleeping area, ordered a new alarm system and placed bars on the windows of the house. Not being able to imagine myself shooting another human being, I decided against purchasing a gun but instead opted for two Labradors, whose ferocious barking belied their gentle natures. You did not have to be resident in the suburbs for very long before learning to fear the approach of an unknown black face at the gate, or twitching awake in the dead of night because there were sounds in the garden. Sometimes a frightened neighbour, convinced that some malign presence was lurking in his garden, would fire a shot into the darkness. All along the road I would imagine others reaching for their weapons as the sound punctured the stillness. The barking of Rottweilers, Dobermanns, Great Danes and my own Labradors would then erupt like a chorus from the gates of hell. In the leafy northern suburbs the price of privilege was eternal vigilance. The poet Shabbir Banoobhai described this suburban fear with immaculate precision in his work 'The Border'.

The border
is as far
as the black man
who walks alongside you
as secure
as your door
against the unwanted knock.

The insidious dread was the direct consequence of a society in which 80 per cent of the wealth was held by just 10 per cent of the population, where the culture of violence and the easy supply of guns had almost obliterated the value of human life, and where the vast battalions of the poor were able to see the other world but enter it only as servants or thieves. To them even the poorest white suburb represented a place of riches, when compared to the misery of the camps. The criminal gangs struck everywhere and fear followed like a plague in their wake. It prompted the richer whites to wonder about their future in the country and consider the possibility of emigration to Australia, England or Canada. For the poor whites whose suburbs were frequently closest to the townships there was no question of being able to leave the country. And it was among this disillusioned class of people that the corrosive effect of the terror was frequently experienced at its most acute.

It is winter in South Africa and the temperatures are dropping fast across the country. In the Cape the first snows have fallen on the mountains at Ceres. Soon the fruitlands and the vineyards will fall silent in this first cold brightness of the season. In the Free State there are thick crusts of ice on the farm dams, and the farm families are gathering in wood and loading extra blankets on to the beds. Up in Johannesburg we are all feeling the chill. The houses of the white suburbs were not built for this cold; they were constructed in the belief that if winter were to be ignored it would quietly disappear and give way once again to the hot, drowsy days of the summer. The cold brings with it force-fields of static. Touch a door, another person, even the curtains, and you feel small electric shocks. Your skin becomes dry and the coldsore viruses that have lain dormant all summer come bursting through the soft membrane of the lips. The rain will probably not appear for another three months. Soon the South African Broadcasting Corporation will be carrying appeals for water conservation. Drought days are here.

But in this huge country it is possible to find summer even in the heart of winter. And that is precisely what the poor whites do. They flock south to the still warm beaches of Durban to winter out. They sleep on the promenade below the palm trees or on the sand where the Indian Ocean rolls in. These are people who in the old days might have come to Durban in the family car, heading for one of the hundreds of guesthouses and hotels that give the city the appearance of a tropical Blackpool or Atlantic City. But now only the better-off whites can afford such holidays. In the days of Verwoerd and Vorster the poor whites would have gone for a fortnight or at the very least a long weekend. They would have found beaches reserved for their exclusive use and neat signs excluding their despised black and brown fellow countrymen from nearly every restaurant and bar. In those long years of apartheid they – the Afrikaner working class – were the chosen ones.

It mattered little whether you were intelligent or stupid, whether you flunked out of school early or became a professor. If you were white and spoke Afrikaans you possessed a passport to plenty. Job reservation ensured that the best jobs in the mines and industry went to whites. The white unions were among the most ardent proponents of racism. They knew a meal ticket when they saw one and fought to ensure that no black came within spitting distance of a white in terms of pay and conditions.

Unless you were a drunk, a habitual criminal or a complete spendthrift it was hard to go too far wrong. The blacks were kept in *place by a ruthless security force and the few incursions made by ANC guerrillas were easily countered by the police and army. Vast white suburbs grew up around Johannesburg and Pretoria. Their inhabitants worked through the week, mostly giving orders, always with a black man near by to do the real physical grind; and then at the weekends came the rugby and the* braaivleis *and the beer and the talk of politics. To outsiders such lives might have seemed dull. But for the working-class whites it had the singular blessing of certainty. After all, Verwoerd had told them it would always be like this: they would have their place in the sun, and the black man would have his, and never the twain should meet. As their part of the bargain they would give up two years of their lives to the army and their sons would do exactly the same. They would also report for camps every year and if needed fight on the border to contain the threat of Communist subversion from the north.*

But when the National Party began to nudge furtively away from absolute apartheid, the commitment to separate nation states, the blue-collar Afrikaner sensed betrayal. The golden thread from which they had hung, suspended above the mass of black South Africans, was beginning to unravel, and with each reform they seemed to come nearer and nearer to that immensity of blackness, that noisy clamouring scrum that threatened their entire existence. They saw the Soweto Riots come and go and waited nervously for the next upheaval and the next cave-in by the Nationalists. For a while it looked to them as if P.W. Botha might hold the pass. They applauded his crackdowns and began to feel secure again. But P.W. went and F.W. de Klerk came in and there was an end of the story. After that it was surrender, surrender, surrender. The black trade unions were the real industrial power now and all the huffing and puffing of their own union leaders could not hide the fact. They began to hear names like Ramaphosa and Naidoo and Molefe more often on the radio. Every day there was news of some new concession. The 'terrorist' Mandela walked free from jail and the ANC comrades were allowed to march in the streets in their thousands. There were strikes and the ANC and Inkatha were at each other's throats. Some of them woke up to find that Indian and even black families were moving into the neighbourhood and, although they threatened action, most of them just sat silently and watched the world they knew and loved disappear.

Worst of all their jobs began to vanish. Retrenchment became a byword in the poor white suburbs. The mines and the big state corporations began to lay off their expensive white workers. It hit blacks badly too but somehow the shame of a lost job did not seem to bite as deeply in the townships and the squatter camps. In black South Africa there was a legacy of struggle and no expectation that the world owed you a living.

These days you can see the poor whites riding the intercity coaches or thumbing lifts to Durban as they migrate out of the winter. A voice seems to say to them: Go to the coast, Afrikaner, and you will find warm currents of air to chase away the bad dreams that torment your days. But there is nothing at the coast. When you walk on the promenade you can see them rooting in the rubbish bins or outside the bars begging for a few cents. They are lost and they know it. In the city of Durban they have set up a refuge centre for the destitute, like dozens of others across the country. It is called the Ark and is run by a group of Born Again Christians. They are serious and devout people and not given to discussing politics. But when I arrive a woman who hands out bedding and food at the Ark comes up and seizes my arm. 'Look at these people. They are broken. They don't know what has happened to their world. They come in here completely unable to cope and so full of shame for what has happened to them,' she says. There is a smell of disinfectant, and armies of small children in bare feet play in the dark corridors. The Christians do their best but there is a sense of profound despair.

There are blacks and coloureds here too, though not nearly as many as there are whites. I hear music coming from a hall and follow some of the residents in the direction of the sound. We find a group of about 200 people singing religious songs. It is a multi-

racial group and a coloured man on the stage is holding up a signboard with the words of hymns. The people are being told that Jesus will save them, but as I look round the room the faces seem heavy and hopeless. Most of the people here will stay for a very long time. Upstairs I find four young white men sharing a tiny room. There are personal belongings stuffed everywhere. Entire lives have been shoved into plastic bags. One of the youngsters – he is at most eighteen – tells me he left his home in Bloemfontein because he couldn't find work. But there was nothing to be had in Durban either and he had washed up here at the Ark. His name is Gert and he tells me that he does not know what to do with his life. He cannot go abroad with his South African passport and in any case his English is poor. Gert would sink without trace in any foreign city. He is an Afrikaner, born and bred, and leaving the country is simply not an option in practical or psychological terms. I ask him how he feels about sharing his life with destitute black South Africans and he thinks for a minute. 'I'll tell you something,' he says. 'There is nothing I can do about it one way or the other. But if my folks could see me they would go crazy.'

CHAPTER 4

To the Bitter End

> *This at least had to be admitted: Africa was*
> *part of them; and they were part of Africa.*
> *Such was God's will for them. Such was his*
> *purpose . . .*

W.A. de Klerk, *The Thirstland*

I crossed the Tropic of Capricorn on an afternoon heavy with
the promise of the first rains. Clouds tumbled and darkened
far above so that all around me the bushveld took on a
morbid grey colour. The noise of distant thunder, like furniture being rolled across the floor of heaven, made the leaves
of the mopane and camelthorn trees, which clung tenaciously
to the parched landscape, tremble. As I drove into the hinter-
land of the storm, the long brown scars of dried-out riverbeds
appeared, the story of the drought years carved into the
surface of the earth. Only far to the west could I see a
glimmering of light splicing its way through the great wall of
cloud. There were mountains over there, great sphinx-like
shapes that hugged the horizon, and beyond them the vast
arid plains of Botswana stretching into the endlessness of
Africa. I stopped the car and stood on the roadside to take
the air, figuring that it would be my last chance before
the storm erupted. Almost next to the highway a granite hill
rose up, huge boulder piled upon boulder, with the dark
mouths of caves beckoning in its upper reaches. The
landscape of the north is full of such curiosities; hills and
small mountains, comprised entirely of rocks, lying where

they tumbled in the lost days of the volcanic age.

The land that rolled beyond the invisible line of the Tropic was tamer in appearance now than it must have been when the wagons of the first voortrekkers rolled and groaned forward in the early months of 1836. The lion and the leopard, the herds of buffalo and elephant that roamed the sacred savannah, were gone, safe only in the make-believe Africa of the game reserves; and the bush itself, though still vast and beautiful, had surely been of wilder appearance then. No high fences, no telephone poles or electricity pylons, no tarred road; only the solitary wisp of smoke rising like a prayer from the roof of some distant farmhouse. I climbed to the top of the hill and perched on one of the smaller boulders, whose surface had been flattened by long centuries of rain. There in the stillness, with the storm in the distance, I began to imagine those old escapists with their bibles and guns, their eyes squinting in the harsh sun and flowing beards clinging like talismans to their chests. In the emptiness of the evening it was possible to imagine the creaking wagons, to hear the rough cries as the cattle were urged forward and to smell the trekker scent of oxen and woodsmoke and rough tobacco. It was to me as if the whispers of history had hidden in the spaces of the wind, waiting for the solitary traveller to give himself over to their old call.

The men and women who had carved this route north were possessed of a blind moral certainty and an acute desire to be free of the civilized corruptions of the British Empire. The trek northward was spurred by the oldest and most elemental of human desires: the need to be free, to be masters of their own destiny. As long as the land rolled ahead with no borders to restrain them, there would always be the hope of salvation. The man who perhaps best evoked the 'holy contagion' of the trekkers, the Afrikaans historian and writer W.A. de Klerk, explained the yearning for space in his novel

The Thirstland. In the book an old Boer woman explains to a stranger the reason for their wandering.

> It will be difficult to trek where there is no water and the sand is thick and the sun beats down. But this is what the Lord has called us to do. So we must trek, come what may. On the other side of the Thirstland is the land we are seeking; the good land where we shall live in peace and happiness for ever.
>
> Why? Do you ask why we trekked, Meneer? There was no other reason but that we had the feeling, the spirit of the trek, as the Lord had given it. It was always our ideal, Meneer.

The trekkers had followed this northward route under the leadership of two men, Louis Trichardt and Hans van Rensburg, at the beginning of 1836. In all about one hundred people spread out in a dozen wagons crossed the Orange River and began the trek away from the British into land that was wild and untamed. In Trichardt's diary the party is described as comprising 'seven households . . . and only nine able shots'. There is one photograph of Trichardt. The face is that of the Boer patriarch: solemn, stern and dependable. In the official histories he is recognized as the man who prepared the way for white settlement in the far north of South Africa, having escaped the Cape Colony where the British authorities had imposed a price on his head for treason. The certain cause of his departure is not known: some said he had incited a border war with the Xhosas; others that he had been found guilty of mistreating servants and stock theft. The real genesis, however, was in the desire to find a place where the *volk* could govern themselves without interference. To men like Trichardt the crown was at best meddlesome, at worst treacherous and malign, forever drawing circles around the Boers, seeking to hem them in and bind them to the Empire.

The British taxed the Boers but still expected them to provide men and horses for raids against native tribes; the British themselves dealt mercilessly with native rebellions yet forbade the Afrikaners from owning slaves; to the horror of the Afrikaners they were even prepared to allow servants to take their masters to court on charges of ill-treatment. This had already precipitated one disastrous rebellion at Slagters Nek in the Eastern Cape, and was certainly a major factor influencing those who decided to join the trek northwards. But these were secondary causes when compared to the growing fear that unless they quit the Cape the Boers would lose their cultural identity. As the Cape Colony began to prosper and develop, and as blacks began to adopt the dress and customs of the whites, the fear that they might be assimilated into the ranks of the native masses began to gnaw away at the Afrikaners, undermining their group identity. This precious sense of a people alone and special before God was still in its infancy, but in the course of the trek, with its thousand hardships and sorrows, the imperative of what the Afrikaner writer Marq de Villiers has called the *volkseie* was forged. This can best be described as the binding sense of themselves, the group cohesion that would withstand the endless trials of the undiscovered land. Piet Retief, another trek leader, in a statement issued on the eve of his joining the exodus, spoke of the *volk* being forced to take their journey in order that they might be allowed 'to govern ourselves, without interference in future'. *To govern ourselves*. The words were to echo down the years.

The Boers saw the trek as an allegory of the flight out of Egypt; the British crown symbolized the Pharaoh, and they were the Israelites whose Promised Land beckoned in the shimmering vastness of the African savannah. To people whose views were deeply rooted in the Old Testament, it was a journey heavy with biblical resonance. They were journeying through a land where the strong survived and the weak were devoured, where a man who did not deliver an eye for an eye could expect no mercy. This is not to suggest that among the ranks of these latter-day Israelites there was anything like agreement on common goals or objectives. In Trichardt's party, for example, there was repeated bickering between him and the older Hans van Rensburg, whose profligacy with ammunition during hunting expeditions enraged the trek leader. They eventually split up and went their separate ways, Van Rensburg paying dearly for the waste of ammunition when his whole party was wiped out by natives near the Limpopo River. Yet in one matter the men were agreed: that behind them lay only enslavement and the destruction of the *volk*, ahead and only ahead the mythic lands of their salvation.

Trichardt pushed on into the wilderness but failed to establish any significant settlement. Eventually, exhausted and hungry, he and a party of fifty-two trekkers and seven servants arrived in the Portuguese settlement of Lourenço Marques in April 1838. Nearly half of the party, including Trichardt, eventually died of malaria. His story underlines the great strengths and weaknesses of the Afrikaners: on the one hand a blind courage to go where others feared to tread and a capacity to endure great privation and suffering; on the other a debilitating fractiousness and a tendency to venture into places and situations that would ultimately defeat them. Trichardt's descendants were to create their own Promised Land but with an immense cost in human suffering. It was nearly five decades before the men who had drawn up the map realized this Promised Land could never be made to work. Now, as their empire began to disappear, the Afrikaners who wanted to trek on were at daggers drawn with those in their tribe who preached compromise and accommodation. As the feared black mass was preparing to wrest the country from them at the ballot box, the voices of history were calling out again: *an own land, a land where we can govern ourselves free from interference*. I had not long arrived in the town of Louis Trichardt, capital of the far north, before hearing the unyielding voices of the new escapists.

The town lies at the foot of the Soutpansberg Mountains, whose forested slopes rise to 1,718 metres above sea level; they once formed a protective barrier between the white settlement and the wild country of the native tribes that stretched north to the Limpopo and the borders of present-day Zimbabwe. These mountains were the castle walls within which Trichardt's besieged descendants constructed the all-embracing theology of apartheid. It is a pretty enough town, though, blessed more by its physical situation than the dull blocks of concrete that make up its core. Beyond the square grid of the business centre the white suburbs ramble pleasingly towards the mountains. They are verdant, thick with flowers – bougainvillaea, hibiscus, flame lilies – which infuse the air with the heady scent of the tropics. Lying in the shade of the Soutpansberg, these suburbs benefit from above-average rainfall. When the rain is poor, the sprinklers come to life and shower the well-trimmed gardens on Eland, Leeu and Munnik Streets. But it is not all so pretty or so privileged in the white town. The houses of the poorer whites have the sad air of places that once knew plenty but are now slowly succumbing to the effects of recession and broken pride. There is a leaking gutter here, a broken window pane there; in one yard an ancient car sits upon bricks while a man struggles to coax it back to life. I have met many of these people at meetings of extreme right-wing groups, and they give the impression of being in the grip of a silent panic, like men who have jumped from a great height only to discover that their parachutes are torn. On the streets of Louis

Trichardt they see a town that is slowly becoming black. The self-conscious Europeanism, the order and the oppressive neatness are slowly being subsumed by an older reality; the declamatory voices of itinerant traders, the jangling guitars of black Africa, are creeping up the main street, threatening chaos and subversion and wild vibrant laughter. The town of Louis Trichardt is returning to Africa.

When the trekkers arrived in this district they used their guns and whips to subdue the native tribes. Their annals are filled with tales of battles and massacres; they had a steady supply of martyrs and their own heroes were soaked in the blood of tribe after tribe. But in time they were to become chronically dependent on those they conquered. The easy access to black labour allowed them to create profitable farms; they switched from being horsemen to driving new Mercedes; swimming-pools were dug in their gardens and they came to enjoy a life that was benevolent beyond their forefathers' wildest imaginings. They still liked to talk of the old days; every year they venerated the trek leaders and urged their own sons to emulate the spirit of the frontier. On 16 December, the anniversary of their victory over the Zulus at Blood River in 1837, they held commemorative services and celebrated the straight aim of their ancestors. They gladly sent their children to war in Namibia and Angola and turned up themselves for regular training sessions with the army commandos. But the men who stood around bonfires drinking beer on sacred anniversaries were not the hardy pioneers who had defeated the Zulus and humiliated the British in battle after battle.

Now, in the face of their greatest challenge, the *volk* were more divided than at any time in their history. The pragmatists were following the statesman-like F.W. de Klerk into a strange new multi-racial future; those left behind, like Koeks Terblanch, were desperately casting about in search of a new

Promised Land. Koeks, who ran the Conservative Party office in Louis Trichardt, was an ardent proponent of the white homeland ideal and spoke in the most vociferous terms about launching a Boer freedom struggle. When I met him he was busily recruiting farmers to join the Afrikaner Volksfront, the right-wing front organization set up under the leadership of the retired army commander General Constand Viljoen. Koeks sat in his poky office above the whites-only barber shop off the main street, patiently dialling numbers for hours on end, urging his neighbours and other farmers further afield to attend meetings of the Front. He had the unshakeable faith of a true believer. Koeks was a small man but broad, with thick arms and a chin that he habitually pushed forward whenever he wished to make a point or express disagreement.

Before I could ask any questions, he wanted me to understand where he was coming from. Thus, our first twenty minutes together were an impressive recital of his family's Boer credentials. His grandfather Josephus had fought nine wars against the black tribes of the Cape before trekking to the Transvaal, where he again took up arms. This time, however, his enemies were the British, who were stronger by far than the Xhosas of the Cape. Josephus was captured in battle and dispatched to the island of St Helena as a prisoner of war. His wife and young son – Koek's father Daniel – were imprisoned in a British concentration camp. Some 27,000 whites, mostly women and children, and 12,000 blacks died in the camps. The deaths among the Afrikaners were to leave a legacy of bitterness that did much to reinforce the determination of later Boer leaders to create a state in which they would never again be subjugated. When a rump of bitter Afrikaners decided to rebel against the Union government in 1914, young Daniel Terblanch was among them. Again they lost and the young man was sent to prison for six months. He emerged with an even greater determination to thwart the pro-British rule of General Jan Smuts. During the war against Hitler, Daniel Terblanch joined the Ossewa Brandwag – the Oxwagon Sentinel. This illegal secret society supported the Nazis and became a focal point for nationalist Afrikaners who resented the influence of the English-speaking business community. Among its members were many men who would later go on to play leading roles in the National Party. While the Brandwag committed itself to supporting Hitler, the real imperative was the one that had so taxed the minds of Louis Trichardt and his fellow trekkers: the need to consolidate the *volk*, to protect them from the pollution of other groups and to create a space where outsiders could never interfere. Within three years of the war's end the hour of Daniel Terblanch had arrived. The Nationalists defeated Smuts and the first all-Afrikaner Cabinet was installed. In the words of the new Nationalist Prime Minister, D.F. Malan, on the morning of 28 May 1948: 'Today South Africa belongs to us once more.'

When he spoke of those days Koeks's eyes began to water. His grandfather, his father and now himself: the unbroken line of struggle. Most of Koeks's four decades of political life had been spent in the National Party, loyally putting up posters and getting the vote out at election time, organizing socials and public meetings, defending the party's apartheid policies to anyone foolish enough to argue with him. When the Nats weakened and began to suggest some form of limited power-sharing with the Indians and coloureds (not the blacks) in 1983, Koeks stuck to his principles and followed Andries Treurnicht into the newly formed Conservative Party. The split with the National Party had meant considerable personal upheaval. Friendships came to an abrupt end, and there were many angry rows with old party colleagues. 'That was hard. You know, we used to have parties at each other's houses all the time and visit, our wives would be always talking. Now that has all finished. If I stop any of them in the street and talk politics, they just walk away from me,' Koeks explained.

His relationships with blacks were, by comparison, much less troublesome. 'Whenever the blacks on my farm got cheeky, I just gave them a good hiding. That always sorted them out. And you know,' he continued, 'they never ever held it against me. It is like children, you have to let the black know where he stands.' Koeks Terblanch believed that the early settlers like Louis Trichardt prayed too much and shot too little; he pointed to the treatment of the American Indians and the Australian aboriginals as laudable attempts at population control. 'I don't hate every black. There are some good blacks. It's just the majority I have a problem with. You know, the black, he doesn't have the same needs as you and me. He is content to lie around all day and let the woman do the work while he sits in the kraal and drinks with his friends. It's not his fault . . . it's his culture. That's the way God made him,' he told me, with eyes as earnest as a missionary's. I noticed that he was wearing a gun. This, he explained, was because he expected there to be a civil war and in any case it was getting damn dangerous in the area, with robberies and murders all the time. There was a woman on a neighbouring farm who had come home to find a gang of blacks in the kitchen. 'You know what those bastards did,' exclaimed Koeks, 'they poured caustic soda down her throat and killed her. Can you believe that for savagery?' I shook my head and this seemed to act as a signal for a further outburst.

'I am telling you now that if they don't give us our own land there will be a war. All we want is to rule ourselves and be left alone. I don't mind if the black comes and works in that land, but he will have to go home to vote in his own country.' Here it was again, the desire to escape, to be masters in their own land, the imperative that had driven the trek and propelled the Afrikaners into the self-defeating madness of apartheid. *Own people, own land. Eie volk, eie land.*

'And where would you like that homeland to be?' I asked, as gently as I could.

'That, you see, is the problem,' he replied. There was a pause and Koeks rose and walked across the office to a wall map. He pointed out the constituencies currently held by the Conservative Party, large chunks of blue that occupied significant portions of the Transvaal and the Orange Free State. These, he seemed to say, might be a good start.

I probed further. 'Would you be willing to pack up and go to some other part of the country if that was what they offered you?'

Koeks paused again and then said he hadn't yet made up his mind on the question. I had the feeling it was a question he would happily avoid for ever, hoping that the war noises might frighten the new rulers into granting the right-wingers an independent state that included the huge swathes of rich farmland they already occupied.

After a few more minutes of delicate questioning I came to the conclusion that Koeks hadn't even begun to think out the ramifications of a *volkstaat*. It was nothing more than the old apartheid ideal dressed up with phrases like 'self-determination' and 'national self-realization', but as impractical and doomed as it ever was. He told me to call again in a few weeks. By then he would have a clearer idea of what exactly was involved.

There were as many different *volkstaat* plans as there were right-wing groups. Literally dozens of them constantly arguing and disagreeing about the borders of the proposed white state. The demands of the AWB (Afrikaner Weerstand Beweging) for a restoration of the old Transvaal and Free State republics was regarded as too extreme and impractical by the Afrikaner Volksfront, which suggested creating an area of independent land in the Northern and Eastern Transvaal that would have Pretoria as its capital. The Front wanted this Afrikaner state to become part of a confederation of Southern African states operating in a similar manner to the member nations of the European Community. Needless to say blacks and Indians would not have voting rights. But the plans always foundered on practicalities. When it came down to it, there were simply not enough Afrikaners willing to sacrifice the good life for an uncertain future in some distant part of the country. And everywhere one looked non-whites were in the majority. It would have been impossible, even with the support of the army and the police, to force millions of black and brown South Africans to leave the parts of the country that the right-wing had designated as homeland territory. Forced removal had been tried before and had failed dismally.

There were others who believed that Afrikaners should buy vast tracts of land and create their own private state. This was attempted in the Northern Cape by Professor Carel Boshoff, a son-in-law of Hendrik Verwoerd, who became the intellectual driving force behind the *volkstaat* ideal. His philosophy was explained in terms of a love for Afrikanerdom rather than a hatred of blacks. Boshoff believed that until Afrikaners learned to live without servants, until such time as they did their own work, they would have no future as an independent people. Although his plans seemed to me to be deeply impractical, I found him to be a sincere man.

While others on the right talked about self-determination, Boshoff and his followers actually went and bought land in one of the most arid parts of the country and set up a homeland. They purchased the old farming town of Orania and appealed to Afrikaners to trek there and build a state where blacks would not be welcome, even as labourers. The project ran into early trouble when white labourers imported to help with construction went on strike, complaining that they did not want to be treated like 'white kaffirs'. But the settlers went doggedly forward. When I visited the area in 1991, it resembled a ghost town of the old West. Dry and dusty and conspicuously empty, Orania seemed far from the vision of an Afrikaner heaven that Boshoff and his disciples had in mind. The people I encountered were honest and hard-working but uniformly gloomy and careworn. Cut off from the world, they reminded me of some obscure religious sect, the kind of people whose children eventually rebel and run wild. One of the men asked me bluntly whether I was a Catholic or a Protestant. When I replied that I had been baptized a Catholic, he was unimpressed. 'That means you couldn't live here. No Catholics, Jews or Blacks,' he said.

I might have been tempted to dismiss the right-wing's blood-curdling threats were it not for my experience in the town of Ventersdorp on the Friday night of 9 August 1991. For several days tension had been building in the right-wing stronghold in advance of a planned public meeting to be addressed by President De Klerk. His decision to go to Ventersdorp was a calculated challenge to the right. Ventersdorp was the home of AWB leader Eugene Terre'Blanche and his neo-Nazi organizations had its headquarters in the town. What happened was a valuable illustration of how dangerous the extreme right could be, and of the naked racism that characterized its paramilitary wing. This is how I remember the long mad night.

It is seven o'clock and the pick-ups and minibuses are still pouring into town. A few moments ago Terre'Blanche strode on to a platform in the middle of the square and started to denounce De

Klerk. The crowd is ecstatic. When a police chopper appears overhead, shining its searchlight down into the centre of the gathering, the men start chanting the initials of the organization. Two thousand voices ring out in unison: 'Aah – Veah – Beah.' It is powerful and for a few seconds manages to drown out the sound of the rotors. Women have set up stalls selling the spicy farm sausages known as boerewors. *They are also selling badges and T-shirts with the AWB insignia: three sevens joined to form a swastika. Almost all of the men and a good many of the women have obeyed Terre'Blanche's instruction and are carrying guns. Some are wearing long pieces of sharpened metal strapped to their arms. I notice gas-masks and canisters of insecticide. There are no blacks to be seen anywhere. A bear of a man – he must be at least six foot six – comes up and tells me to put away my tape-recorder. 'If you don't, I'll shove it down your fucking throat,' he warns. Of course I comply, and edge away in the direction of the police lines. They have drawn up around the municipal hall where De Klerk is due to speak. Lines of razor wire have been rolled out and the area is completely sealed. Behind the wire are several lines of policemen and dogs that bark fiercely every time a stranger approaches. Some right-wingers have strolled up to the wire and seem to be chatting amicably with the police. A young sergeant examines my press pass and allows me through, pointing in the direction of the hall, from which the sound of accordions can be heard, blaring in competition with the chanting of the right-wingers. At the entrance to the hall a woman is handing out stickers that bear the message* I LOVE F.W. *alongside a large red heart. 'You have to wear one if you want to get in,' she says, smiling and pressing a sticker on to my chest. Some of the men are having a barbecue. The same ruddy farmer's faces, the same* boerewors, *the same language as the men on the other side of the wire. But these men are believers in compromise. They would be badly beaten or worse if they appeared on the other side of the wire. Inside the hall the audience is already seated. There is an air of expectancy, though whether this is because* of the President or the barbarians at the gate it is hard to tell. Security men have already been through the list of invitees, but a final check is being made just in case. Men with walkie-talkies are moving through the hall, scrutinizing every face, on the look-out for potential trouble-makers. There is a commotion outside, the sound of a helicopter. In what seems like a few seconds the President has arrived and is being ushered to the front of the hall. People are on their feet, clapping and cheering.

But the clamour from the other end of the street is growing; voices are being raised and the dogs are barking in one furious chorus. I rush outside and make my way through the barrier, circling around to the rear of the right-wing crowd. There are about 2,000 people gathered in front of the police line. They are singing 'Sarie Marais', an old Boer song. Some are spitting at the police and shouting traitor. One of them asks what radio station I work for. Knowing that the words 'BBC', with their vague connotations of empire, can infuriate right-wingers, I tell him that I am an Irish radio reporter. 'Irish, eh,' he says, pulling me away from the crowd towards Voortrekker Street. 'You are OK here, we won't trouble you. Just do this much for me . . . give me a number for the IRA. We need guns and explosives, my friend.' Before I can answer, a loud cheer rises up from the centre of the crowd. Terre'Blanche has arrived near the barrier. We rush back and I lose the would-be terrorist in the mêlée. I try to get behind a wall at the Ventersdorp Hotel but am pushed into the centre of the crowd. They are heaving forward now, and the men at the front are spraying insecticide into the eyes of the dogs and their handlers. I can see Piet Skiet Rudolph, scion of the right, lifting a baseball bat and striking at a dog. The police finally crack. They launch volleys of tear-gas, and the lights go out. Somebody has tripped the master switch for the town. There is wild cheering and rocks are being thrown. More tear-gas, and I am knocked over. The police charge and we are all running. As I come around the corner, I hear the sound of automatic-rifle fire. I can see to my amazement and horror a taxi with a black family inside being surrounded by right-wingers. There is a man, a woman and small child. Right-wingers are scrambling over the vehicle, smashing in through the windows with batons and striking at the occupants. I can see that the woman is hysterical and the child is jumping around on her lap. I want to be sick. Then the police come storming around the corner. There is more shooting and they clear the right-wingers away from the van. A young cop – he can be no more than eighteen – holds the racists at bay and rushes the family to safety.

Other blacks are not so lucky. In panic a van carrying a coffin for burial ploughs into a crowd of AWB men. They open fire, pumping the coffin full of bullets. A right-winger is killed in the collision. A dead black man lies sprawled beside the vehicle. Another is wounded. When an AWB ambulance arrives, it refuses to treat the wounded black. While this is happening I am running across a field, caught between the police and right-wingers. A man emerges from the shadows and points a shotgun at my stomach. 'Moe nie skiet nie,' I shout. 'Please don't shoot me. I am a foreigner.' He looks at me with contempt and tells me to get back to where I belong.

More tear-gas grenades explode. I am blind and retching, staggering up the street, when a hand reaches out and pulls me into a doorway, out of the line of fire. Through the fog of gas I see the face of the Associated Press Bureau chief, Barry Renfrew. In the middle of the road a policeman is lying with blood pouring from a bullet wound in his leg. The helicopter is back and the wounded man is stretchered away. By now the police seem to be in control. The streets are free of right-wingers. The street where the worst of the battle took place is littered with cartridges, broken glass, spent gas grenades. In the Jewish old-age home – the only place where I can find a phone – the woman manager wants to know what was going on. When I tell her the AWB was causing trouble she sighs and offers me a drink. The good news for F.W. de Klerk is that the meeting went ahead. The bad news is that three people, two right-

wingers and one black, are dead. Scores of people have been injured. Later that night I am driving with colleagues back to Johannesburg. A whisky bottle is passed around, and the warm liquid sweeps back, numbing our raw throats. The lights of Johannesburg appear, vast and glowing in the distance, and we pass a long convoy of police vehicles. There are row after row of men inside the darkened coaches, but they seem to be sitting in silence. The driver of our car switches on the radio. Bob Marley is singing 'No Woman, No Cry'. As our car speeds through the platteland, hurrying towards home, we join in the chorus, singing: 'Everything's gonna be all right, everything's gonna be all right.' This last is hard to believe.

For a long time after Ventersdorp I wanted to avoid right-wing rallies like the plague. They frightened me just as much as the townships. It was not that they were likely to pitch up with a tyre and want to burn you; it was more the constant feeling of menace and the sure feeling that they hated your liberal guts. I know that most of my colleagues felt this way about the right. We would attempt to palaver with them, persuade them of our desire to see their point of view, but we didn't really fool them. They knew that most journalists despised the right-wing and sought to portray them as barbarians. Given the way they behaved most of the time, it was a relatively easy task. Presuming he/she agreed to be interviewed, the average AWB member would, for example, explain how blacks were mentally subnormal, how their simple wish was to drink and copulate all day, how they had the same body smell as sheep and stole whenever the boss's back was turned.

Going to cover right-wing meetings was like taking part in a circus: part menace, part farce. Leading the parade would be Terre'Blanche on his plumed horse, a fat man on a sweating animal; behind him the ranks of the black- and khaki-clad stormtroopers and the burly women of the ladies' commando; and, swarming all around them, *us*, the footsoldiers of the mass media. But Terre'Blanche was not the fool he frequently looked. For one thing he appreciated the simplistic understanding of the South African conflict common to many of the large television networks. To stay in the limelight that he craved, and to remain out in front of the plethora of other right-wing groups, Terre'Blanche needed to be seen as the Big Man by his followers, the one whose voice could be heard booming and bellowing across the airwaves of the world. To that end he became a master at putting on a good show at rallies and delivering apocalyptic warnings that no other right-wing leader could match for their ferocity and power. The comparisons with Hitler, which he publicly scorned, were in fact carefully cultivated. His black-clad Iron Guard was blatantly imitative of the SS; the khaki-clad Aquila wing of his movement a copy of Ernst Röhm's Brownshirts. But if his skills as a demagogue were second to none, Terre'Blanche was a political illiterate. His stated demand was for a restoration of the old Boer republics of the Transvaal and the Free State, a position so ludicrous that not a single credible right-wing leader supported it. His main success was in whipping up the fears and passions of his supporters, his words inciting them to acts of racist cruelty against defenceless people. Those who flocked to the ranks of the AWB frequently came from the poorest sections of white society, where the effects of recession were most severely felt and for whom the collapse of apartheid represented a disaster from which recovery was impossible. These people were at the bottom of the ladder, and if they could be certain of one thing it was that no black government would give a damn when they slipped off. They were, quite simply, poisoned with fear.

As the country moved inexorably towards elections, the

ranks of the far right swelled. The police estimated that there
were at least eighty different organizations, some of them
tiny and insignificant, others well-armed and dangerous.
Weapons began to disappear from military arsenals and training camps sprang up around the Transvaal and the Free State.
And as always when the far right went to war, it was
ordinary black civilians who paid the highest price. The
number of racist attacks increased: minibus taxis were ambushed; bombs exploded on railway lines used by black
commuters; cars were stopped on lonely roads and the occupants shot dead. A black barman in a hotel in rural Transvaal
explained it to me this way: 'They are like the Ku-Klux-Klan
up here. Except you know them all and they know you. I
even serve some of them in this bar, but if they catch me out
on the streets after dark then I am dead meat. You can talk as
much as you like about a new South Africa, but to me it's
just bullshit. I am still a kaffir up here and they do what they
like.'

Samuel Kanagha made the mistake of falling into the hands
of the racists. In his case they were men he worked with. His
story began as a simple one of cops and robbers. Samuel was
employed as a guard with a Johannesburg security company,
one of the big companies that was thriving in the fearful and
crime-ridden atmosphere of the transition years. One evening
money was stolen from the company safe. It was around
£15,000, a considerable sum in South African terms. Suspicion fell on the black workers, principally on Samuel. The
court records give no indication as to why he in particular
was singled out by his white co-workers. Perhaps he was the
kind of black man who answered back or was 'cheeky';
perhaps he simply looked suspicious. At any rate no evidence
was ever produced that might have linked him to the robbery.
Several of the white staff were former members of the
security forces and held pronounced right-wing views. Three

of them – Johan van Eyk, François Oosthuizen and Heinrich Gerber – decided that they would interrogate Samuel in their own way. Both Van Eyk and Gerber had been officers in Koevoet – the counter-insurgency unit that earned a singular reputation for brutality during South Africa's bush war in neighbouring Namibia. The white men in these units were generally regarded as being to the right even of Terre'-Blanche. On a clear autumn morning they bundled Samuel into a car and drove out of Johannesburg along the super-modern highway in the direction of the dormitory town of Benoni. Soon they passed the mine slag-heaps that dot the landscape of the East Rand. These dumps loom out of the landscape like mountains on some stark, lifeless planet and are the result of the deep burrowing in the earth, the hungering after gold that gives dull little towns like Benoni and others along the Reef a reason for existing. The area was originally a wide expanse of scrubland on which the mine dumps and acres of suburban bungalows were imposed, as the Wit-watersrand was developed in the closing stages of the last century. Gold hunger brought with it the demand for a large pool of native labour, the forefathers of men like Samuel Kanagha and the millions of other blacks who now live in townships spread out around the city of Johannesburg. They are the people who gaze out at us like dejected shadows from the grainy photographs of those years. It is unlikely that the foreign tourist travelling to and from the Kruger National Park or to any of the other scenic delights of the Eastern Transvaal will see the townships; but they cannot miss the mine dumps that the wide, terrified eyes of Samuel Kanagha saw on that autumn morning.

He was taken to a disused dump, out of the public eye, a place where a man's screams would be lost in the emptiness of the veld. The court records do not tell us what was said in the car, so we can only imagine the scene: a black man and three white men, the black accused of a serious theft, the whites determined to make him admit to it. In a car behind were two other black guards from the company. Their duty, it appears, was to watch out in case the mine security force happened along. The lead car pulled up on waste ground, and Samuel was hustled out and tied up, arms and legs bound so that he could not move or threaten his interrogators. Somebody went back to the car and produced an electric-shock machine and a plastic bag. Lying on the ground, Samuel would have seen this happening: muscular white men chatting to one another in Afrikaans, setting up the machine and wires with which they planned to extract the truth from him. One of the whites tied a rope around Samuel's feet and put the plastic bag over his head; he felt himself being dragged along and then hoisted on to the branch of a tree.

Within a few minutes the interrogation began. One of the white men pulled Samuel's trousers down and placed electrodes on his genitals. The shocks started: waves of pain that convulsed the black man's body. Soon Samuel was begging for mercy but he still refused to admit to any crime. He did not do it, he told his tormentors again and again. The interrogators were becoming thirsty, so they paused and one of the black guards was sent off for drinks. Among the whites there was laughter and bantering. This was hard work and the day was warm. Eventually the drinks arrived and Samuel begged for something to cool his thirst. He pleaded for mercy again, but they laughed. In fact these men knew that the worst was yet to come.

Of the three only Oosthuizen was feeling any inkling of humanity. He offered Samuel something to drink. We are not told from the records of the court what the reaction of the two black guards was. In the story told to the judge they seem to hover in the background. The white men eventually ran out of patience. They began to place wood and sticks under their victim's head. Somebody produced a lighter and the dry wood crackled into flames. Van Eyk, Oosthuizen and Gerber stood back and watched their victim twist in agony as the fire gathered force. They and the black guards could hear his screams but nobody else could. One of the whites pumped several bullets into the dying black man; another cut off his right hand. This bizarre mutilation was never explained at the trial. There was speculation, though, that the hand might have been a trophy that was later abandoned in panic. A schoolboy found the limb on a suburban street in Benoni. The taking of such grisly prizes was common during the bush war in Namibia.

By nightfall Samuel Kanagha was dead. He had endured a day of unspeakable terror until life finally abandoned his wounded flesh. At the conclusion of the court case the accused were sentenced to periods of between ten and twenty years for his murder. With good behaviour they could be free, having served less than half of those sentences. Had three blacks been accused of murdering a white in such a horrific manner, they would have been sentenced to death. People died every day in South Africa. Nobody had a monopoly on the exercise of murder. Blacks killed blacks, whites killed blacks, blacks killed whites. Yet there was something about the murder of Samuel Kanagha that stood apart. He died at the hands of men who must have regarded him as little better than an animal; men who took their time with the killing, who carried it out in front of black witnesses and who never even bothered to cover their tracks. It was a crime that reeked of contempt, of the arrogant assurance that the murder of a black man did not really matter in a society that had for centuries reduced such people to the status of farmyard animals. All three were products of a security system that revelled in the casual use of brutality with the black underclass. It was the system that allowed Steve Biko to be beaten senseless and then driven for more than a thousand kilometres while he lay dying on the floor of a Land Rover, the system that permitted the habitual torture of detainees and the establishment of innumerable hit squads whose task was to eliminate enemies of the state.

All of this, it should be remembered, was presided over by men who felt they were doing their duty for the *volk*. From the highest-ranking Cabinet minister to the lowliest policeman, the ultimate goal was the same: to prevent *them* from ever rising up and driving the masters into the sea. The savagery of the apartheid system, the brutal security measures it demanded and the extreme right-wing views it created were the product, more than anything else, of fear – fear that those who had for so long been stamped on might someday come to inflict the same on the *volk*. While F.W. de Klerk and his ministers spoke in terms of boundless optimism about a new South Africa, the attitudes that they as Cabinet members had done so much to create were still poisoning the body politic. The 'new' nationalists might well pat themselves on the back for leading the country away from apartheid, but they could not as easily escape the dangerous legacy of their abandoned philosophy. Those who had not joined their trek towards reality were spoiling for a fight and inflicting pain on any black man unlucky enough to cross their path.

Yet it would be a gross injustice to suggest that all of the Afrikaners who opposed De Klerk's decision to move away from apartheid were fascists in the manner of Terre'Blanche. While the AWB made excellent television, their antics overshadowed the majority of Boers who waited fearfully and silently on their farms, scanning the horizon for the first signs of the advancing storm. The bulk of such farmers whom I encountered were decent, hard-working people. One did not have to like their political views to be able to respect their

sincerity and their commitment to the land. That they prof-
ited from the apartheid system is beyond argument: they
supported the mass evictions, the homeland system and the
ruthlessness of the police. But in securing a place in the sun
on the back of other men's sweat they were no different
from the huge business conglomerates which ardently proclaimed liberal views. In many ways they remind me of the
dour Protestant farmers of County Antrim, possessed of a
powerful sense of self-reliance and a flinty determination to
hold fast to the land of their forefathers. Like the Ulster
Protestants they are outnumbered and live perpetually in fear
of the destruction of their sacred group identity. They watch
bewildered while the men who once urged them to worship
apartheid scramble for their places in the new power elite;
this they see as a conspiracy of political convenience from
which they, the stolid farmers with their antiquated views,
are shut out.

Boet van Rensburg is one such man, a creature of the land
for whom the distant city represents the same vision of
corruption and weakness that the Cape represented for Louis
Trichardt and his trekkers. On the telephone Boet told me
that the last journalist who visited him had wanted him to
take out his gun and shoot in the back garden. He wanted me
to understand that he was not prepared to do this. 'Only
come if you are prepared to give a true picture of me,' he
said. I promised that I would and two hours later found
myself driving down a dirt road in the direction of Boet's
farm. He had planted blue gum trees along the side of the
road, and they leaned over to form a protective arch, shutting
out the harsh glare of the sun. The farm was set in the
platteland, the flatland, which rolls east of Johannesburg for
several hundred miles before tumbling down into the hot,
subtropical lands of the lowveld, a place of great citrus
plantations and game reserves that run up to the border of

Mozambique. The poet Peter Sachs has described this great sweep of country beautifully in the poem 'Machadadorp':

> The ground is thick with dew. Around us open contours
> of this cattle and wheat country
> play out to each soft
> amber range, a low horizon
> broken only by a line
> of smoke, a stand of blue gums
> in a darkening cleft.

I came to a stop outside a bungalow of brown stone that appeared to have been extended haphazardly in several directions. A tall, broad-shouldered man with grey hair, wearing khaki trousers and an ancient pullover, strolled out to meet me. Behind the silver-rimmed glasses Boet's blue eyes regarded me with what I imagined was a mild wariness as he proffered his hand and invited me inside for coffee. 'The rain has been threatening all day but no sign of it yet,' he remarked as we walked towards the house. There were fat clouds the colour of slate marshalling to the west, and Boet was hoping that by dusk they would purge themselves over his fields of maize. The drought of the previous four years had crippled several neighbouring farmers and good rains were badly needed if the mealies were to flourish and the bankers were to be kept from the front door.

In the dining room I noticed a large family bible perched on the side dresser, and above it a painting of a tiny whitewashed cottage, tucked into the folds of a huge mountainscape. Boet said the cottage was similar to the one his parents had lived in before they trekked out of South Africa in the bitter years that followed the end of the Boer War. Defeated and almost penniless, they had crossed the Limpopo on their ox-wagons and trekked for several thousand kilometres to what was then Northern Rhodesia, where they established a farm deep in the bush. 'Everything went well for them up there. The rains were good and the crops prospered and they had no trouble with the blacks. And then what happens? Then the British just up and hand the place over to Kaunda. After that it was time to get out. The country just started sinking down and my ma and pa uprooted everything and came back to South Africa.' They had settled here on the platteland and had worked the land, building up the farm into one of the most prosperous in the district. In due course the old people handed the farm on to Boet, who was now equally determined that it would go to his son Boet Jr. He stood up and pointed to some photographs high on the wall that I had not noticed until then. There were grandparents and uncles, a brother and cousins. All of them were dead, many having succumbed to TB or malaria on farms that were hundreds of miles from the nearest hospital. Their sad, lost faces spoke of hard lives and long journeys back and forth across the wilderness, journeys away from fear and hunger into the endless promise of the open spaces.

Boet wanted me to understand that he did not hate blacks. He would never dream of calling them kaffirs, he did not physically ill-treat them, and he looked after their housing and medical needs and the education of their children. 'I just don't want to be ruled by them. Just look what happened to us up in Northern Rhodesia. They'll do the same here. Just you watch. And when the people are starving and the place is falling down around them, then they'll come running to us to save them,' he said.

Boet began to tell the story of an Englishman of his acquaintance who had made common cause with the blacks in Rhodesia, inviting them to his home and socializing with them. 'We used to have lots of arguments with him and he would never understand our point of view that the blacks had their side of the fence and we had ours. Then one night he arrived at my garden gate, shaking with anger and saying we should shoot the whole lot of them. Now, that is the kind of thing I would just never agree with because I understand them. Anyway, I told him to come in and I poured a whisky. You know what it was that happened? It seems they were at a party and some black fellow made a pass at his wife. And I can tell you after that my friend was a changed man. He left and went back to England soon after.' *Ah, the foolishness of outsiders*, he seemed to be saying, *they will never understand our Africa until it jumps up and bites them in the backside*. The story was intended to be a vindication of the ideals of segregation. That people of all colours made passes at other people's wives and husbands all the time was a point I felt sure would be lost on Boet, so I said nothing. Boet van Rensburg was plainly terrified of the ANC, convinced that the black squatters who were beginning to appear on his neighbours' farms would some day come and claim his vast acreage as their rightful inheritance. No amount of soothing words from Nelson Mandela could convince him otherwise. For Boet listened to the other voices, the chants from the townships of 'Kill the farmer, kill the Boer', and in them he heard his own requiem. He did not want a war and he did not want to trek off to some new white homeland. Even if they could find one with no blacks living there, the legacy of earlier wanderings had convinced him that the time had come to stay put. He would fight only if they came to take his land. 'It's a lot easier to talk about a war than it is going out and fighting it. People should be very careful about threatening war. It's an easy way to lose everything overnight. But if they were to come here and say '"Give us the land", then I would take up arms because I would be protecting my place and my family.' It was clear from what Boet was saying that for him the group imperative was giving way to the demands of more personal concerns. The tribe had been split in two: De Klerk and his followers went one way, while the conservatives like Boet fractured into splinter groups that argued bitterly among themselves, victims of the old tendency towards schism. Apartheid had been devised in part to counter these schismatic tendencies, to bring the Boers together and to divide and weaken their enemies. But in its mad unworkability it succeeded only in tearing the tribe apart, leaving men like Boet van Rensburg bewildered and lost, children of a fantastic illusion that was turning to salt in their mouths.

Boet took me on a tour of his farm. We visited a huge henhouse where he delivered an impressive imitation of the noise of the birds. They belonged to his daughter-in-law. On this farm everybody contributed something. Out in the pasture, among the fat cattle, Boet pointed in the direction of a distant power station. 'There was a time,' he said, 'when you could see as far as the horizon and there would be nothing. Now we have that station and those mines over the other side. And you know what happens when the industry comes ... the people follow it. That's when you get squatters and robbing. You know, my neighbour, he just put up a new livestock fence. When he came out the following morning it was gone. And who is going to compensate him for it? De Klerk or Mandela? Agh, you can forget it, man. Those boys just want to feather their own nest. They don't give a damn about us.'

In the dairy, with its gleaming new milking machine, a black man named Lucas was hosing away the cow dung that had accumulated on the stone floor. Boet asked him if he was happy with his work. 'Oh, yes, baas, very happy,' the black man replied. And what he did he feel about all this politics? Lucas said he wasn't really concerned with politics. But he was afraid that after the election the *tsotsis* from the city might come and cause trouble. Boet turned to me and smiled. He had that 'I told you they don't really worry about politics' look on his face. Maybe Lucas really couldn't care less about the elections, but, confronted by two white men on a farm in the Eastern Transvaal, it would have been damn hard for him to sing the praises of Mandela. I thought there was a sullenness and a wariness in his manner that suggested a very different Lucas to the compliant, faithful worker whom Boet envisioned.

Before I could leave, Boet insisted that I come back to the kitchen for more coffee and meet his wife, June. She was a portly woman of about fifty, with a warm, soft face that carried a look of eternal concern. As she went about the business of boiling water and collecting cups, a tiny blond grandson wandered in from the garden and demanded coffee. Boet scooped the child up and sat him on his lap. 'Now you must say please to Ouma if you want your coffee,' he gently chided the boy. June van Rensburg went over to where her husband was sitting and ran her hand through the little boy's hair. 'If you really want to know, it is them I worry about, the children. We have had our lives, but what is going to be left for them?' she said. The grandmother then went back to the kettle and the job of making coffee and said no more.

Besides the question of what might happen to their land, the Van Rensburgs were deeply fearful of a new concept that seemed to crop up all the time on radio and television discussions. It was called *affirmative action* and the idea, according to the politicians, was to level the playing field and give blacks an even chance on the job market. But to Boet it seemed more like a way of keeping whites out of jobs, especially Afrikaners who came from the rural areas and did not go to university. If his grandson did not – God forbid – decide to settle on the farm, then he would have a hell of a tough job getting into the civil service or the police or any of those other institutions that had provided generations of Afrikaans boys with employment.

By the time it had come for me to leave, the clouds were directly over the house and the first large drops of rain began to play hopscotch on the tin roof of the veranda. It sounded as if stones were dropping from the heavens. Boet smiled and remarked that the downpour might be a good omen. 'Who knows? It might be a sign. In this country you can never tell.' I said goodbye with offers of yet more coffee ringing in my ear and ran to the car. The potholes on the dirt road were beginning to fill up with water, and I drove slowly towards the highway. In the mirror I could see Boet standing and waving as the rain came down around him, like a great curtain falling steadily on the last months of the white empire.

Back in Louis Trichardt. It is night and I am sitting in the living room of a young Church minister. His name is Dominee Gerhard Botha. He is quietly spoken, a handsome man in his early thirties. There are pictures of two blond children and a dark-haired woman on top of the piano and several children's drawings. Outside the cicadas have begun their ratcheting, grinding chorus. The Dominee is a worried man, fearful for the future of his people. He came here from the Orange Free State, but it is clear he does not feel at home among the Afrikaners of the northland. 'This is not just a conservative town,' he says, 'it is an AWB town. There is an awful lot of fear here.' He tells me more and more women are coming and complaining of their husbands getting drunk and beating them, there is a growing gun culture, and the men are becoming more macho by the day. Dominee Botha is a liberal by the standards of Louis Trichardt and he walks a fine line in his sermons, preaching social justice but carefully avoiding any form of party politics. He wants to get out of here, to go back to his own people. I have the impression that this frightened town is starting to close in on him. He tells me that the greatest fear of all is the fear that the Afrikaners have of themselves: the gnawing worry that in spite of the mythology they may not have it in them to survive the new multi-racial future. He believes that in the long term they probably will. The Dominee supports De Klerk. 'It is the only way we can survive. We have to come to terms with the world we live in, not the one we would like. Remember most of us are just ordinary people who want to be left alone to get on with our lives. We are not all fascists,' he says with a smile. More than anything he wants me to understand that his people, his Afrikaners, are people of Africa. They will not be going anywhere. There is no question of them running back to Holland. That was left behind centuries ago. Driving away from Louis Trichardt, through the desolate emptiness of the bushveld, no other car for miles, I struggle to decide which of the voices of the town I should heed: Koeks Terblanch, with his intimations of the apocalypse, or the gentle Dominee, who believes in the possibility of an Afrikaner rebirth in a non-racial society. But there is no answer, the future is hidden. Approaching Pietersburg at one o'clock in the morning, I think of the words of Afrikaans novelist André Brink: 'Such a long journey ahead,' he wrote. 'Not a question of imagination but of faith.'

CHAPTER 5

The Land of the Dead

> *There is a land of the living and a land of the dead, and the bridge is love, the only survival, the only meaning.*

Thornton Wilder, *The Bridge of San Luis Rey*

Although I could not have imagined or predicted it that night during my long drive back from the far Northern Transvaal, the ultra right-wing was just weeks away from the act of self-destructive, arrogant stupidity that would drain the will of its support base and remove for ever the threat of a widespread uprising against the incoming government. Yet for me the events surrounding the first and last major military action by the right-wing were to have devastating personal consequences, leading to the death of one of my closest friends and colleagues and propelling me into a long period of melancholy and questioning. They were to prove my darkest days in South Africa, days when my belief in the foreign correspondent's trade was severely tested and my worry over the future of the country at its most intense.

In those final rain-drenched days of February 1994 the far right represented much more of an unknown quantity than most journalists cared to admit. We would talk about the fascists endlessly, assessing their military capability, examining the mad maps for a white homeland as if there might be a grain of political possibility lurking somewhere between the arbitrary grid lines. Although we suspected them of being little more than overblown bullies who had little stomach for a fight, we could not be sure. Thus it became the accepted wisdom among the international press corps that while most of the AWB's supporters were oafish loudmouths, there was a minority on the right that was well-armed and dedicated enough to seriously disrupt the election if it sought to do so. There were endless rumours about former reconnaissance commandos* of the South African Defence Force (SADF) training groups of men in the mountains. It was even suggested that large groups of German and Croatian rightists had appeared in the country to put steel into the backbones of their South African counterparts. Throughout the months of January, February and March speculation about the military intentions of the right-wing increased. Although there were increasing signs that the pragmatists led by General Constand Viljoen wanted to ditch the AWB and take part in the election, the General continued to talk in two languages: one suggested joining the democratic process as a strategic alternative that would allow Afrikaners to argue the case for a white homeland from within; the other hinted at a joint course of political and military action. His press officer, a tense and obsessive young man named Stephen Manninger, had taken to carrying an automatic rifle and a pistol in public, and spoke alternately of the need for dialogue and of his willingness to fight against the 'Communist-dominated ANC'. Yet, like many of the thinking rightists, Manninger was beginning to understand what had long ago dawned on the leaders of the National Party: the demographic reality made it inevitable that black men and women would someday rule South Africa, all of South Africa. It was now a case of having to get the best deal possible within the parameters of that reality.

*An elite unit of the South African army that acted as a long-range scout and sabotage group during the bush war in Angola and Namibia.

But even if most of us did ultimately believe in Viljoen's common sense and reluctance to go to war, the signals were vague enough to leave many journalists in a state of open confusion. The doubts were to be dispelled during a few insane days in the death of the Republic of Bophuthatswana.

The 'republic' consisted of six pieces of territory said to represent the traditional homeland of the Batswana tribe, South Africa's second-largest language group. These islands of land were scattered across the provinces of the Transvaal, the Orange Free State and the Cape, and surrounded by the white South Africa upon which Bophuthatswana was politically and financially dependent. The fractured 'republic' had as its president one Lucas Manyane Mangope, a greedy and despotic tribal chief who crawled and stamped his way to the top with the help of South Africa's security establishment. For them he represented the perfect puppet: a man who was quick to denounce racial discrimination but who was equally willing to praise the notion of 'separate development' as a means to achieve peace and prosperity. Mangope was given a flag and a capital, Mmabatho, with its own parliamentary buildings and the great symbol of African pride, an independence stadium. Crucially the President of Bophuthatswana was given his own security forces, with scores of South African advisers to help him crush any internal dissent. In appearance Mangope looked like a man whose face was in the process of melting: the flesh sagged from his high cheekbones, while his lips seemed to curl outwards and down. His great dead eyes exuded contempt for the lesser beings who flitted in and out of his charmed circle. When he spoke it was with an unusually (for an African despot) soft and restrained voice, a voice that was both pompous and bored, which regarded the public explanation of his government's actions as an unnecessary and time-wasting exercise.

Lucas Mangope was born in 1923 into an old chiefly family in the North-western Transvaal, and on reaching the age of twenty-one he inherited the title of leader of the Mathlathowa clan of the Tswana tribe. Upon leaving school, Mangope studied as a trainee teacher and taught in schools throughout the north-west, an experience that should have given him ample insight into the wretched condition of black education. Between the years 1952 and 1959, the formative years of apartheid, Mangope travelled from school to school and would have seen the steady destruction of black lives as the authorities moved to enforce the various acts that defined where the majority population could live and what work it was entitled to do. But while the oppression of those years prompted many to join the liberation movements, propelling themselves towards death, jail or exile, Mangope opted for the inside track. He went back to his home region of Motswedi and inherited the chieftainship upon the death of his father in 1959. From then on it was a straightforward climb up the apartheid ladder from Chief of the Tribe to President of the Republic of Bophuthatswana.

The 'country' became formally independent in 1977 – the same year Steve Biko died in police custody – and Mangope's Bophuthatswana Democratic Party won every seat in the National Assembly. The vast majority of the population of this new republic refused to vote; having been stripped of their South African citizenship overnight, they were not about to endorse the move by voting for the fictive republic dreamed up by the apartheid master planners and their local puppet. The President quickly made it clear that he would brook no serious internal opposition. Supporters of the ANC, members of the trades union movement and students all found themselves facing the guns of Mangope's thuggish security forces. For its part, the ANC set out to destabilize the Mangope regime using the tactics of ungovernability that had caused so much trouble for Pretoria.

The campaign came to a head on the morning of 10 February 1988, when Mangope was confronted by soldiers and placed under arrest. Together with his senior cronies the President was taken to the Independence Stadium to await a decision on his fate. It was a fatal misjudgement by the coup plotters. Within hours the SADF came steaming into Mmabatho, crushing the coup and freeing the President from his captors. There followed a purge of the armed forces and government departments, with anyone suspected of disloyalty being summarily dismissed.

With the release of Mandela and the unbanning of the ANC in early 1990, Mangope's lease on power began to run out. Implicit in the whole process of negotiation was the principle that a united South Africa would emerge at the other end. Thus, while he took part in negotiations, Mangope could never have been in any doubt that the process signalled the end of his toy state. As the ANC and the government reached deal after deal, Mangope moved into an alliance with the white right-wing and Chief Buthelezi, arguing for an ethnic constellation of states and continually blustering about his determination not to be intimidated. He had as his chief negotiator one of Southern Africa's inveterate political carpet-baggers, the toupee-wearing Rowan Cronje, who had been a former member of the UDI (Unilateral Declaration of Independence) government of Ian Smith in Rhodesia and who had subsequently served in the administrations of Transkei and Ciskei (two of the other nominally independent states set up under apartheid). Cronje presented a genial and reasonable face to the media and might well have signed up for the elections had he been able to persuade Mangope that there was more to be gained than lost from such a course of action. But Mangope deluded himself into believing that the alliance with Buthelezi and the far right and the power of his own security forces could hold the day.

Just months before the polling day Mangope opened an embassy in the Baltic republic of Latvia, to add to those he maintained in London and Washington. But of all the remaining members of the conservative Freedom Alliance he was the most vulnerable: his territory was scattered across South Africa, his patrons in Pretoria had deserted him and, unlike Buthelezi and General Viljoen, he had negligible political support. Mangope bought the loyalty of his civil service and his security forces; when they began to realize that an ANC government was inevitable and that their pensions and jobs were in danger, they promptly turned on their benefactor. Thus it was in the final weeks of March 1994 that a wave of strikes, encouraged by the ANC, began to cripple the homeland administration and prepare the way for Mangope's downfall.

All morning the reports have been coming in and by now both myself and John Harrison are in a state of mounting anxiety. 'I knew we should have gone in yesterday,' says Harrison, who is pacing up and down the hallway. 'It'll take us at least three hours to drive to the bloody place and I'll never make it in time for the nine,' he adds before disappearing into his office. I check the wires again and notice that the South African Press Association is now describing serious rioting in the centre of Mmabatho and its twin town of Mafeking. Upon hearing this, John jumps up from behind his desk and shouts out, 'There is nothing else for it — let's just hire a plane and get the bloody hell up there.' In a matter of minutes this is organized and we are en route to Lanseria Airport. The BBC news television crew is already in Mmabatho and filming the disturbances. John had sent them ahead the previous day.

Once inside the cramped interior of our four-seater plane, John begins tapping his fingers on the case of his lap-top computer. 'I just hope to God we make it in time for the nine,' he says. We climb through several layers of black cloud and the pilot warns that there is a storm coming from the north, the very direction in which we are heading. The plane begins to jump and bump, and I bang my head against the roof. John is giggling now, noticing the expressions of pure panic on the faces of myself and our two colleagues, Chris McGreal of the Guardian *and Joan Leishmann of the Canadian Broadcasting Corporation. 'Don't worry, Keane, we'll be fine,' he says. Heartened by this, I turn to him and say that I am never afraid in his company. 'As long as you're here we'll be fine,' I tell him. 'If you keep saying it, then it must be true,' he replies. We have given John the nickname 'Basher' and suspect that he is secretly proud of it. It is a nickname bestowed because of his determination never to allow anybody or anything to stand in the way of his getting the story.*

Soon the plane is circling above Mmabatho, and we are straining our eyes to see if there are any burning buildings or crowds on the streets. From where we are, all seems to be quiet. Inside the airport terminal – with its customs hall for Bophuthatswana's foreign visitors – there is no sign of activity. Mangope's police and customs officials appear to have abandoned their posts. The white manager of AVIS tells us not to worry but warns us to take care of the car. 'You won't be going near any townships, now, will you?' he asks. We lie and tell him all we want to do is drive around Mmabatho and Mafeking. John has already jumped into the car driven by his crew. They are Glenn Middleton, a blond and cheery cameraman, and Jerry Chabane, the sound recordist. Chabane is a native of Soweto, a quiet but tough operator who is Middleton's best friend. Together with John they have covered some hair-raising scenes of violence in the past few months.

We drive in convoy into Mmabatho and then split up, the television crew going to the hotel to allow John to view their footage, and myself, McGreal and Leishmann heading into the town centre. There is debris all over the streets, up-turned rubbish bins, huge rocks and acres of broken glass sparkling under the afternoon sun. Groups of youths are hanging around the street corners. A police van pulls up just in front of us and a sergeant jumps out. He grabs one of the youths and starts to beat him. But the others push forward and begin to remonstrate with the policeman. He listens to what they are saying, frees the youth and then retreats into the interior of the armoured car. We hear the sound of tear-gas being fired and suddenly a group of people comes surging around the corner pursued by another armoured vehicle. I notice little puffs of smoke coming from the window of the van. 'Fucking rubber bullets,' shouts McGreal from the back. We have all seen what these lumps of hard rubber can do to people's heads and so we make a bee-line for the ANC offices.

At the door we are greeted by an extraordinary apparition: a woman in a mini-skirt and fish-net stockings wielding a huge shotgun. She introduces herself as 'Comrade Sis' and welcomes us inside. The office is crammed with excited young men. They are speaking in Tswana, but the gestures and the English words scattered here and there – police, tear-gas – make it obvious that they are expecting an attack on the building. Suddenly there is the sound of rocks bouncing against metal, followed by loud bangs and cheering and then the searing presence of tear-gas. A police van pulls up outside the door and a voice on a megaphone begins calling on the occupants of the building to come outside. Comrade Sis fingers the shotgun nervously. 'Just let them come,' she says, assuring me that at close range the blast from her gun would stop several policemen in their tracks. She tells me there are several more guns in the building. The tear-gas is now beginning to choke us. We cannot see it, but our eyes are streaming and our lungs are beginning to heave.

The police eventually pull back from the building. Rioting in another part of the city has apparently relieved the siege of the ANC building. Outside on the streets the crowds have set up barricades of burning rubbish and tyres. Thick black smoke is rising into the sky, blending with the dusk, and the mood is changing. Whenever the police appear the crowds melt back into the side streets. No sooner have they disappeared than the road is thick with angry chanting youths.

Both McGreal and Leishmann are veterans of Central America's wars and like me they have witnessed countless riots and civil disturbances. This, however, is different. There is a viciousness, a madness in the air, that makes us all nervous. Anything can happen on these streets. Bophuthatswana is in limbo-land — half way between the oppressive rule of Mangope and the clutch of the future. Nobody is sure what the rules are, if there are any rules. We ask a police sergeant, 'Who is in charge here?' He pauses for a few seconds and then answers, honest and confused. 'I don't know. Me . . . I really don't know.'

We drive to the township of Montshiwa outside the capital. There are army checkpoints everywhere. They seem to have sprung up within hours. On the road outside Mmabatho we meet a Reuters TV crew. They are friends of mine from Johannesburg. Mark, a white South African, and Frank, his black sound recordist, have been badly beaten up. They are in a state of shock. Mark tells us how the army and police dragged them out of the car and laid into them with batons and rifle butts. Mark warns us to keep tape-recorders and cameras well hidden. 'These guys are crazy, man — just keep your heads down,' Mark calls out as we drive away. There are several checkpoints on the road to Montshiwa, all of which we manage to negotiate safely. There are hostile stares and endless questions but we are left unmolested.

On the outskirts of the township our car is surrounded by several hundred youngsters. I notice that many of them are carrying petrol bombs and rocks. A large trench has been dug in the middle of the road. The mob is very angry and we are being told to produce our ID documents. We hand over ANC press cards and this mollifies the crowd. Behind us Ken Oosterbroek, a photographer from the Johannesburg Star, is being given the same treatment. Ken is a *cool customer and produces his ID and smiles his way through the roadblock. Within six weeks Ken will be dead – shot dead in another township – but on this morning he cannot see into the future, and he is able to joke and laugh with us about the crazy situation. When we get out of the car kids surge around us, shouting, 'Phantsi, Mangope, phantsi' ('Away with Mangope, away'). The leader is a youth of about eighteen. 'Mangope, he must just go now. We never elected him and we don't want him. Tell him, you can tell him from us he must just go,' the unofficial spokesman says. One of them waves a petrol bomb in my face. 'You smell that. You like that,' he says before reeling back into the crowd, laughing aloud. It is time to leave.*

Back at the hotel that evening I met John Harrison in the bar. He was excited, talking about the rumours that were circulating of a major march by students and civil servants the following day. But later I watched him having dinner with Glenn and Jerry and he seemed strangely quiet. There was none of his usual jocular banter. I put it down to him being tired. At forty-eight he acted and worked like a twenty-year-old, hauling himself from townships to press conferences to interviews without drawing a breath. Most of the time he seemed to blast his way through, without appearing to feel the effects of his punishing work schedule. Except occasionally he would crash, hiding himself in a dark room until the effects of the savage migraines he suffered went away.

John had covered more wars than anybody else in the South African press corps. He had been in Vietnam and Uganda, had covered the fall of Nixon and the rise of Thatcher. Having started his career on local newspapers, he became a domestic and later foreign correspondent on the *Daily Mail* and the *Daily Express* before moving to the BBC, where he rose to become Chief Political Correspondent. His blunt nature and fierce honesty made him an unsuitable candidate for the chumminess and double-talk common to the Palace of Westminster, and when the chance came to go back into the field in South Africa, he jumped.

Having spent much of his childhood on the move because of his father's job in the army, John knew what it was to have to prove himself again and again in new environments. In South Africa he seemed to have found the perfect niche. It was a place that gave plenty of scope to the determined individual, and John blossomed, completing project after project and always planning another. Although he was a bright, curious man, he had an instinctive suspicion of intellectuals and was inclined to present the tougher side of his nature all too often. This was to the detriment of the sensitive and thoughtful part of his personality, which I had encountered in the quieter moments away from the job. Yet his no-nonsense attitude was something I and many others had reason to be thankful for on more than one occasion. In the heat of battle he could make you feel safe as no other individual I have known could manage. With John one felt secure. His presence was powerful, domineering, and seemed to cast a huge screen around those who travelled with him into the townships or to right-wing rallies. I had seen him dispatch young toughs in the townships with a clip around the ear, order spear-carrying warriors to stop intimidating journalists and, in one unforgettable moment, physically lift Eugene Terre'Blanche's bodyguard out of the way when he tried to prevent John from interviewing the neo-Nazi leader. He could be infuriating – driving his camera team as hard as he drove himself, arguing relentlessly – but his courage and generosity overcame any defects in his personality.

Like myself John felt an intimate attachment to the South African story. It went beyond the ordinary interest of a journalist to the degree that the country's transition to democracy became a personal passion. He lived and breathed the story; for him it was a magical tale, a human drama in which he played the honourable role of participant/historian.

Unlike so many others in our profession he did not regard the death and horror as vehicles for his own advancement. The massacres and the stupid waste horrified him, touching the core of his being. Because he was one of life's outsiders, perhaps because he had found himself on the receiving end of taunting and discrimination as a child, John identified with the suffering of the impoverished, the voteless and the abused. He was at his best reporting from the marginal zone, from the edge where the lost and the broken hovered, their voices striving to be noticed. I knew from our many private conversations that he was looking forward to covering the elections as the biggest story of his career; for somebody who felt the story so intensely and who detested oppression as much as John did, the first non-racial election was an event to be savoured.

That night John went to bed early, stopping at my table to say goodnight and to make arrangements for coverage on the following day. The next morning students from the University of Bophuthatswana began to arrive at the hotel, some of them talking excitedly about demonstrations that were being planned for that afternoon. John was among the first to head off in the direction of the university campus, a sprawling complex of hideous blockhouse buildings close to the city centre. By the time I arrived the rioting was in full swing. Clouds of black smoke were drifting across the campus from piles of burning rubbish, groups of students were roaming around armed with iron bars and rocks. The police made occasional sallies but retreated again under a hail of rocks.

A car pulled up and was immediately surrounded by the mob. A woman inside began to plead for her life. Someone in the crowd had recognized her as a government official. She began to cry hysterically. 'Out, out . . .' the mob shouted, shaking the car from side to side. A window was smashed and a youth reached in and began to beat the woman around the head. I threw caution to the wind and began screaming at them to stop. The crowd turned and some of the youths began to shove me backwards. 'Go away, man . . . this one is not your problem,' a student who was wearing a balaclava shouted into my face. Suddenly the car bucked forward, surprising the crowd who jumped out of the way, giving the woman a few vital seconds to accelerate. She drove with the fear of one who could sense her life was seconds away from being extinguished. As the car sped on to the centre of the road, the crowd began to pound the vehicle with a barrage of rocks. I saw one of them crash through the passenger-seat window and bounce off the woman's head. Blood spurted out and the car zigzagged for a few moments. But her fear was greater than the pain and she managed to drive out of range, the car shuddering to a halt at a police roadblock further up the road. The police reacted with fury and began to advance down the road in armoured cars. Rubber bullets and tear-gas rained on to the campus. I jumped behind a wall, coughing and choking, but at least out of the range of the police guns.

I kept looking out for John, remembering our midday appointment and hoping that he had managed to get some footage of the riots. A photographer hiding behind the wall with me said he had seen John earlier, when the police launched their initial assault on the university. John had apparently filmed the action and then made a break to the nearby town of Zeerust to feed the story in time for the BBC's lunchtime news. After spending several hours at the university, I decided to return to Johannesburg to collect some clothes and equipment. It was clearly going to be a long, difficult period and I was running out of clean laundry and tapes. Before checking out of the hotel, I tried to telephone John's room. The line was engaged and because I was in a hurry I decided not to walk up to the room and say goodbye.

It is late afternoon and I have left Mmabatho well behind. The weather is stiflingly hot and I roll down the car windows to feel the rush of air. It carries the haylike scent of the mealie fields and I feel myself coming back to life. The land here is endlessly, relentlessly flat, pushing off into the distance for hundreds of kilometres, the tedium of the view broken only occasionally by the giant towers of grain silos and the even more occasional herd of cattle.

Somewhere south of Lichtenburg I notice a strange apparition in the distance. Because it is dusk, a time of a thousand shadows on the highveld, I am not sure if the distant convoy is what I think it is. Perhaps it is a line of delivery trucks on the way to Botswana or a huge pipe heading for one of the mines. But as the convoy comes closer, I notice that it is made up of SADF vehicles. There are troop carriers with fifty-millimetre cannons as well as smaller armoured cars with light machine-guns. The convoy comes alongside, I slow the car and shout to a black military policeman who is riding scout on a motorbike. 'Are you going to Bop?' I call out. He smiles and shouts back that they are going to sit on the border. 'We are on stand-by,' he says. At this stage I have to decide between going on or returning to Mmabatho straight away. I decide to keep going, reasoning that I am now so close to Johannesburg that it would make more sense to push on, collect my equipment and then race back.

By the time I get to Joburg it is dark and the radio news is talking about a fresh upsurge of rioting in Mmabatho. 'I can see people lying on the ground bleeding . . . this surgery is packed with the wounded' a reporter on Radio 702 is saying. As I walk into the office I can see my colleague, producer Peter Burdin, busy taking notes. He is white-faced and shaking his head. On seeing me, he looks up and mouths some words. 'John is dead,' I think he is saying. But he must be referring to somebody else. He puts the phone down and there are tears in his eyes. 'John is dead, mate . . . a car crash outside Mmabatho. I can't believe it, I just can't believe it,' he says. I feel as if I have been kicked in the stomach. This is an idea I am not prepared to accept. It is as if my whole being rejects the notion that big, strong, loud, energetic John is dead. Peter is shaking as he tells me what he knows. There has been a bad accident outside Mmabatho. John and Glenn Middleton were rushing to the feedpoint. The car overturned as they went round a sharp bend. John died immediately. Glenn is in hospital but his injuries are not serious. The voice at the other end of the phone talking to Peter belongs to a woman who witnessed the immediate aftermath of the crash. She heard a huge bang and ran out on to the road from her house. Although concussed and shocked Glenn had managed to give her the number of the office. In a few minutes Glenn's wife Treacy arrives at the office. She is crying. A policeman has called her to say that John is dead and her husband is in hospital. 'What is happening?' she asks me, but I am unable to tell her. She gives me the name of the policeman and I call him. The facts are as the woman explained. John died immediately, his skull crushed when the car roof caved in.

At John's home the door is opened by his wife, Penny. She is one of the softest, kindest people I know. When she sees me and family friend François Marais the expression on her face changes. I can see that she senses something and has been seized by fear. 'What is it? Something has happened to him, hasn't it?' she asks. We do not know what to say, so we place our arms around her. 'Something very bad is after happening. There's been a car crash,' I say. François picks up: 'It was a very, very bad accident.' We go into the sitting room. 'Don't tell me . . . I don't want to hear you say it,' says Penny. 'I won't say it, Pen. I won't say it,' I reply. And so we sit there, the room becoming emptier and emptier by the minute, the huge presence of John Harrison sucked out of the atmosphere. Friends of John and Penny begin to arrive in ones and two. The telephone rings and a familiar voice asks for Penny. 'Please tell her it is Mr Mandela,' the man says. Later President De Klerk's office rings. Soon every room in the house is full of people speaking in hushed voices; this is not real, this is a house suspended in a place of shadows.

The night seemed to last for ever. After calling the rest of the BBC staff together, I decided to drive back to Bophuthat-swana in order to retrieve John's body and to bring Glenn Middleton back to a place of safety. The news reports coming out of Mmabatho and Mafeking suggested a rapidly deteriorat-ing situation; there were huge crowds on the streets, the police and army seemed to have split down the middle with rival factions exchanging fire. Nobody knew where Mangope was holding out. There were even rumours that he had fled to neighbouring Botswana. What I knew for certain was that the body of my dead friend and an injured colleague were lying in the middle of a battlezone in a hospital that could be overrun at any moment. And so in the early hours of the morning I headed back for Mmabatho with Milton Nkosi and two Canadian colleagues who volunteered to come along and help. It was a spectacularly starry night and we could see for miles across the veld, the lights of distant farmhouses blending into the canopy of the sky so that earth and heaven seemed to be one great portrait that spread before us.

We entered Mmabatho at around three a.m. and found the streets deserted, only a few soldiers milling around the main police station. The hospital was situated on the outskirts of Mafeking – the old Boer War siege town that lies directly adjacent to Mmabatho. It was a small building, more like a rural dispensary than a hospital catering to the needs of thousands of people. The main ward was filled with people who had been wounded in the previous day's fighting and a solitary nurse was making her rounds. She directed us to the room where Glenn was sleeping and told us we could take John's body away once the police had given the necessary clearance.

Glenn was bruised and severely concussed. We left him to sleep and went off in search of the police. At the main station a nervous guard cocked his weapon and advanced menacingly. Only the earnest pleading of Milton persuaded him that we were seeking their assistance and not planning to overrun the station. Inside several exhausted, red-eyed policemen sat slumped on the hard wooden benches of the charge office. We explained our desire to remove the body and they listened patiently. 'You must come back in the morning. Can you not see we are overstretched?' one of them asked. The police force was at this stage struggling to make up its mind which side to join in the battle for Bophuthatswana. Some of the rank and file had already gone over to the ANC side, but the officers, like the men sitting in the charge office, were still loyal to Mangope. They had seen him survive the previous coup and were reluctant to put their careers, and possibly their lives, on the line to join an adventure that might yet be crushed. The memory of Mangope's purges of the security forces after the last uprising was fresh in the minds of the commanders, many of whom were promoted to fill the vacancies created by purged officers. The atmosphere inside the station was becoming tense and I sensed a growing impatience on the part of the man who had been answering our questions. We left offering profuse gratitude and promised to return in a few hours to talk to the day shift.

At the hotel I slept for perhaps an hour and then woke up with a start, after dreaming that I could hear John's voice calling out above the sound of bullets and explosions. He had been shouting my name and telling me to follow him. It was the sound recording of some moment in the past suddenly hurled into my dreams, some fragment of a sentence uttered in a township long before when John was running hard and fast, blind to the future, to the death that was preparing to overtake him.

Now I was awake in the strange lost hours before the dawn, and could hear only the gentle sound of African birdsong on the patio outside my room. The light began to seep under the curtains, grey and uncertain at first, then flowering into the full bright glory of a late-summer morning. Much of what happened later that morning has, thankfully, been lost to memory: I can remember a protracted debate with the police about the removal of the body; a steady stream of wounded arriving as the battle came closer and closer to the hospital; the road to the airport – our only exit – blocked by rioting mobs; and finally the helicopters arriving to take us out. The first chopper was driven by a former airforce pilot. He had seen the mobs on the road as he circled above Mafeking. 'Shoot the whole fucking lot of them,' he said, 'that's what I would do. It's the only way, my friend. What is happening to this country?' Glenn and his wife Treacy, who had also arrived at the hospital, left on the first flight.

As soon as they had vanished into the sky, I went to the morgue to help lift John's body on to a stretcher. We could not find a body bag, so we wrapped him in blankets. How can I say what it felt like, this preparation for the journey home? Outside the mobs roamed the streets and soldiers were firing wildly, while here in a small concrete hut my friend slept an endless sleep, his energy and vigour now drained away. Now that I could see that mighty life force reduced to stillness and silence, I was forced to accept that John Harrison was indeed dead. Dead. So hard to say the word much less accept it.

There was no time for reflection just then, however. The sound of gunfire was louder and I could hear the cheering of the crowds coming closer. With the help of some hospital porters we quickly loaded John's body on to the second helicopter. As the chopper lifted us up above the hospital, far above Mmabatho, I could see the smoke of burning barricades and the figures of the rioters like ant-people milling about in the streets below. And then we found ourselves over the veld, crossing the fields of green mealie plants and the farmhouses of the Western Transvaal as the chopper flew east in the direction of Johannesburg.

There is something timeless about this journey. The chopper is a dream floating above the great flat spaces of the platteland. I am crammed in next to John; I can feel his arm wedged into my ribs, but I do not believe he is dead. We pass over herds of cattle and they run from the noise, the wap-wap of our rotors. Then we are crossing over an African village; there are mud huts with corrugated tin roofs and rusting cars lounging in the field alongside. Children rush out and wave at us; they are smiling and jumping, delighted by this great silver bird in the sky. I want to shake John and hear him laugh. He loved the innocence of children and these sweet angels in their ragged clothes are waving for him. 'Wake up, Johnny,' I say to myself. 'Can you hear them? Can you hear them?' But we sail on through the sky and behind us the children become specks on the horizon; they are like fragments of all the hope and possibility lost in the moment of John's death, and though they reach out to us, though they call his name on this late-summer wind, we cannot touch them or hear their sacred voices. We are lost.

By the time I had returned to Johannesburg with John the situation in Bophuthatswana had deteriorated dramatically.

The South African Army was reported to be preparing an invasion plan, but there were reports too of a mass gathering of right-wingers in Ventersdorp, the headquarters of the AWB. There had also been a call on the right-wing Radio Pretoria for a general mobilization of Afrikaner Volksfront members. These were General Constand Viljoen's supporters, many of whom had gained their military experience during South Africa's bush war in Namibia and Angola in the seventies and eighties. Lucas Mangope, now hiding out on a farm in fear of his life, had called on the right-wing to do the same job the South African Army had done several years before: save his government from the wrath of the people. To the right-wing the call had a powerful resonance. Mangope was their kind of black, content to buy the idea of a Tswana nation state and an Afrikaner state on the simple basis that it guaranteed a life of wealth and power that a democratic settlement would never grant him. Though they would never say it openly, the President of the Republic represented the perfect Uncle Tom and if his republic were allowed to fall the whole allied concept of a white nation state would be severely, if not permanently, damaged.

That night, on farms across the platteland, men loaded supplies and ammunition on to pick-up trucks and set out for Ventersdorp. By early morning a convoy of some 400 right-wing vehicles were heading in the direction of Mmabatho, about two hours' drive from Ventersdorp. This was to be the great adventure. The men in the convoy felt confident. They were armed to the teeth with shotguns, sniper rifles, automatic weapons and pistols. As far as they knew the Bophuthatswana security forces would support them. Their view of the potential opposition was shaped by the master–servant relationship on their farms. Well-fed and muscular, they could not imagine the scrawny boys of the Bop townships being any match for them.

The right-wing army was a divided force, however. The Volksfront men tended to look down on the AWB, partly because of a genuine distaste for the neo-Nazi apparel and rhetoric, but also because many of Viljoen's supporters thought themselves socially a cut above Terre'Blanche's stormtroopers. Viljoen attracted the big farmers and the intellectual right-wing; Terre'Blanche drew his strongest support from among the ranks of the poor whites and the smaller farmers who had most to lose from the economic and political upliftment of the black majority. To add to that was the very real contempt for Terre'Blanche felt by Viljoen himself and several of the other generals who made up the command council of the Volksfront. To them the AWB leader was an oaf and a bully. Unlike Viljoen he had never led men in combat, had never really known the reality of war. He drank too much and his much publicized affair with the English-speaking columnist Jani Allan was just the kind of business to mortify the stolid Calvinist souls of the generals. In short, they regarded him as a fool, albeit a dangerous one.

The cracks in the right-wing alliance were to be glaringly exposed later in the day. But for the time being a semblance of togetherness was maintained. On arriving in Mmabatho, the right-wingers headed straight away for the airforce base, where Mangope had arranged for them to rendezvous with some of his senior officers. As the dawn came up, the main runway was witness to the extraordinary spectacle of right-winger marchings and drilling while others roared around in pick-ups. They began to patrol Mmabatho and Mafeking. All this time the South African Army stood on the border, awaiting instructions from Pretoria. Almost everybody in Bophuthatswana knew that once the SADF did move in, the trouble would end. It had a reputation as a no-nonsense force and easily outgunned the right-wingers, the Bop security forces and the ANC's young militants. The explanation advanced for the delay by political and military sources in Pretoria was that Bophuthatswana was still a constitutionally independent state (in terms of South Africa's constitution, that is) and a military invasion could take place only if Mangope requested it, or if his government ceased to function and exist. There were others within the military establishment who suggested to this author that the decision to wait may have been prompted by a desire to see the right-wing humiliated on the streets of Mmabatho and Mafeking. Whatever the reason, the delay helped contribute to the bloodshed and chaos that were to engulf the two towns later that morning.

The trouble began when sections of the Bophuthatswana Army refused to co-operate with the right-wing army. Weapons that had been promised to the white army were refused and racial insults were exchanged between rival groups at the airforce base. Finally, under pressure of invasion from Pretoria Mangope was forced to issue a statement calling on the right-wingers to withdraw from Bophuthatswana. As the news was filtering through, a blazing row erupted at the base between leaders of the AWB and Volksfront contingents. Jannie Breytenbach, brother of the poet Breyten and a former special forces commander, publicly denounced the AWB and accused them of being unfit for military duty. Amid a welter of bitter abuse and angry gestures, some of the right-wingers began to trickle out of Mmabatho. As they left, one group of AWB members encountered an ANC crowd that was dancing and toyi-toying at the side of the street. Someone in the AWB convoy opened fire. Within a few seconds units of the Bop Army that had been following the AWB attacked the right-wingers. One car was hit while the others sped away. After a brief firefight the occupants of the car – all of them wearing the camouflaged uniforms and swastika-like insignia of the AWB – rolled out on to the ground. One was dead, the two others wounded. The survivors lay in the dust, pleading with journalists to get an ambulance. They said they had come because Viljoen had given an order for general mobilization. For more than half an hour they lay there being photographed and filmed by a large contingent of journalists. No ambulance came. 'For fuck's sake, will you please get an ambulance?' one of them pleaded. It was strange beyond words for black soldiers to see uniformed white men lying on the ground like this, begging for help. A friend of mine who witnessed the incident told me he was afraid to go for assistance. The soldiers were angry and he was convinced they would have killed him had he moved. Then suddenly a soldier walked up to the AWB men and shot them dead at point-blank range. He screamed as he opened fire. It was a terrible moment and yet inevitable. The belief that blacks would melt away in the face of white firepower, that a white South African somehow carried an aura of untouchability when he confronted a black in battle, was punctured for ever. Right-wingers who had heard about the execution went storming out of town, shooting at black civilians as they went. Three were gunned down in cold blood within hours. White journalists who approached the right-wingers were badly beaten up.

The departure of most of the right-wing contingent sparked off a major bout of looting in the centre of Mmabatho. A huge shopping complex known as MegaCity, reputedly owned by Mangope's Cabinet ministers, was picked clean. I watched thousands of people swarm out of the building carrying suites of furniture, whole sides of beef, washing machines – everything that could be carried. A lone soldier fired a few shots in the air, but the Bop Army had clearly given up any hope of stopping the looting.

After I had been there about an hour a rumour began to sweep through the crowd. The South African Army was on the outskirts of the town. They were coming this way.

People began to flee, some of them dropping their valuables as they raced across the car-park in front of MegaCity. I was driving back across the city in search of the South Africans when a group of armed men jumped into the road and began levelling their rifles and motioning for me to stop. I put my head down and accelerated through. In retrospect it was a foolish thing to do, but I was frightened and tired and felt certain they wanted to kill me. The combination of fear and deep anger over John's death had filled me with a kind of desperation. I wanted to get this story over and done with, to get the hell out of Bophuthatswana as quickly as I could. Luckily they did not shoot and I made it through to see the first South African columns rolling into Mmabatho. Groups of locals waved and cheered as the armoured vehicles drove into town. That night I watched them escort the remaining right-wingers out of town. The men who had entered Mmabatho swaggering and boasting now crept out of town under the protecting guns of the South African Army. It would be hard to conceive the depth of the humiliation felt in right-wing circles as a result of the débâcle in Bophuthatswana.

The following day General Constand Viljoen called a news conference in Pretoria and announced that he would henceforth refuse to take part in military actions involving the AWB. It was only a short step to a final split and a further announcement a week later from Viljoen that he would participate in the elections. Terre'Blanche was left isolated and humiliated. His boast that he would 'level the ANC with the grave' was shown up for the hollow flourish of rhetoric it really was.

Mangope was removed from power and two administrators – one black and one white – were installed in his place. The make-believe country set up to prove that apartheid could work had disappeared. There was jubilation on the part of the ANC, which had worked so hard to engineer Mangope's downfall. The President himself retreated to one of his many farms, muttering about court actions. Unusually for an African dictator ousted by popular revolt, he was neither killed nor imprisoned. He was left to a sullen silence and the enjoyment of the vast wealth he had appropriated during his years as supreme ruler of the supreme bantustan.

The overthrow of Mangope by a combination of people power and South African intervention was to have a profound impact not only on the right-wing, splitting it irrevocably, but also on the politics of Natal, the country's bloodiest battleground. The collapse of the homeland regime was watched nervously from Ulundi, capital of Chief Buthelezi's KwaZulu homeland, where rumblings of secession and rebellion had been growing since Inkatha's refusal to sign the interim constitution the previous November. It was there that the next great acts in the death of the apartheid state were to be played out.

Bophuthatswana has fallen. Mangope is a bad joke from the past and everyone is shifting their focus to Buthelezi. But John Harrison is still dead. It is a week since the battle of Mmabatho, and we have gathered in Johannesburg to bury our colleague. It is a hot day of brilliant sunshine and mourners arrive in small groups at a small Anglican church in the northern suburbs. As we sit in the church, blissfully cool after the heat outside, they begin to play a tape of his favourite songs. I listen to Jagger sing 'Hey you, get off of my cloud', and I can see John elbowing his way to the front of the crowd at a news conference or shoving some heavy out of the way as he creates space for Glenn to film. In front of us John's wife, Penny, sits flanked by their sons Paul and James. Behind us is Glenn Middleton staring straight ahead, his gaze focused on a stained-glass window behind the altar. There are prayers and words of praise for John. The minister talks about the tragedy of John never seeing a democratic South Africa. He asks everybody to pray for peace. The cleaners from the BBC offices stand up and begin to sing in sweet, mournful voices: 'Senzenina, senzenina' ('God, what have we done to deserve this'). Although I have heard this hymn at countless funerals, today for the first time it reaches deep inside me. It is with difficulty, struggling to find a steady voice, that I go to the pulpit and talk about the life-force that has been taken away. 'He was not a human being, he was a force of nature,' I say. But what can anyone add to ease the pain of this most final goodbye? He was doing the job he loved, but there was so much more he wanted to do. Yes, it is surely a glorious thing to witness the birth of democracy in South Africa. But I cannot at this moment, looking at John's coffin, at his grieving widow and sons, have any belief in the world I have chosen to live and work in. And although I am ashamed to admit it, I have begun to fear for my own life. I look at the coffin of my friend and feel afraid for myself, as if the thousand risks we had taken together were adding up and my turn would come soon: perhaps in some wretched township; or at the hands of the neo-Nazis or in the hills of Natal; or maybe like John it would be a death of chance on a road somewhere. There would be tributes from my managers and colleagues, my wife and family would be heart-broken, but South Africa and all the other news stories in the world would go on, with men and women risking their lives to report them. And would a single reporter's death be worth it? Damn sure it wouldn't.

Filing out of the church into the sunlight, we listen to a flautist playing 'Amazing Grace'. But I feel nothing like grace. In fact I am gripped with hatred for the country. Although this is not noble to admit, I am sick of its insane and savage violence and the nightmares it gives me. As for the holy trade of the foreign correspondent — I have begun to doubt everything we represent. I am possessed by the feeling that the reporting of South Africa has become a commodity, a three-minute simplification of 300 years of history wrapped up in well-worn phrases. Journalists race around in search of civil war, secretly happiest when they sign off from some hell-hole where the bodies are stacking up and the omens of apocalypse are most vivid. I am sick to the teeth of the war stories, the flak jackets and all the attendant bullshit. Why did we all do it? Why do people like John and me and countless others race around townships and battlezones? I am still searching for the answer but I know that pursuit of the truth is only one part of the equation.

In the evening we are standing in John's garden, surrounded by a host of memories. The sky is low and overcast and the rain will come soon. People are drifting around with glasses of wine, seeking comfort from one another. I want to cry but no tears come. I want to cry for John and all the dead of the past three years but the emotion stays bottled up inside. I am lost and angry and confused and John Harrison is dead and gone for ever.

One last memory: three weeks before John's death and we are in Natal on the way to a funeral. A group of teenagers has been murdered while campaigning for the ANC. As usual John has gone ahead to get some shots at dusk. I am on the road with Milton when we see a car stopped in the middle of the road, its hazard lights flashing and headlights beaming straight ahead. 'Don't fucking stop, don't stop . . . it could be a fucking ambush, just keep going,' shouts Milton. I accelerate but notice as we approach that the car is John Harrison's. He is standing in the roadway. Glenn and Jerry are there too. Just in front of their car is the body of a black man. He is naked from the waste upwards and his body is covered in blood. I stop the car and talk to John. He tells me they came across the body in the road a few minutes beforehand. The man had been badly beaten and was dead, but the few cars that were on the road would not dream of stopping. Only John did. 'You can't leave the poor bastard lying there like that, can you?' he asks. He gets a blanket from the boot of his car and places it over the dead man. A few minutes later a police van comes along on a routine patrol and they remove the body. 'Sometimes this fucking country . . .' John says, but I lose the end of the sentence as he walks away into the dark towards his car.

CHAPTER 6

Among the Zulus

I do what I do because the politics of negotiation are in all reality far more potent as a force of change than the politics of violence.

Mangosuthu Buthelezi,
evidence to Parliamentary Committee
on Foreign Affairs,
London, 20 June 1986

My supporters are now angry. The South African government and the ANC are making deals behind our backs. If this happens Zulus will not listen. I see at the very least massive civil disobedience in Natal, and at the most civil war.

Mangosuthu Buthelezi,
speech reacting to ANC/government
agreement in December 1993.

Chief Maphumulo's brother lurched towards me, holding out a piece of half-cooked goat's meat. 'This you will eat. Eat it now, now,' he commanded. I took the dubious morsel and slowly lifted it to my mouth. As I began to chew the sinewy flesh, he pressed his head close to my right ear and whispered, 'Do you know something, Mr Foreigner? Do you know what they call me here?' I had to admit that his local name was unknown to me. He stood back and smiled, rubbing his stomach and giving me a contemptuous stare. 'My name, Mr Foreigner, is a name everyone knows around here. It is the name of Simon ... Simon the Killer. You see if people is cheeky with me I get a bush knife and I cut them down. That way they is not cheeky with me. Yes, yes ... Simon the Killer is the Chief's man here among the people.' I gulped down the vile meat and told Simon that he had a most interesting name. 'You must be a very strong man, a strong man indeed, Simon,' I offered.

He shrugged his shoulders and adopted what I can only describe as a pose of murderous modesty before reaching down to the fire and taking up another piece of meat from a blackened grill and offering it to Milton. As a city dweller more used to the cuisine of Johannesburg's restaurants, I had little doubt that Milton found the meat as revolting to the taste as I did. But as ever in dubious situations he was the picture of pleasantness and courtesy. His surname, 'Nkosi', is a Swazi name and closely related to the Zulus. This and his relentlessly charming manner frequently helped to smooth the way on our journeys through KwaZulu/Natal. While Milton engaged Simon in polite conversation I wandered over to the fire, where the women of the kraal were busy cooking the meat and boiling rice and pumpkin. They spoke among themselves but simply smiled and stared blankly when I asked questions. It was clear that Simon did not approve of my attempts to engage the women in conversation. He came over and gave me what I interpreted as a dirty look before presenting me with yet more of the appalling meat. I strongly suspected that he knew I hated the goat's meat and had decided to punish my transgression by offering me yet more of it.

The feast was being prepared to celebrate Simon's thirtieth wedding anniversary. His family of eighteen children were among the guests. A group of his cronies sat inside a mud hut away from the women, drinking and chewing endlessly on the meat. They were all tough men too, Simon assured me. I gazed into the gloomy interior and was met by a battery of sullen stares. An old man next to the door told me they were discussing local matters and did not want to talk politics with an outsider. I stepped back into the sunlight where Simon the Killer was waiting. His family kraal was set among a series of tumbling hills upon which tiny beehive-shaped huts clung like barnacles. It was the Africa of the imagination, a tableau of the pastoral and primitive that suggested quite the opposite of the murder and misery for which the valley had become infamous. This was the case throughout Natal, which I had come to regard as the most beautiful of South Africa's provinces, the least white and the least regimented. One could drive from the pounding surf of the coastal region, with its mountainous sand dunes and coral reefs, into the feathery fields of sugar cane, on through small villages with their Indian trading posts and Zulu-speaking white farmers in shorts and knee socks, up into the hill country north of the Tugela, where the women still wore the traditional wide skirts, bright-coloured headgear and neck bracelets of old Zulu tradition and the young girls still walked about bare breasted without a trace of inhibition, where the hold of the chiefs on the lives of ordinary people was as powerful as it had been in the days of King Shaka a century and a half before. Chief Maphumulo's 'subjects' – for that is what they were – did not wear the traditional Zulu garb. The close proximity of Pietermaritzburg had left the valley susceptible to modernizing influences. Most of the young men had worked in the city at one time or another, and it was close enough for them to visit and meet their more radical counter-parts from the townships that ringed Pietermaritzburg. Never-theless the crushing of a previous rebellion left the residents of the valley disinclined to go against the word of Chief Maphu-mulo or his brother Simon the Killer.

I travelled first through Pietermaritzburg, with its colonial town hall and monuments to the lost age of the pioneers, and

then through the ragged section of town, where the minibuses
gathered to carry the black workers into the townships and
villages that extended beyond the white territory. About five
miles beyond Pietermaritzburg the first sign for Table Mountain appeared, pointing off in the direction of a deep valley
where the long stems of the sugar cane waved gently in the
breeze, rather like the tentacles of a forest of sea anemones
floating back and forth in an underwater current. The territory was now almost solidly Inkatha, the ANC elements
having lost the battle for control three years previously,
driven out by the guns and spears of their plentifully armed
opponents. The ruined houses of the ANC people were now
homes to armies of goats that munched the weeds and the
elephant grass that had come sprouting up with the summer
rains. What had happened here was in effect a political
pogrom. The ANC members were of the same ethnic group,
in some cases members of the same family, as the Inkatha
faction. But opposition was not something the Chief tended
to tolerate, and when the ANC began to flex its muscles and
recruit the youth of the area, a political 'cleansing' was
ordered. This was similar to what had happened across wide
areas of territory controlled by Inkatha, where the comrades
of the ANC attempted to organize and demonstrate against
the rule of people like Maphumulo. The ensuing war made
Table Mountain one of South Africa's most infamous killing
grounds

Having waited for nearly an hour and chewed as much
goat's meat as I could endure, I asked Simon again when I
might be able to meet his brother, the Chief. 'Oh, he is the
most important man in the valley. You will have to wait. He
is busy visiting his people,' Simon responded. Themba, the
young Inkatha official who had accompanied me to Table
Mountain – it was deemed unsafe by Inkatha for me to travel
alone – apologized for the delay and began to lecture me on

the customs of the rural villages. He was a soft-spoken university-educated youth who had lost patience with the ANC when it launched the campaign of school boycotts in the late seventies. Because he came from a desperately poor rural background, Themba's family struggled to provide him with school uniform and books. His daily journey to school involved a two-hour walk each way. For Themba, education was the one route away from the poverty and the hopeless horizons of his village. When the ANC comrades at his school told him to stay away, he rebelled and turned up anyway. He was beaten up and received a death threat for his defiance and was forced to move to another school. The journey there was even longer. Themba wanted me to understand that he respected the people of his village even though they were illiterate and unsophisticated. The point was that he wanted something better, a career and an income that would allow him to improve his mind and do something positive about the conditions his people lived in. 'But I don't want to do that by ditching out everything I was brought up to believe in. Our traditions are important and we cannot forget them,' he said. His voice rose above the murmuring and laughter of the feast taking place around us. As a young man who was intensely interested in politics but who was alienated from the ANC because of his experiences at school, Themba looked around for a political flag to follow. He found his standard bearer in Chief Buthelezi, whose message of Zulu pride and liberation through constitutional politics made perfect sense. Themba joined the Inkatha Youth Brigade and continued with his secondary education. He was now a leading official in the movement in KwaZulu/Natal and studying at night for a degree in business administration.

Our conversation was sharply interrupted by the wild ululation of the women in the kraal. 'That is for the Chief. He has arrived,' said Themba who stood up and motioned in the direction of a pathway leading up above the kraal. Simon, who had until that moment adopted a lordly, casual air, straightened his shoulders and began marching around the compound, giving orders and waving his hands in the air. 'The Chief is here. He here now, now. You come with me, I bring you to his *induna*,' Simon said, as he joined us on the walk up the hill.

A man with an automatic rifle appeared and smiled. He was the Chief's bodyguard and had been sent down to look us over. He appeared satisfied that we were not carrying weapons and led us in the direction of a modern bungalow, outside of which were parked several cars. I stopped to catch my breath and noticed that Simon had turned around and was heading back towards the kraal. 'He's going back for the beer,' the bodyguard explained. Themba smiled and urged me to hurry along. The Chief did not like to be kept waiting. Upon reaching the top of the hill, another bodyguard appeared and beckoned me forward. 'Put your hands over your head,' he ordered. 'Now you must approach the Chief with your hands in the air and say: "Wena undlovu" ["Behold the great elephant"].' Although it sounded like a party trick I thought it wiser to comply, and with hands in the air Milton and I approached the Chief.

Perhaps it was something in our expression, or the way we pronounced the tribute, but the Chief exploded into rage when we walked up to the circle of men in whose midst he was sitting. 'Get back, down there, over there . . . get back and show respect,' he barked. The bodyguard grimaced and pointed to a spot about ten yards from the circle. 'You people are just a bunch of shits . . . you think that I am some kind of fool that you can come wandering in here and treat me like this. This is my valley. Did anyone say you could come here? Did they? Did they? What fool said you could come here? Show me this fool,' the Chief screamed. Milton translated slowly and nervously, and the bodyguard began to tiptoe away behind us. 'You come here now,' he called out to the bodyguard. The man with the automatic rifle came up and knelt in front of Chief Maphumulo. As he did so, one of the men in the circle began to berate the bodyguard. The Chief rounded on both of them. They were to stop humiliating him in front of the outsiders. He motioned to a clump of trees and ordered both men to go there and wait until he had finished talking to us. The two sidled meekly away. I had not seen such a display since school when errant members of the class were ordered to stand with their faces to the wall. Themba approached, hunched over with his hands clasped in front of him like a man who was about to pray. He had hardly started speaking when the Chief rebuked him. Why had we been brought to the area without his permission? Did we think we could just walk in here unannounced? Themba did his best to explain and apologize but was eventually told to keep quiet. I cringed for him and decided to follow Milton's example and stare straight at the ground, keeping absolutely silent. And then salvation, in the most unlikely form, came tumbling into the middle of the group.

She was a huge woman in a bustling dress with a raucous voice and I guessed from the familiar manner of her approach to the Chief that she was his wife. It was also obvious that she was drunk. The Chief stood up and began to laugh. Just then the woman twirled around and nearly fell on top of Themba. Everybody laughed nervously. She jumped up and down and began shouting the Chief's praises. He laughed uproariously when she started to rail at the bodyguard and adviser who still skulked behind the trees. I began to dread that she would focus her attention on me. The Chief, a tall thin man, threw his arms around his wife's waist and lifted her into the air. It was a formidable show of strength, given her considerable frame and weight. The entire group applauded as the

Chief walked out of the circle and deposited his wife next to the front door of the bungalow. When he came back to us he appeared to have undergone a definite transformation. Friendly now, he called Milton and myself forward to his chair, where we were invited to sit on the ground and ask questions.

Before we could say anything the Chief began to give a speech. 'The ANC . . . you see the ANC . . . you see that Mandela. I'll kick his fucking arse if he comes here, I can tell you. I am Chief Maphumulo. They'll have to cut my fucking head off if they want to come into this place.' Milton translated rapidly, his voice consciously lower than the Chief's. There was to be only one speaker here and he was the man gazing down from the chair. Although I felt like a fool squatting on my haunches before this bully of a man, I was much too frightened to do anything other than nod appreciatively as he spat out a stream of hateful abuse about Mandela. The Chief blamed it all on De Klerk's government. They were a bunch of liars. They had sold out to the ANC and now they wanted him to give *his* valley away. 'It's bullshit, man. It's bullshit,' he exclaimed. The British were to blame too. The Chief knew John Major's name and appeared convinced that he too had sold out to the ANC. This was a view entirely consistent with that of Mangosuthu Buthelezi and had clearly been passed down the line to the rural henchmen like Chief Maphumulo. There was one thing he wanted me to know above anything else, though. There would be no election in the valley. 'Tell me where they would hold it here without my authority?' the supreme ruler of Table Mountain demanded to know. He was sure there would be no voting in his area. They could send in the SADF if they wanted, but they could not make his people vote if they did not want to.

Chief Maphumulo stood up and asked me to walk with

him in the direction of the enclosure where his herd of fat
black cattle were grazing. Away from the others he softened,
becoming almost lyrical as he described what the valley
meant to him. 'This is my people's place. This is the land of
our fathers. Do you expect me to hand all of this over to the
ANC? Surely you do not expect such a thing of a man like
me,' he said. He told me he had spent a great part of his life in
the cities, working in a steel factory outside Johannesburg and
coming home once or at most twice a year with money for
his family. He had been among the great host of migrant
workers whose toil and sweat had helped to build the South
African economy. But although he had lived in the black
townships around Johannesburg during the worst of the
apartheid years, Chief Maphumulo saw his destiny not in the
terms of universal suffrage and economic equality demanded
by the ANC but rather in the ancient rights of the chief. His
security lay in the knowledge that he was strong enough to
ward off any challenge to his authority. In the old days it
might have come from the leader of another clan in the area.
Now it was coming from the young comrades of the ANC,
the people whose modernist ideas represented the single greatest threat to the feudal world of the Chief. Under the existing
system he enjoyed absolute obedience. He could dispense
patronage and punishment without fear of contradiction. His
cattle were the fattest in the valley and the steady flow of
gifts – cattle, goats, beer – ensured that he never lacked the
essentials of real wealth in rural Zulu society. The Chief was
a prominent member of Inkatha. But I had the feeling that
his membership of the party was a pragmatic and not an
ideological choice. For him Inkatha was the party of tradition-
alism, the party most likely to guarantee his continued pride
of place at the top of the social structure in Table Mountain.
He felt that Chief Buthelezi – great grandson of Cetswayo,
the mighty warrior king – understood him and men like

him. Buthelezi was the guardian of a way of life that had served Chief Maphumulo's interests well. In return he could be relied upon to deliver the numbers at Inkatha rallies and the warriors for the battle with the ANC. At the level of Chief Maphumulo the argument had nothing to do with Buthelezi's demands for a federal system or the enshrinement of the rights of the individual. Nor had it very much to do with pride in his Zuluness. The virulent Zulu nationalism espoused by Inkatha in the months before the election allowed men like Maphumulo, local warlords and kings of their own areas, to cast a political cloak around what was ultimately a determination to preserve their powers of patronage, their power of life and death over vast numbers of people.

When I left the Chief, he warned me to take care in the weeks ahead. Bad things were happening everywhere and the election could be a very bad time indeed. I was welcome to come back but I should make arrangements before entering the valley. The Chief did not want me to be mistaken for a trouble-maker or a spy. It was nearly dark when we left the kraal and I switched on the headlights, anxious to avoid hitting any of the numerous human beings and farm animals that drifted out of the shadows. A man jumped out in front of us about twenty yards ahead and raised his hands. It was Simon the Killer. I slowed to a halt and rolled down the window. Simon pressed his head into the car. 'I just wanted to say goodbye to you, that is all. Goodnight, Mr Foreigner,' he said and backed away into the darkness.

The man to whom Maphumulo and his brother owed their allegiance, Mangosuthu Buthelezi, was the ultimate chief. He was Prime Minister of KwaZulu and Minister of Police, leader of the Inkatha Freedom Party, and uncle and traditional adviser to the Zulu king, Goodwill Zwelethini. It would be an understatement to say that most foreign correspondents based in South Africa disliked Buthelezi. Loathing came closer to describing the feelings of many. Yet he was a more complex and certainly more politically astute figure than was ever generally accepted. Born on 27 August 1928 into the Zulu royal house, he was the brightest and most ambitious of the young royals. Although he was much too far down the line of succession to become king, Buthelezi – who became leader of the largest family clan in the Zulu nation in 1957 – set his sights on achieving prominence through politics. As a student at Fort Hare University – the country's pre-eminent political nursery – Buthelezi was a contemporary of Mandela and Robert Sobukwe, the founder of the Pan-Africanist Congress. He was expelled from the university because of his ANC activities. When he returned to Zululand he took up a prominent part in the ANC, which his uncle Pixley Seme had played such a major role in founding. It was the accepted route for a bright and politically aware young man. Other Zulus who had helped to build up the ANC included John Dube, A.B. Xuma and the Nobel Laureate Chief Albert Luthuli; it seemed natural that Buthelezi would follow in their footsteps.

Upon taking over the leadership of the Buthelezi clan – the biggest in Zululand – he began to see himself more and more as a leader in his own right, and not dependent on the ANC for patronage. After the banning of the ANC in 1960, Buthelezi began to carve out a political future as a leader in the impoverished lands set aside for black use under the apartheid system. He began by opposing the proposals for a black territorial authority in what was to become KwaZulu on the basis that it encouraged the divide-and-rule politics of the white state. But by 1964, with the ANC's leaders imprisoned or in exile, Buthelezi accepted the proposal for what was later to become a homeland government and was elected its chairman. Watching this from abroad, the ANC leadership grew increasingly suspicious of Buthelezi, believing that he intended to create a personal power base in KwaZulu and to abandon the concept of using his position to launch a second front against apartheid from within South Africa. As the years progressed the rift between Buthelezi and the ANC became wider and the old friendships became strained. As the leader of KwaZulu, Chief Buthelezi was given a state salary; his police force relied heavily on the South African security police for information and training, and ensured that the ANC was given a difficult time on the ground in KwaZulu during the seventies and eighties. The KwaZulu Assembly became little more than a rubber-stamp parliament for Chief Buthelezi's Inkatha, the movement he founded as a counter to the ANC in 1975.

The ANC crucially misjudged Buthelezi when it began to portray him as a stooge of the apartheid regime. He was autocratic, arrogant and contemptuous of opposition; he manipulated Zulu tradition and the royal house to ensure that the interests of Inkatha and the Zulu nation were seen to be one. When it came to issues like sanctions and disinvestment from South Africa, his views were at one with those of Pretoria. He denounced any form of radicalism and condemned the ANC's armed struggle. His organization took money from the security police and it sent its members for training by the special forces as members of hit squads. But for all this Mangosuthu Buthelezi was anything but a stooge. Other homeland leaders like Lucas Mangope or the Matanzima brothers in Transkei were consumed by the need for self-aggrandizement and saw their positions as passports to eternal plenty. For Buthelezi it was never a question of personal wealth. I am convinced that power, the compulsive desire to be *the* top man, motivated by vanity and ANC-inspired paranoia, was at the root of his incredible political drive. He was shrewd enough to realize that the 'independence' offered

him by the Pretoria government would never work in the
long run and he duly rejected it. When P.W. Botha mooted
the idea of a national council for blacks in the eighties,
Buthelezi refused, saying no black of any substance would sit
on such a council until Mandela was released. Again the
Chief knew what would be workable and what would not.
For him to sit down with P.W. Botha while the ANC
remained outside would have been foolish; no agreement
reached in such discussions could have been made to stick
without Mandela's imprimatur. Buthelezi knew this and
stayed well away from the proposed council. At the root of
the ANC's hatred for Buthelezi was the simple proposition
that those blacks who were not with them in the struggle
against apartheid were most definitely against them. By comparison the organization had an indulgent attitude towards
whites like Helen Suzman, who argued for precisely the same
things as Buthelezi – federalism, free enterprise – and who
did so from within the white parliamentary system. Although
Mrs Suzman and every other liberal member of parliament
accepted salaries from Pretoria, they never faced anything
like the opprobrium directed at Buthelezi. His crucial political
mistake – as the ANC saw it – was to divide the anti-
apartheid struggle by agreeing to work within the system and
to inspire loyalty by appealing to the tribal pride of the
legions of impoverished, dispossessed rural Zulus who made
up Inkatha's support base. To the ANC – which encompassed
every tribal group in the country – the notion of tribal
politics undermined everything contained in the organization's Freedom Charter, the seminal document of the liberation struggle that pledged to establish a South Africa free of
racial and social barriers.

Of course from Buthelezi's perspective it made perfect
political sense to evoke memories of the glorious Zulu past,
with its warrior kings and long list of martial exploits. His

people were among the poorest and most illiterate in the country; they lived on land that was overgrazed, under the rule of chiefs who, like Maphumulo, frequently operated like feudal lords; and they were instinctually suspicious of the slick comrades with their talk of a brave new socialist world. By summoning up visions of the imperial past and hinting that such an age might come again, Buthelezi appealed to the sense of injured pride of a people who had watched the colonists steal their land and banish their kings. He encouraged the warlords* to strengthen their grip in the urban areas and used the patronage of the KwaZulu government to reward his supporters. A loyal party hack could find himself quickly promoted through the ranks into the government; the disloyal could find their names on death lists. Some of the gunmen were members of the KwaZulu police which was regarded by many independent observers as a fiercely partisan force. Those who discovered that their names were on lists had the choice of fleeing or of waiting for death. As the editor of the Johannesburg *Sunday Times*, Ken Owen (certainly no fan of the ANC), put it, Buthelezi's rule became a reign of terror.

Buthelezi's vanity grew with the years and he encouraged the growth of a Buthelezi personality cult in KwaZulu. Arriving at the Prince Mangosuthu Buthelezi Airport in Ulundi, capital of KwaZulu, one was confronted in the arrivals area by a beaming portrait of the Chief. To reach the legislative assembly one travelled along the Mangosuthu Buthelezi Highway, perhaps stopping off at the Holiday Inn to visit the Buthelezi Conference Room and to admire the

---

*Men who control large areas of Natal because of their capacity for violent action against their enemies. The majority give their support to the Inkatha Freedom Party.

photographs of Buthelezi and his nephew the King in the lobby. I have vivid memories of Inkatha Party congresses and rallies where fawning chiefs and party officials queued up to present Buthelezi with gifts; it was explained to me that this was part of Zulu tradition, but the atmosphere reeked of small-town sycophancy. When Buthelezi scowled, the party hacks scowled; when he clapped and laughed, they fell over themselves to join in. I formed the impression that he inspired a great deal of fear as well as loyalty among his black acolytes. Some of them – like Ben Ngubane and Frank Mdlalose – were among the brightest politicians in the country, but they invariably seemed cowed by his presence at press conferences or other public occasions. The whites who joined Inkatha were a different and far more disparate collection. Some were so-called 'white zulus' who nurtured visions of Buthelezi as a noble warrior chief; some were former security-force members suffering from obsessive anti-Communist paranoia; others were committed to the anti-apartheid cause but frightened by the ANC's perceived radicalism; still others were big farmers who had at first feared Buthelezi but who later came to regard him as the greatest hope for the preservation of their vast estates and privileged way of life. The predominance of whites in leadership and public relations roles within Inkatha encouraged the belief that Buthelezi was at best a puppet of establishment interests, at worst a calculating opportunist determined to frustrate the wishes of the ANC.

But in portraying him as the ally of apartheid and the creature of Pretoria, the ANC made two important mistakes: it made it increasingly difficult for its own supporters to accept the day when compromise with Buthelezi might be necessary and it lulled itself into believing that he had no significant constituency, that he really was on a par with the self-serving money grabbers who ruled the other homelands. To a large extent the ANC was paralysed by loathing of

Buthelezi to the degree that many in the leadership were unable to make a calculated assessment of his strengths and weaknesses. The propaganda directed against him by ANC surrogate organizations during the eighties was virulent, to put it mildly: at one point the ANC's voice in exile, Radio Freedom, described the Inkatha leader as a snake whose head had to be crushed. He was repeatedly characterized as a sell-out and suffered the indignity of being chased away from the funeral of the PAC leader Robert Sobukwe in 1978. To a man who so acutely needed the affirmation of others, who bridled at the slightest insult to his dignity, the ANC's campaign of vilification was nothing less than a declaration of war. The incipient paranoia that lurks inside most insecure men and women – and I believe Buthelezi is a fundamentally insecure man – came rushing to the surface. He became obsessed with frustrating the ambitions of the ANC and with securing a base for himself that would survive the end of white rule. Thus, when the South African government – which had led him to believe he was a natural ally in any future election – began to make deals with the ANC, Buthelezi's response was furious. He saw enemies everywhere and became more sensitive and hostile by the day.

We are making our descent to Ulundi Airport. Below us the Umfolozi is in full flood; a wide and swiftly flowing river, it is a rich brown colour, fat with the soil that has been washed away on its journey from the hills of Zululand down towards the Indian Ocean several hundred kilometres away. As the plane descends the heat fills the cabin; we can see another group of journalists on the tarmac unloading equipment from a light aircraft. It is less than two months away from the election, and we have come here to see if the Inkatha Freedom Party is about to commit suicide. There has been speculation all week that Buthelezi will formally withdraw from all talks and finally rule out participation in the election. The problem is that he has – like the *ANC* – pulled out of talks before but has kept on talking. We have been fed a diet of deadline after deadline by the *ANC* and the government; they tell us the 'democracy train is leaving the station' and warn of dire consequences for those who do not climb aboard. But nobody believes in these deadlines any more; we have all made fools of ourselves too many times, reporting yet another crisis, to run the risk of telling our newsdesks that the time really has come, the talking really is over.

Nevertheless we have all trooped obediently to Ulundi because Buthelezi, however much the media may dislike him, always provides good copy. These days the whiff of čivil war and the hint of a Zulu rebellion are never too far from the Chief's lips and his predilection for appearing in public accompanied by spear-carrying warriors dressed in skins guarantees the attention of television networks and photographers. Today he has dispensed with the warrior hordes. The atmosphere is stiff and formal and all is not well in the Inkatha camp. There is not the usual fawning and grovelling. Some senior members of the party have done the unthinkable and taken to the floor of the congress to call for Inkatha to take part in the elections. There is a great deal of sensitivity and none of the usual sources are speaking. A man called Phillip Powell, former member of the security police and now trainer of Inkatha's military wing, physically obstructs a cameraman who tries to film some armed supporters of Buthelezi. Powell is one of the seriously unpleasant people with whom Buthelezi surrounds himself; he is feared by the *ANC*, whose supporters have already tried to kill him.

Inside the tent they have draped posters of Buthelezi everywhere; there are signs calling him the 'Father of Negotiations' and the 'Prince of Peace'. The temperature is soaring towards forty degrees Celsius and people are beginning to wilt. They have been up all night debating whether or not Inkatha should take part in the elections. Ziba Jiyane – a leading member of the pro-elections faction – is stopped by the press as he prepares to enter the tent.

Jiyane is bright and articulate; he only joined Inkatha earlier in the year, having been a member of the Pan-Africanist Congress in exile in Tanzania. He has been telling any delegate who will listen that a political party exists to fight elections, not to boycott them. But before he can open and speak to the press two of Buthelezi's close advisers appear on the edge of the group of journalists. Jiyane decides that he cannot speak to the media after all. He says that he is a democrat and will abide by the will of the party. He excuses himself and goes into the tent, which is now a sauna. Youths at the entrance undo the overhead flaps and a torrent of water comes gushing down. It is the sweat of the exhausted delegates, rising through the canvas and collecting in pools.

Most of those inside the tent are black; they wear khaki shirts and black berets on to which have been pinned Buthelezi badges. There is a group of old women to the left of the platform. I can see that at least three of them have fallen asleep. They are rudely woken by a younger woman who is some kind of party official. As she turns around, I notice that it is Gertrude Mzizi, Gertrude from Tokoza, warrior queen of the hostel dwellers who is still surviving in spite of the best efforts of the ANC self-defence units. I call out to Gertrude but my voice is suddenly drowned by clapping. Buthelezi has come into the tent. People are on their feet cheering. This is genuine emotion; in the past I have seen party congresses where Buthelezi is routinely hoisted on to the shoulders of his delegates, smiling and waving as they sing his praises. Today he simply goes straight to the stage. But instead of a political speech we are to be given a special treat, the compère tells us. A fashion show. An Inkatha special fashion show. With that, a black American bounds on to the stage and introduces himself as Mr Simpkins. He tells us his company has the franchise for the Inkatha 1994 catalogue. 'Ladies, if you will,' he says, pointing to the right-hand side of the platform. The women enter to loud cheering. 'This is the special wrap which has the face of the Chief Minister,' Mr Simpkins tells us. The women twirl and dance, the smiling face of Mangosuthu Buthelezi draped across their bodies. There are T-shirts, posters, hats, everything on to which the great man's face can be stencilled. He enjoys the display, chuckling to himself. The KwaZulu ministers and party officials beside him chuckle as well. When it is all over the Chief stands up and thanks everybody. His speech is short and to the point. The IFP will not be taking part in the elections unless the ANC and the government back down and grant KwaZulu federal status, taking into account as well the position of the Zulu king as constitutional monarch of the area.

This is an increasing theme of Buthelezi's. He knows the King – whom he privately treats like a political junior – is revered by millions of Zulus. If Buthelezi's argument with the ANC and the government can be turned into one between them and the Zulu nation, his hand is immeasurably strengthened. He spends his time warning the ANC not to bring the King into politics, when the monarch has become a virtual spokesman for Inkatha. But because the King is revered by the majority of the tribe, the ANC and the South African media tend to pull their punches about this shameful manipulation. There are gentle nudges to the Zulu royal house, warning it that there are perceptions of favouritism towards Inkatha. It is less a case of favouritism than of complete subordination of the monarchy by Buthelezi. He, after all, is the man who took the King to court and publicly humiliated him when he attempted to set up his own political organization back in the seventies. It is widely said that the King detests Buthelezi but that his fear is much greater than any temptation to rebel. A cousin of the King's, Prince Petrus Zulu, who was rumoured to be close to the ANC, has been murdered outside his home in recent weeks. In this part of KwaZulu only a fool openly challenges Buthelezi and Inkatha.

After Buthelezi's speech people file out of the tent, half stupefied by the heat. They clamber on to buses that will take them home to the furthest corners of Zululand. Those getting on the buses know the journey can be dangerous. Attacking coaches packed with the *enemy – whether they are armed or not – is a speciality of both sides in KwaZulu/Natal's brutal war of attrition.*

Buthelezi invites us to a press conference in a government-owned hall close to the marquee where the congress has been held. I always feel uneasy attending his press conferences. You know that no matter how straightforward the question the response will be informed by suspicion and hostility. Thus when someone asks, 'What is your bottom line in negotiations, Chief Minister?' Buthelezi tells him to read his policy document. When Buthelezi is asked whether or not he believes civil war is a danger, he tells the questioner not to put words into his mouth.

I ask him how he can – as an opponent of apartheid – justify being in alliance with white right-wing group that want to set up a state based on the colour of people's skins. 'They have committed themselves to non-racialism. It is we who made them do that,' he informs me. I point out that a volkstaat as proposed by the right-wing involves giving citizenship to people who are white and denying it to non-whites. How could that be non-racialism? 'I told you they have committed themselves to non-racialism. It is there in the constitution of the Freedom Alliance,★' he says, becoming increasingly agitated. I decide to put my neck on the line and attempt a further sally: 'Surely there is a complete contradiction here, Chief Minister?' He gives me that cold contemptuous stare I have come to know and fear. 'The contradiction is in your eyes, Mr Keane.' The supporting cast of party officials chuckle appreciatively and I retire defeated. Buthelezi produces a kind of group nervousness among journalists. It has two effects: some, like my courageous colleague John Carlin ('Are the KwaZulu police not your private army?'), go for the jugular and ask the difficult questions; others sit

★The conservative grouping that came together to oppose the ANC and the National Party in the run-up to the elections. It included Inkatha and the white right-wing Afrikaner Volksfront.

quietly, jotting down everything he has to say, and then join in
the chorus of guffaws when Buthelezi launches into a verbal
assault on the questioner. There is a temptation that I have felt
with other difficult subjects to simply announce that I did not
come to listen to childish and petulant guff and then, with a look
of dignified resolve, walk out of the press conference. I have
never succumbed to this temptation and do not do so on this
occasion.

It is beyond dispute that Buthelezi received a diabolical press.
This was in a large part due to his own irascibility and
reluctance to accept any challenge to his stated view of the
world. I am sure that the sight of a young reporter standing
up and questioning his political judgement must have infuriated him. The whole manner of how KwaZulu was run, the
tactics of fear and patronage and the links with the South
African security establishment, all helped to make him a
distinctly unlikeable public figure. In contrast to the ANC
leadership, Buthelezi's efforts to cultivate a relationship with
the media were infrequent and characterized by reticence and
hostility on both sides. The fact that he had become, for the
majority of the media, such a disliked figure tended to
frustrate rational analysis of his demands. He suffered too
because the majority of South Africans wanted a peaceful
settlement above all else. If this settlement failed to live up to
Chief Buthelezi's demands for federalism, then that was his
misfortune; there could not be any turning back. The overwhelming desire to move quickly towards elections, with all
the compromises this involved, was shared by the South
African media, which tended to row behind the general
political consensus. Most South African newspapers and journalists represented the views of a centrist, pragmatic audience
that increasingly came to regard Buthelezi as a spoiler who
stood in the way of a speedy and peaceful settlement. Thus

the fine print of his demands for federalism was too often overlooked. True, his record in KwaZulu indicated the very opposite of the liberal democracy he publicly espoused, but that did not entirely invalidate his arguments about what constituted real federal powers. He was correct in pointing out that at the end of the day the central government could rule the roost on the important issues like taxation and policing. If it came to a serious dispute on the core issues, big government had the power of override. When F.W. de Klerk told Buthelezi that he had achieved a federal constitution, the latter was correct in pointing out that the document agreed in November 1993 was far from federal. But even if the media as a whole failed to give due credence to Buthelezi's analysis of the constitution, the overall picture they portrayed of a vain and intolerant man, of a leader more concerned with the preservation of his own power than with anything else, was largely correct.

A classic case in point was Buthelezi's behaviour at the signing of the National Peace Accord in Johannesburg's Carlton Hotel on 14 September 1991. It was supposed to be a day of national reconciliation, a feel-good day when the leaders would publicly commit themselves to the peace process and shake hands for the cameras. Imagine, then, the surprise of the policemen guarding the entrance to the Carlton Hotel when they saw a host of Zulu warriors approaching in full cry on the morning of the fourteenth. The group – which eventually numbered several thousand – was carrying spears, clubs and knives, and was openly hostile to black passers-by. Inside, the gentle tinkling of the delegates' coffee cups was drowned out by the arrival of the chanting Zulus. When Buthelezi and the Zulu King arrived they were greeted by wild cheering. The demonstration had clearly been organized on Buthelezi's instructions and it set the tone for the day. Instead of the Accord being launched in an atmosphere of peace the main leaders bickered with one another in public, while the warriors entertained themselves by chanting and occasionally clubbing innocent bystanders. It was not the action of a man who had come to the Carlton to place the interests of South Africa first.

What had infuriated Buthelezi on that day was the perception that the Nationalists, having led him to believe he was their natural ally, had now dumped him in favour of the ANC. When he arrived at the signing ceremony for the National Peace Accord, Buthelezi knew that De Klerk and Mandela were making plans to move against the Zulu-dominated hostels around Johannesburg. Later, as the ANC and government worked their way through several sets of negotiations and breakdowns, finally reaching agreement in November 1993, Buthelezi drifted further and further away from the process – rightly convinced that, while his views would be listened to, it was the desires of the Nationalists and the ANC that were regarded as most important. Here was a man who had been fêted by Thatcher, Reagan and Kohl as a bulwark against extremism, a defender of Western democratic ideas and a champion of free enterprise. He had been photographed with the great and good, had been welcomed in the world's capitals, and encouraged to believe that he was a political player on a par with the most important South Africa could offer. With Mandela's release from prison this illusion was shattered. Now it was De Klerk and Mandela, the immortal double act that was going to save South Africa, while he, Buthelezi, was being given the role of minor player, a little duke who hovered in the wings waiting – in T.S. Eliot's words – to 'swell a progress, start a scene or two'. Buthelezi wanted a troika of leaders to share the limelight but the ANC in particular wanted to consign him to the dustbin. To them the idea of giving Buthelezi equal status with the hero of Robben Island was inconceivable. The ANC had scores to settle with Buthelezi and in any case believed that he was a regional leader first and foremost, not a political figure of the eminence of Mandela or De Klerk. This the Nationalists were increasingly willing to play along with. Privately, senior National Party figures sneered at Buthelezi and disputed his claims to have the support of millions of people. To the great coalition of interests that came together in the last months before the elections Mangosuthu Buthelezi represented an obstacle that would have to be persuaded to come on side and, if that failed, subjected to all the coercive power of the state.

I remember a particularly vivid illustration of the changed National Party attitude towards Buthelezi. It was just days before Christmas and the new interim constitution had sailed through parliament. The MPs were heading back to their constituencies before the advent of the new year and the long election campaign. Yet another final attempt was being made to bring Inkatha and its right-wing allies into the process. One evening as the talks were finishing, I went for a drink with a senior government minister and one of the country's leading intelligence officials. We settled down with a couple of large whiskies poured by the intelligence man, and the Minister launched into a weary diatribe against Buthelezi. Every time he thought he had made a deal with Inkatha, Buthelezi pulled the rug out from under him. What made it even more difficult was the fact that the Inkatha team was itself divided. The Minister made the familiar case that white hard-liners were preventing the more moderate blacks like Dr Ben Ngubane, a doctor and a sophisticated negotiator, from reaching a deal. 'And even when we do get them to agree to something, Buthelezi says no. Tell me how we are supposed to please him, will you?' he asked.

I put it to the Minister that what Buthelezi seemed to want

was a guarantee that his personal power base in KwaZulu would be preserved whatever agreements were reached at national level between the ANC and the National Party. At this point the intelligence official – a man of known ruthlessness and pragmatism – cut in: 'What he wants he cannot get.' The words were left to float in the air for a few seconds before the Minister spoke again: 'The process will go ahead with him or without him. He has to realize this. Most of his negotiators would accept a deal in the morning, but they are afraid of him.' The intelligence man rose to refill the drinks. He apologized because there was no ice. 'What will happen, then,' I asked, 'if he does try to stage a rebellion, if does try to secede?' The spy master placed the drinks on a small coffee table and looked at me directly. 'Anybody who attempts to obstruct this process through the use of force will be crushed. We would have no hesitation.' He spoke in the quiet manner of those who are not inclined to make idle threats. The Minister nodded his head quietly.

It is a fortnight away from polling day in Natal, and the killing is escalating to levels that terrify the leaders of the ANC and the National Party. Suddenly the brave talk about a free and fair election seems to be evaporating. I have spent my time here in Natal travelling from one murder zone to the next. One morning recently I visited Solomon Mzolo, the ANC organizer in Greytown in the northern midlands. He is a sprightly sixty-year-old with a goatee and bright, enthusiastic eyes. His part of town is now an Inkatha-free zone. Chief Buthelezi's supporters were driven out long before the election campaign began. Solomon points to a row of burned-out houses. 'That was where the Inkatha people lived,' he explains. He is completely unsentimental about this political eviction. The houses are directly across the road from his own home. He must have known the people who lived there, but he displays no emotion when he describes the battles that led to their departure. He

*then tells me how his own son was shot dead by Inkatha. 'The kids
came to me and said my boy had been shot . . . so I drove up the
road and I saw his body lying there. He was dead by the time I got
there.' Solomon says he is not bitter but that he is just as prepared
as Inkatha to take up arms and fight. He is proud to be a Zulu, but
he regards himself as South African first and foremost. Solomon
rejects the rule of the chiefs.*

*I follow him on his canvass of some of the houses in the
neighbourhood. The knocking on doors and the asking for votes are
just formalities here. Everybody will be voting ANC, he assures
me. But at the first house we come to the woman won't come to the
door. A voice from inside says the baby is sick and the mother
cannot come to the door. Solomon gives his name. 'How can I be
sure it is you?' she calls back. Solomon laughs out loud at the reply
and this seems to persuade the woman to open the door. She is small
and very young, perhaps as young as nineteen or twenty, and her
baby is crying in a cot that is wedged next to a sink. There is a
portrait of Mandela on the wall and below it the words* NOW IS
THE TIME. *Solomon tries to get the woman to explain why she
supports the ANC, but it is clear that she is concerned by my
presence. We leave her with profuse thanks and apologies for the
disturbance. Before I leave the township, Solomon calls together a
group of ANC supporters and addresses them about the need for
vigilance. Then they sing freedom songs, finishing with the haunting
'Hamba Kahle Umkhonto we Sizwe' ('Go Well, Spear of the Nation')
in honour of Solomon's dead son. I give Solomon some BBC pens
and badges for his family and promise to come back and see him
after the election. 'This is a really great time. How often do you
get the chance to live through something like this?' he says,
smiling and laughing as I drive away.*

*Three hours after my visit Solomon is addressing an election
meeting in Greytown. At least two gunmen enter the hall and walk
up to where he is standing and open fire. He is hit several times and*

dies instantly. Solomon Mzolo, born under white rule, died under white rule.

The ANC in Natal was dominated by the presence of a septuagenarian Stalinist whose public utterances frequently embarrassed the national leadership. Harry Gwala was short and round, and his arms hung limply by his side: this was the result of motor-neurone disease, which had caused paralysis in both his arms. Entering his office, one always made a mental note not to offer a handshake. A young ANC member was always on hand to turn the pages of his diary or to answer the phone. But when Gwala opened his mouth to speak the physical infirmity was obliterated from the hearer's consciousness. He spoke slowly and with great deliberation, pausing before he mentioned the name of Buthelezi so that he could muster the entire force of his lungs and blow out the name as if he were belching away some vile inner gas.

Harry Gwala was not a likeable man. He was hard and bitter and wedded to Stalinism, a political ideal that had sent millions to their deaths and that denied the freedoms Gwala claimed to cherish. He was the kind of black politician who terrified whites. Gwala had not forgotten or forgiven the nearly twenty years he had spent in apartheid's jails and the torture he had endured at the hands of the security forces. His communism was uncompromising: the social democracy preached increasingly by the South African Communist Party appalled him. On the walls of his office were portraits of Lenin and Marx, and his speeches were heavy with Stalinist rhetoric. When Gorbachev was ousted by Soviet hardliners in August 1991, Gwala praised the plotters. In Gwala's ideal South Africa the dictatorship of the proletariat would have been absolute, with the ideologically impure lining up for re-education. The Zulu traditionalists of Inkatha would have to hide away their tribal skins and drums.

newspaper interview Gwala openly declared war on Inkatha: 'Make no mistake, we kill Inkatha warlords. Why be apologetic about it, when they come to attack us, we offer them no bibles. We believe in a just war. The difference between us and Inkatha is that we do not kill women and children. We hit hard on those who target us.' But of course Mr Gwala's supporters did kill women and children. One of the worst episodes of the Natal violence occurred when a group of ANC supporters ambushed the children of an Inkatha tribal leader in Table Mountain in March 1993. At least two gunmen opened fire on the pick-up truck carrying the children to school in Pietermaritzburg. Six children were killed in an ambush that was calculated to strike terror into the hearts of the Inkatha supporters in the area.

Harry Gwala believed firmly in the philosophy of an eye for an eye. Although ideologically far removed from the Inkatha warlords, Gwala seemed to me to be a prisoner of the same 'kill or be killed' psychology that infected the politics of Natal. He viewed the national leadership of the ANC as soft and corruptible, too willing to compromise and unwilling to share the dangers experienced by its beleagured supporters. He was warned to tone down the vehemence of his public utterances on more than one occasion. After one particularly bitter clash with the Johannesburg head office, Gwala reportedly described Mandela as a tyrant. Yet in the region Gwala was revered by the young and the old, by Communist and non-Communist. To a people who were under siege he appeared as a man of courage and candour, someone who lived with them at the front-line and who could be depended on to confront the enemy. Although I found his political views archaic and was depressed by his willingness to condone violence, Gwala had one blinding virtue: honesty. In a country where bland platitudes choked the political atmosphere, Harry Gwala was a breath of cold, acidic air. When the elections came closer and the level of political violence began to spiral in Natal, Gwala and other regional leaders began to press Mandela for dramatic action to be taken against Buthelezi. On the ground Gwala began to prepare his supporters for the possibility of civil war.

It is dusk, a beautiful hazy end of summer evening and the interior of the car smells of sweat and potato crisps. Empty Coke cans are rolling around on the floor. We have been driving around Mpumalanga for the past hour searching for the football stadium and are on the point of going home. Then I notice dust rising up from behind a hill about 200 yards away. We stop the car and roll down the windows. There are voices chanting and the sound of feet stamping in rhythm — one two, one two, one two.

Within minutes we are standing among several hundred young men and women, their faces and clothes caked with dust. They are running laps around what must have been a soccer pitch. The goalposts and the markings are gone and rubbish is piled on the concrete stand. As the group moves around and around, the dust begins to obscure the individual bodies, until all we see is a long shape circling in the fading light. A shot rings out and the shape collapses on the ground. The gunman is running with the group, testing their reflexes. Barely a few seconds pass and they are up and running again. This goes on for at least half an hour and then they form into groups of ten and practise marching. It is the old Soviet goose-step and the marchers chant: 'Forward to victory with the comrades of M.K. Forward . . .'

The youngsters are being put through their paces by a short, thin man who gives his name as Comrade Zero. His eyes tell us that he is not a trusting type, and he soon makes it clear that he regards our presence as intrusive. 'But we have permission. It has all been arranged,' I tell him. He is, to put it mildly, sceptical. I tell him that Harry Gwala and the press officer back in Pietermaritzburg have given us permission to come out and watch the training. 'It will really screw things up if we have to go away and say you guys turned the press away,' I add. This last suggestion of trouble with head office seems to penetrate his consciousness. There is a brief discussion in Zulu with another young man and we are duly given permission to film and interview the would-be soldiers. 'These people are from overseas. They are from the BBC – from the British Broadcasting Corporation – and they will not harm you by writing anything bad. You can talk to them . . . it's OK,' he tells them.

These are Gwala's soldiers, young Zulus who turn up every morning at six o'clock and again in the evenings to take part in what is described as 'self-defence training'. They are doing it because Inkatha are doing it, Comrade Zero says. All over Natal on this lovely evening there are groups of young men being trained in the arts of war. Inkatha has set up a big camp in the Umfolozi Game Reserve, where a former security policeman is giving instruction in the use of automatic rifles and shotguns. These are war preparations. Phillip Powell likens his own men to the Vietcong and warns the ANC against trying to conquer KwaZulu.

The world's media have descended on Natal. You cannot drive into a township here without meeting television crews. The bar of the Marine Parade Holiday Inn begins to fill up with voices exchanging the latest rumours and scare stories. Many of the journalists are old Bosnia and Somalia hands who have come down to Natal in anticipation of a new civil war. Given the current political atmosphere, the media focus is not surprising. The political talks are going nowhere. A peace summit between Mandela, Buthelezi and De Klerk has ended in bitter recriminations. ANC election workers are being killed throughout the province. In one of the worst episodes a group of youths handing out voter-education pamphlets are abducted, tortured and forced to lick the backsides of their tormentors. Then they are told to lick their own blood from the floor of the abandoned schoolroom that is the torture centre, before being bundled into the bush and shot dead. Up in Johannesburg

Buthelezi's supporters stage a march through the centre of the city that ends in the worst gunbattle ever seen in a metropolitan area. After a day of madness fifty-three people are known to have died. A state of emergency is declared in Natal, and the army moves in with armoured cars and heavy machine-guns.

But the training in Mpumalanga is different. This is supposed to be the model township, the one part of Natal where peace agreements between the ANC and Inkatha are holding. The local leaders of the two organizations have attended peace rallies together and there hasn't been a political killing in the township in well over a year. If they are training for war in Mpumalanga, then things are heading for a dangerous pass, I tell myself. Although there are no guns on display here, it is common knowledge that both sides in Natal have plenty of weapons. The guns come in across the Mozambique border. The soon-to-be demobbed soldiers of Renamo and Frelimo are flogging their weapons to anyone with the money to buy.

Comrade Zero is a veteran of Angola and tells me he is passionately opposed to war. 'I have seen what it does to people. No water, no electricity, wounded children and orphans . . . all of that I have seen and I don't want it to happen here,' he says. Comrade Zero says he is training the young people to protect democracy. If anybody tries to prevent the election going ahead, the young men and women of the township will be there to ensure that people can cast their votes. But over in the Inkatha section of the township there are other youngsters who think the election is an ANC/Communist plot to seize power. They are talking about their own war of liberation. Doesn't that worry Comrade Zero? 'Not really,' he says, before wandering away to talk to his troops. He does not come back and I get the impression that he is tired of our presence and our bothersome questioning. As we are getting back into the car, Comrade Zero trots over. He has one last comment. 'Nothing will stop us from voting. Nothing,' he says.

But the sharp increase in the levels of violence in Natal was matched by a quieter, unseen shift in the politics of the region. There were, for the first time within Inkatha, voices openly questioning the wisdom of Buthelezi's actions. Much of the discontent was emanating from parliament, where Inkatha had won several recruits among white and Indian MPs who had originally seen Buthelezi as the great black hope, a powerful force for free enterprise in the face of a socialistic ANC and a National Party contaminated by its racist past. The MPs who had seen Inkatha as a natural home for those wanting to extend their constituencies were now worried. They had begun to question publicly the wisdom of an electoral boycott. One of the senior white recruits told me privately a few weeks before the election: 'This party is bigger than the Chief Minister. It is about a lot more than him.'

But even more worrying for Buthelezi were signs that the Zulu king was at last responding to the pleadings and the offers of financial security emanating from the ANC. The Chief's gravest tactical mistake was to elevate the King to a position of such political importance that his dependency on Buthelezi and the KwaZulu government was diminished. By telling Zulus that they owed absolute loyalty to their monarch, Buthelezi was placing his nephew in a powerful position: the Chief was suddenly to discover that the man he thought would be his puppet in perpetuity had a voice of his own and a constituency of several million Zulus who regarded him, not Buthelezi, as their supreme leader. Playing the Zulu monarchist card, evoking images of a new invasion of Zululand, might have served to whip up opposition to the ANC and the government among Buthelezi's supporters. But when Mandela's men offered the King a constitutional guarantee of his position and, even more importantly, a promise of life-long financial security in return for support in the elections, the monarch was seduced. He joined the increasingly vociferous group around Buthelezi who were demanding that Inkatha and the KwaZulu government participate in the elections. He had staged his major hope on securing a postponement of the elections, during which time foreign intermediaries would hold talks with the major parties in the hope of securing agreement on the constitution. But the foreign mediators – Lord Carrington and Henry Kissinger – had no intention of taking the blame for postponing South Africa's march to democracy. When their mediation effort collapsed, Buthelezi was finally isolated: he had to choose between retreating into the hills and taking up arms, or coming into the electoral process at the last minute. He chose the latter.

All morning the buzz has been growing. De Klerk's PR people have told us to get to the Union Buildings in time for a press conference before midday. The ANC's head office is keeping silent, but I eventually manage to track down a contact in the intelligence department. 'He is coming in. He has caved in completely. We can't fucking believe it, man. He has abandoned all the demands. Everything goes on ice until after the election,' my contact reveals. The source says that a Kenyan politician, Washington Okumu, has been shuttling between Ulundi and Pretoria, stitching up a deal that allows Buthelezi to save face and the elections to go ahead.

It is one of the hottest days of the autumn and, as we drive towards Pretoria, the great north road shimmers and seems to buckle and warp ahead of us. Outside the Union Buildings a huge crowd of journalists has gathered. There must be nearly 200 people here. Even though most of us have had the story confirmed by our sources, there is a sense of disbelief. The last three years have been lived under the shadow of Buthelezi's threats of civil war. We took those threats seriously, we had seen the horror of Natal's civil war close up, and few can quite believe that the nightmare is about to end. Since Buthelezi decided to boycott the elections in March, 700 people have been killed, and the East Rand townships have again become battlezones.

But today is the beginning of something special, a vault out of the stupidity and selfishness that have been Buthelezi's trademarks. He enters the conference room at the Union Buildings with Mandela and De Klerk and the fat Kenyan political consultant who has done the dealing. It is De Klerk who speaks first. He is calm and controlled, and it takes about thirty seconds before he utters the words that bring Buthelezi formally into the election. An agreement has been reached that allows the Inkatha Freedom Party and the KwaZulu government to participate in the elections. The head of the Independent Electoral Commission, Judge Johan Kriegler, is making the necessary arrangements. Stickers bearing the name of the Inkatha Freedom Party will be attached to ballot papers. Buthelezi has exactly one week to canvass. Both he and Mandela make speeches that for once manage to avoid giving offence to either side. De Klerk looks tired but very, very relieved.

All of this I am relaying to London as it happens. A presenter asks me how I feel and I respond in a suitably detached manner. I speak of the great sense of relief that most South Africans will feel now that the prospect of a civil war in Natal has been well and truly removed. But how do I feel personally? I can tell you, dear reader, that I am ecstatic. I feel the way the air feels after one of those great summer storms on the highveld: there is freshness, clarity and lightness. As the news starts to circulate, South African friends telephone me to ask if it is really true. They are overjoyed, like prisoners who have been told that their convictions were unsound. The three leaders have told them: 'You are free to go. You may leave this place of imprisonment and walk out into the golden lands of promise.'

Of course Buthelezi has lost a great deal by waiting so long. He has abandoned all of his demands for a federal constitution. They are to be discussed again after the election. What he has settled for in the final analysis is the constitutional guarantee for the Zulu king and little more. But it doesn't seem to matter today. The political balance-sheet will no longer be written out in blood. Who wins what and how much? Who cares? The frightened people of South Africa — the ones who have been buying up foodstuffs and ammunition, who have been planning to leave the country — are breathing deep sighs of relief and allowing themselves the gift of hope. But something else has happened on this glorious morning. The apartheid dream has finally died. Make no mistake about it. This is the moment when the concept of ethnic nation states has been finally destroyed. With Buthelezi's acceptance of a unitary state, the far right has been exiled to the far reaches of the political wilderness. No longer can they claim that the Zulus are allies in the fight for a constellation of race-based states. Today there is time to laugh and feel good about South Africa.

CHAPTER 7

Nelson, Frederik and the Last Mile

In spite of my criticism, Mr De Klerk, sir, you are one of those I rely upon . . . we are going to face the problems of this country together.

Nelson Mandela in televised debate
with F.W. de Klerk, April 1994

A man of destiny knows that beyond this hill lies another and another. The journey is never complete. As he contemplates the next hill I hold out my hand to Mr Mandela in friendship and co-operation.

F.W. de Klerk to Nelson Mandela,
April 1994

Today I became a human being once more.

Elderly Sowetan voter to the author
at Orlando West polling station,
26 April 1994

The platform was crowded with journalists and diplomats. ANC officials were flitting to and fro, examining passes. A green one got you into Mandela's carriage; the ordinary yellow ANC press pass was good enough only for the train carrying the second division of party leaders. I had a green pass and was swept into the carriage among a pile of clambering, heaving bodies. I was pushed into a seat and found myself sandwiched between the Lebanese Ambassador and a security guard. The carriage bristled with weapons. Next to one of the doors leaned a young member of Umkhonto we Sizwe cradling a shotgun that was almost as long as his body. He practised mean stares on everybody who went past. 'I don't care who you say you are, if you don't have the pass you are not coming on board,' a voice shouted from amid the throng surrounding Mandela. But another louder voice came back. 'We are from ABC Television. Don't you understand? We are from ABC Television and we want to talk to Mr Mandela,' he said. I looked around and found the source of the demand, a middle-aged black man who was standing on the platform and thrusting his head into the carriage. He was a few yards away from Mandela, but his view was being obscured by the formidable figure of Gill Marcus, one of the two main spokespersons for the ANC. I wanted to shout and warn the American that trying to persuade Gill Marcus to allow you to speak to Mandela without an appointment was as futile as trying to hold back the sea. But the poor fool blundered on, and when the train pulled away he was still standing on the platform, shouting into the air, his words lost under the locomotive groan of the carriages as they moved south out of Johannesburg Central.

A puppeteer walked up to Mandela and began to speak. He was carrying a Kermit the Frog puppet and was clearly part of the show arranged for the benefit of the cameras. Kermit began to ask Mr Mandela about the importance of voting. Why was it so important for people to exercise their franchise? The ANC's official camera crew moved in to capture this moment of contrived humour. Mandela obliged with a few bland comments and the ever beatific smile. The stills cameras clicked and clicked like cicadas. The last time I rode on a train like this I was travelling to Soweto to produce a radio feature on the train violence which was killing hundreds of people. Gun- and knife-wielding gangs routinely ran amok on trains, shooting and stabbing and hurling passengers out of windows. I remembered that journey as an exercise in raw fear, both that of the passengers and my own. Although I emerged unscathed from the experience, it left me with little inclination to ride the rails again.

But on the Mandela express there was ample protection. The carriages behind and in front had been set aside for ANC supporters. They cheered and stamped noisily as the train left Johannesburg with its horn blaring. Policemen had been deployed at every station along the route. We moved slowly through the southern suburbs of Johannesburg, past the second-hand car showrooms and the mechanics yards, past the Portuguese cafés and the run-down hotels and the empty factories and the mine dumps high and dusty in the near distance. The security guards were tense as we passed through the southern suburbs. This was poor-white territory and the sight of a train flying the ANC colours might have tempted one of the right-wingers in the area to take a pot-shot. But we left the white city and entered Soweto without incident. The only brief moment of fright came when thousands of balloons in the ANC colours were released into the air. A group of township children who were playing near the station grabbed at the balloons and began to explode them. The staccato crackle resembled the sound of automatic weapons and Mandela's security detail jumped into action, throwing a defensive shield around their leader and preparing to draw weapons. Then the guards noticed one of the children laughing hysterically. Everybody relaxed and the procession moved away from the station behind a troupe of African dancers and singers. They were the only sign that this was the election launch of an African political party. Everything else on that morning of cameras and shouted questions resembled the banality and blandness one associates with the campaigns of small-town politicians in America. There were no great crowds of people here, there were none of the township youths who make up the majority of ANC audiences. Although we had come to Soweto to witness the launch of the ANC's election manifesto, with its promises of jobs and houses and health, there was no sign of the people for whom the document had ostensibly been written. The South African poor were not on the invitation list.

A string quartet was playing inside the huge conference hall that the ANC had hired for the occasion. The notes of Vivaldi floated above the throng of journalists, diplomats and party officials. Here and there an American voice could be heard, nudging and advising the organizers of the launch. This was not the ANC I had known over the previous three years. I had come to expect conferences where thousands of people danced and punched the air, events of sweat and emotion, and not the perfume-drenched tedium of this occasion. There were tables of savouries and two bars. Glossy information packs had been placed on each seat. On the walls the pledges of the ANC's Freedom Charter – the organization's seminal document – had been painted on to gaudy murals whose brilliant pinks and yellows overpowered the message. Somewhere on the wall the Congress was declaring its basic tenets: the land of South Africa belongs to all the people and so do the mines, the hospitals, the schools. But it did not really matter. As I say, there were no ordinary people there to read the slogans. I did notice a few faces from the ANC's township structures. They were wearing suits and some carried mobile telephones.

After the ritual singing of 'Nkosi Sikelel' iAfrika', Mandela was welcomed on to the stage. Over the next half hour he outlined the ANC's plan for the reconstruction of South Africa. In any ordinary election the delivery of a manifesto that promised houses, jobs and education for all would have attracted significant attention. But when the speech was over there was no rush to file stories. There were a few questions about what it was all going to cost but nobody pushed Mandela on the issue. Perhaps it was because we all knew that the promises and the policy were not the point of this election. We had come here merely to witness the official starting point and found it a moment devoid of drama or a sense of history. Had the ANC produced no manifesto at all there would have been little protest among its support base. All the organization needed to produce was the face of Nelson Rolihlahla Mandela, at rallies, in newspaper photographs, on posters and on television. And that was the real point of the train journey and the lavish reception: a photo opportunity at which the party could dole out free drinks and food to the media and the diplomatic corps. The ANC was an organization of numerous component parts. It embraced capitalists, Christians, Communists, fundamentalist Muslims, liberal intellectuals and old-fashioned African nationalists. In the very truest sense of the word the Congress was a broad church within which countless views and arguments were able to struggle and compete. But when it came to the question of the election, the ANC and its policies seemed to take second place, subsumed into the aura that surrounded the great national hero, the edifice of struggle and majestic defiance that was Nelson Mandela. From the moment in March when the first posters began to appear carrying the face and beaming smile of Mandela, the ANC's campaign was to be directed primarily at reminding every single black South African that he, Madiba,* had given up the best years of his life to secure their freedom. Now was the time to repay the debt.

---

*This was the clan name given to Nelson Mandela.

The campaign is a couple of weeks old and Mandela is criss-crossing the country at a furious rate. I have been following him from township to village to city, day in, day out. The media posse gets bigger all the time. There are more and more Americans. Having largely ignored South Africa for the past few years, the big networks are back. This is the kind of event they understand. The prince released from prison will soon become king. In the weeks ahead hundreds of journalists will go wandering around white farms in search of men with guns; they will trawl the townships in search of the militant youth; there will be stories about whites planning to pack up and leave or hoarding food and ammunition, about blacks who are reported to have 'impossibly' high expectations. All of this you can take with as large or small a grain of salt as you wish. For my part I find most of the network reporting — with a few honourable exceptions — to be tired and clichéd. I recognize the stories and many of the characters. I have interviewed most of them myself in the past. There is fear among whites and anticipation among blacks, but I do not get the feeling that my neighbours are about to hurl themselves aboard Jumbo jets, or that the black servants of the northern suburbs are sharpening machetes in anticipation of 27 April. Every time he addresses a press conference Mandela is asked about meeting the expectations of blacks. By the middle of the campaign he appears to be bored senseless with the question. The response is the same on every occasion: 'We are telling our people not to expect the earth but their expectations are not unrealistic. They have the right to expect that a democratic government would work to provide houses and jobs and basic healthcare, etc., etc. . . .

What impresses me everwhere I go is the extraordinary patience of blacks, the willingness to accept that the world will not change overnight. I have spent more time than most of the visiting correspondents travelling through the squatter camps and the townships. The people are not fools. At least 50 per cent of those I speak to say they know Mandela can't deliver overnight. Like Patience

Ndhlovu, a woman in Alexandra township who lives with her nine children in a one-room shack. I visit her a week before the election and she welcomes me inside with an offer of tea. When I ask what she wants for the future she responds, 'All I want is that Mandela should try for us. That is all. If he can try, then he will be doing more than the whites ever did.' She then gets up and opens a suitcase and pulls out a framed photograph of Mandela. 'He is like Jesus Christ for us. He is our saviour,' she says.

In Soweto at the last but one rally of the campaign, one of the country's top black musicians, Sipho 'Hotsticks' Mabhuza, explains the ANC's appeal to me like this: 'It is like a religion with people here. That is the only way you can understand the ANC. People have been following it all their lives and before them their parents and their grandparents and so on back all the way to the beginning. It is a thing which is beyond politics and up at the top you have Mandela. You feel proud to belong to something like that. If I can I will be the first person to vote for Mandela in Soweto. Man, I would like that.'

Sipho's children have come with him to the rally. There are several hundred men with spears and axes, but the atmosphere is relaxed and friendly. People clear a path when the ANC pensioners arrive. They are brought to the front of the crowd and given seats with a good view of Mandela. Most of them joined the organization around the same time as their leader. Remember the twenty-seven years in jail, they are told repeatedly. These people do not need to be told. They have known the worst of apartheid and want to see it buried once and for all on 27 April. When Mandela arrives the crowd erupts. Photographers and cameramen are swept out of the way by the security guards. There is shooting in the crowd. It is the kind of wild firing that you expect to hear in an Afghan village when the bandit chief arrives. Mandela is furious and admonishes the crowd. He is like an elderly schoolmaster and they hear him out respectfully. How can he go and ask the security forces to be just and fair when his own supporters behave in such a fashion? There is no more shooting. Mandela can say these kinds of things. He can lecture them at length and know that when the day of decision comes there is only one choice: the broad smile and the letters ANC. *Although the PR men and women have taken over the campaign, milking every moment for contrived photo opportunities, something of the real Mandela always manages to beam its way through the fog. Like in Durban, in the middle of the embattled township of KwaMashu. There are perhaps 10,000 people gathered in a soccer field. For many of them the journey to and from the field is fraught with danger. The buses must pass through Inkatha strongholds and make easy targets for gunmen. At the end of a long speech under a savagely hot sun, Mandela looks into the crowd and says: 'I love each and every one of you. I wish that I could gather you all up and put you in my pocket, so that when I am feeling lonely I could look inside and see your smiling faces.' The crowd erupts into wild cheering. They believe him.*

It is difficult for the foreign correspondent to exercise anything remotely resembling real detachment when it comes to writing about Nelson Mandela. He is one of the few world leaders whose goodness is taken for granted and who can be truly said to have a heroic aura. Having followed Mandela's footsteps since he was released from prison, I would be less than honest if I did not admit to a deep admiration and affection for the man. I am confronted always by the simple mathematics of his life: twenty-seven years behind bars; twenty-seven years in which his mother and son died without his being able to say goodbye or to attend their funerals, twenty-seven years in which his wife drifted away from him and became a dangerous bully, twenty-seven years separated from his children. All that time because he had chosen to pursue an ideal universally accepted: the right of all human beings to live as equals with their fellows in the land of their birth. There was nothing terribly complicated about his political philosophy when he came to the fore of the ANC in the late fifties and early sixties. Along with other members of his generation like Oliver Tambo and Walter Sisulu he was suspicious of Marxism and the white intellectuals who led the South African Communist Party. 'The exotic plant of communism cannot flourish on African soil,' he was quoted as saying in 1950.

Nelson Mandela simply looked around and saw that in the country of his birth he was a third-class citizen. He once told a story from his early days as a lawyer in Johannesburg. One day a secretary in the office offered Mandela some tea. When the tray came he noticed that amid the cups was a mug that looked decidedly ancient. The secretary explained that the mug was for him because it was used by other blacks in the building. The cups were for the whites. For a young man who had grown up in one of the foremost chiefly houses of the Transkei and been educated in the university of black nationalism, Fort Hare, the incident was a pointed reminder of the degree to which apartheid had reduced blacks to a position of subjugation, irrespective of their education or background. The journey to Robben Island would take another few years, but the political consciousness that would lead Mandela into armed struggle and eventually jail was being formed. When he was sentenced to life imprisonment in 1961 it was almost as if he had known that his entire life had been a preparation for the moment of ultimate sacrifice. Thus the evidence of eyewitnesses and fellow prisoners shows that when the sentence was announced, when the prison van drove away, when the door closed on that first night on Robben Island, Mandela did not weep or cry out. Having visited his cell on the island, I am awestruck, humbled by his sanity and immense capacity for forgiveness.

I had only been resident in South Africa for a few months when the Prisons Department invited a group of journalists to visit Robben Island. The political prisoners had all gone and only a small number of so-called 'ordinary criminals' were still in residence along with large flocks of seabirds and penguins. The last visit by journalists had been in the late seventies, when Mandela and the other Rivonia trialists were still working the lime quarries and sewing mail-bags. One of the correspondents on that trip, Rodney Pinder of Reuters, was coming back with our small group. He remembered catching a distant glimpse of the political prisoners as they made their way to work. But they were to remain hidden for the rest of the visit while the government PR man sang the praises of the prisons system. The day chosen for our visit could not have been worse. I had been woken during the preceding night by the sound of a thunderous downpour. Table Mountain had disappeared behind a wall of cloud and the wind drove the rain hard against the window of my hotel room. By dawn the rain had eased off slightly, but the wind continued to howl around Cape Point, pushing huge waves across Table Bay. From the safety of the harbour Robben Island looked like a dark scar on the horizon, a place of exile and oppression whose bleak shores glowered back at us in the first grey hours of the morning.

We reached the island after a stomach-wrenching journey bouncing across the waves in the same prison boat that brought Winnie Mandela and other prisoners' wives to see their husbands over nearly three decades in jail. Again the mathematics. Try to imagine it. Year after year for twenty-seven years – through winter days when the Cape winds howled themselves hoarse and on into the long summer when the beaches across the bay filled with white bodies and the sun beat down relentlessly on the backs of Mandela and his fellow prisoners. The warders wore immaculately pressed uniforms and greeted us like old friends when we stepped off the boat. We were shepherded around the island. They were happy to point out the different kinds of seabirds and the flora, and to regale us with the island's history as a place of banishment. It was almost as if they saw themselves as tour guides. The cruelty and the pain were somehow unconnected with them.

After inspecting almost every inch of the island we were eventually taken to the block that had until so recently housed the political prisoners. There was a great deal of barbed wire here and several look-out posts, though nobody was likely to have wanted to risk swimming to freedom with the cold sea, the currents and the great white sharks that infested the waters of Table Bay. The door to the political cellblock opened with a ringing echo, and we followed one of the warders along a narrow and poorly lit passageway. He was under instructions not to talk about Mandela or the others, but once inside the cellblock he relaxed and began to point to the different cells. 'That was Sisulu's and over there was Ahmed Kathrada's and there,' he said, pointing to our right, 'that one there was Mr Mandela's.' I noticed that I adopted a more respectful tone when referring to the most famous of the former inhabitants. Mandela's cell was physically exactly the same as the others but the memory of its former occupant filled it for me with a powerful sense of loss. I imagined the long empty years as they piled up outside the tiny cell window like sad, ragged leaves. The cell was seven feet square. There was just enough space for a small bunk bed and a tiny desk. For a man of Mandela's imposing height the cell must have been a hellish place. I think I would almost certainly have gone mad within weeks in such a place. However you stood, whichever way you faced, the cold stone walls seemed to close in. Writing of prison, Mandela commented, 'the prison is above all punitive. It operates to break the spirit, to exploit weakness, undermine strength, destroy initiative and process an amorphous robot-like mass.

The challenge is how to resist.' If you looked through the window it was possible to see the sky and the great battalions of clouds that rolled across it on this winter's day. One of the most moving letters written from jail by Mandela describes looking out the window and dreaming of the world beyond that had been lost to him: 'Early one morning, I looked out through the window and the eye could see eastwards as far as the distant horizon. The power of the imagination created the illusion that my vision went much further than the naked eye could actually see. I could survey vast regions behind the long mountain ranges where I have never been.'

Yet his experiences of prison were something Mandela was profoundly disinclined to sentimentalize when he spoke to journalists. Whenever I attempted to coax out his real feelings during interviews, he would lapse into a well-rehearsed spiel about the collective nature of the experience, how he and his fellow prisoners drew strength from each other and how they learned about the changing world outside from the younger men who were rounded up during the upheavals of '76 and '86. He told one interviewer shortly after his release from prison, 'We met remarkable people in prison who enriched our lives. We also had the opportunity of reflecting on past mistakes and planning how we would handle problems when we were released from prison. It was a rewarding experience.'

That he would be released from prison was something Mandela never doubted. Those close to him say he was always possessed of a sense that he was born to lead South Africa. Although he frequently takes pains to present the ANC struggle as a group effort, his sense of himself, of his ability and mission to lead the struggle, is profound. His outstanding personal characteristic is the calm dignity that enabled him to overcome the determined efforts of racist prison warders to humiliate him. I believe that his knowledge, his absolute conviction that blacks would one day be free in

South Africa, allowed him to remain without bitterness. The man who knows that he is right and that he will ultimately triumph is far less likely to be vengeful and malicious than the one who is condemned by the dynamics of history to be an eternal third-class citizen.

Writing from jail in February 1985, when he rejected a conditional offer of freedom from P.W. Botha, Mandela gave perhaps the clearest exposition of his political convictions. The speech was read to a crowd of 10,000 people in Soweto by his daughter Zindzi.

> I cherish my own freedom dearly but I care even more for your freedom. Too many have died since I went to prison. Too many have suffered for the love of freedom. I owe to their widows, to their orphans, to their mothers and their fathers who have grieved and wept for them. Not only I have suffered during these long, lonely, wasted years . . . I cannot and will not give any undertaking at a time when I and you, the people, are not free. Your freedom and mine cannot be separated. I will return.

The Messianic tone – *your freedom and mine* – might have been worrying in any other leader. The world is filled with the ruins of countries where the leader has seen himself as the embodiment of all the people. But in Mandela's case we are dealing with a fundamentally decent and good man, not a dictator. Although prone to flashes of autocratic behaviour, Mandela is a democrat to the core of his being, and his lack of bitterness continues to astonish even those who are his political opponents. I remember once standing with a group of journalists who were having drinks with F.W. de Klerk when the subject of Mandela came up. The two had recently been involved in bitter controversy over the question of township violence, with Mandela accusing the National Party

leader of having blood on his hands. De Klerk was fairly
frank and admitted that the personal relationship between
them had deteriorated. But then he put down his drink and
folded his arms, thinking for a second before continuing.
'What I do find astonishing,' he said, 'is Mr Mandela's
extraordinary lack of bitterness. That is astonishing.' It was as
close as I had ever heard De Klerk come to admitting the
scale of the crime he and other National Party politicians had
committed in keeping Mandela in jail for nearly three
decades.

The highest price Mandela paid was the loss of his family
life. From the helpless vantage point of prison he watched his
wife become increasingly power drunk; he heard the rumours
about her adultery and then the stories concerning her football
team, which was terrorizing the people of Soweto. All of this
he heard and was powerless to prevent. For a man who was
acutely conscious of his own dignity, the stories of adulterous
relationships must have been the worst form of emasculation,
perhaps worse than anything the state could have thrown
against him. Although he was only too well aware of the
cruel measures being employed against his wife by the state –
banning, detention and harassment – Mandela was realistic
enough to know that not everything could be blamed on the
actions of the state. In her excellent book *The Lady* Emma
Gilbey lists the men suspected of having been Winnie's
partners at different stages of Mandela's imprisonment. Mandela was not blind to what was going on, certainly in the
latter stages of his jail term. How the knowledge of this
affected him in prison we will never really know. His survival
behind bars was to a large extent dependent on the submerg-
ing of personal feelings and the immersion in what he describes as the 'collective experience'.

Only once did I get a glimpse of the pain behind the
dignified mask. The week after he announced his official

separation from Comrade Nomzamo, as he publicly referred to Winnie, I was granted an interview with Mandela at the ANC headquarters. The marriage had publicly come asunder following a spate of allegations about Winnie's involvement with a young lawyer and persistent rumours about financial misbehaviour in the Social Welfare Department of the ANC, which Mrs Mandela headed. Nelson Mandela was uncharacteristically subdued during the interview. We spoke about the current run of political happenings, his feelings on the violence and the progress of negotiations. At the end I asked whether he would answer a question on his personal life and he agreed. How was he feeling these days? What was the predominant emotion? Calmly but with great sorrow in his voice, he spoke about the pain of separation, the effect on his children and the trauma of being forced to choose between loyalty to his wife and the liberation struggle. When he had finished speaking there was silence. I felt as if I had reopened a wound, and although Mandela is a public figure and the question had to be asked, I felt clumsy and intrusive. He is one of the few politicians I know who is capable of creating such emotions.

Those close to Mandela say he initially felt a huge weight of guilt because of Winnie, believing that he might have kept her out of trouble had he not gone to jail. But over time, as more and more allegations of her wrongdoings came to light, he seems to have become much less sentimental. I remember witnessing one of their first public encounters shortly after the break-up. They were both attending an ANC conference in Soweto. Winnie was standing with other Women's League members at the front of the hall when Nelson entered. He walked over and said hello and she responded politely. There was no embrace, no physical contact of any kind. 'How are the children?' Mandela asked. 'They are fine,' she replied and that was the end of the conversation. The atmosphere was frosty and the scene one of the saddest I had witnessed in my time in South Africa. In the months that followed Winnie was to find herself frozen out of the inner circle that surrounded Mandela. The people she had persecuted for their opposition to her wrongdoings, like the Secretary General Cyril Ramaphosa, were firmly back in the driving seat. It was as if she were an errant daughter whom Mandela had decided to disown publicly. She was an exile within the leadership of the ANC. And although Winnie was to stage a political come-back with the help of township radicals, taking over the leadership of the Women's League, she would never again belong to the charmed circle of black South African leaders seated at the right hand of Nelson Mandela and fêted by the world.

That she made a come-back at all was a scandal in itself. A convicted child kidnapper whose name was widely linked to other abuses, Winnie Mandela should never have been allowed to take up any office, much less present herself as a candidate for the ANC in the elections. For an organization that promised good government and transparency, it was an appalling mistake to put Winnie's name on the list of candidates. At a press conference held to announce the ANC's new year message John Carlin of the *Independent* asked Mandela how he could justify having a convicted criminal on his list of candidates. Mandela's glib reply was that Winnie had been the choice of the people and that was not something the ANC could interfere with. It was a serious error of judgement that highlighted one of the ANC's less pleasant attributes: arrogance. The handling of allegations into torture in the organization's camps in Angola during the 1980s was another case in point. In spite of the fact that a commission of inquiry into abuses at the camps named several leading ANC members as having been actively involved in torture or at the least turning a blind eye to the practice, the organization refused to say publicly what action had been taken against the accused. In fact most of those involved were promoted. Mandela tried to claim later that the simple fact of holding an inquiry at all and then publishing the results and the names of the accused was a moral victory for the ANC. It was, he said, more than the South African government had ever been willing to do when confronted with allegations over human rights abuses. But that is a generous interpretation of the ANC's lack of action. Mandela must have known that by refusing to take tough steps against people who had been involved in vicious cruelty against prisoners, he and the ANC were quietly condoning what had happened. It also made a mockery of the ANC's repeated claim to stand for transparent and accountable government. What Mandela and his colleagues knew, of course, was that whatever stink the press created did not really matter at the end of the day. The black people of South Africa would vote ANC whether or not any steps were taken against the perpetrators of the abuses.

As a political organization the ANC can give the impression of being strangely contradictory. On the one hand Mandela and a few senior leaders exercise an extraordinary degree of influence over the policy and direction of the movement. Nowhere was this more apparent than during the negotiations for a new constitution when, particularly in the latter stages, Cyril Ramaphosa wrote party policy as he went along. Yet on the other hand the ANC can appear to be acutely responsive to the demands of its constituency. The collapse of negotiations following the Boipatong Massacre in 1992 is a good illustration of this. Under pressure from the militant youth who were demanding guns to fight their enemies, Mandela announced that the ANC was pulling out of constitutional talks with the government. But appearances deceive. In reality the talking went on, with Cyril Ramaphosa and his opposite number in the government, Roelf Meyer, working away at the fundamentals of an agreement that would get negotiations back on track. Thus it could be confusing for ANC supporters to listen to the public rhetoric of the organization and contrast it with what was happening in the negotiations that they read about in the daily newspapers. Above all the ANC was ruled by pragmatism, the art of the possible. It had learned the hard way that overthrowing the government by force or civil disobedience was not possible. However unpopular it might have been with the more radical elements, the senior leadership knew that the only viable route to a democratic future lay in power-sharing with the whites. The ANC was able to walk the tightrope between the militancy and anger of many of its supporters and the compromises needed to secure a constitutional agreement because of Mandela and the twenty-seven years. No supporter, however militant, could stand up and tell Mandela that he did not represent the wishes of the people. Although once out of prison he portrayed himself as the good and faithful servant of the people, he was in fact their Messiah.

We are in Durban again, gazing out at the waves crashing up the beach and the figures of surfers scything along the surface of the water. It is Sunday, 23 April, and Mandela is coming to town. The ANC's last rally is to be held here in Natal. It is both an attempt to ensure the biggest possible ANC vote in the most embattled region of the country, and a message for Buthelezi. 'This is Mandela's country,' the ANC seems to be saying. I cannot really believe that this is the last rally before liberation. I have grown tired of such events. There is nothing new to say. Rally after rally. Liberation song after liberation song. A sea of clenched fists and a thousand and one chants of 'Amandla'. In these final days there is a very real sense that the leaders are going through the motions. Everybody knows the ANC will win the election; we are just betting on the margin. Will they make the crucial two thirds majority that would allow Ramaphosa and Co. to write the new constitution on their own? But anybody who knows South Africa realizes that even a two thirds majority will not give the ANC a completely free hand. The whites still control the army, the police, the civil service and big business. Trying to force a new constitution down the throats of such powerful interest groups would be a recipe for national suicide. All of the senior players are tied into a power-sharing agreement even if there is an ANC landslide. Reality dictates that South Africa will be ruled by a coalition. Therefore this election is less an act of pure politics than a benediction for the entire nation. It is about the breaking of psychological chains – the bondage of fear; the fear that led whites to deny the humanity of blacks, the fear that led blacks to regard whites as supermen. Yes, there is tension and fear in the air right up to polling day. But greater than anything is the sense of excitement. Across South Africa ordinary people are being faced with a real choice for the first time in their lives. It is ultimately – for black, white, Indian and coloured – a choice between freedom and the bondage of the past. They are being asked to place their 'X' beside different parties but the election is about much, much more than the ANC, the National Party, the Inkatha Freedom Party. It is about the power of forgiveness and the capacity to look beyond the bitterness of the past, it is about healing a bloody history and claiming the gift of hope.

On this autumn morning in Durban a gorgeous orange sun has come up behind the ocean to welcome Mandela, the President in waiting. But the same sun is shining in Ulundi and Pretoria and across the vast spaces of the interior. The theme of this last rally in Durban is 'One Nation, Many Cultures'. Already Mandela is acting like the President of the entire nation. It has not always been a good-tempered campaign. Frequently Mandela has had to upbraid his own supporters for driving their political opponents out of the townships. The National Party produces a blatantly racist document for distribution in the Cape. It portrays intolerant blacks seeking to obliterate the coloureds. After protests the document is withdrawn. And the right-wingers have been planting bombs in a last desperate attempt to derail the elections. There are murderous attacks in Johannesburg and Germiston, and a bomb goes off near the international departures lounge in Jan Smuts Airport. At Terre'Blanche's last press conference before the election a black journalist from the United States is beaten up and ejected. Other reporters and cameramen are threatened. But the Durban gathering is peaceful and celebratory. There are Indian musicians and Zulu tribal dancers. There is township jazz and the inevitable poems of struggle. And above all there is Mandela. When he arrives, a tall figure in a flowery shirt and sunglasses, the huge crowd erupts into frenzied cheering. The scaffolding in front of the stage is swaying dangerously. There are people sitting in every tree in Kings Park where the rally is being held. At times the old man's words are drowned out by the cheers of his supporters. But they hear him when he tells them it is time to leave the past behind. They must go out and vote but always remember that they belong to one nation, one South Africa. As we are driving back to the hotel, through the good-natured crowds, it occurs to me that is the last rally of its kind before liberation. Here in the city of Durban, on a balmy autumn evening, the ANC's struggle against white rule has formally ended.

It should never be forgotten that the experience of a genuinely democratic election was as unique for whites as it was for their black and brown fellow countrymen. F.W. de Klerk might have participated in numerous elections but this was for him the first genuine experience of democracy. He is possibly the most astute politician I have ever encountered, certainly the toughest. In possessing this latter quality De Klerk was precisely the right man for his time. South Africa did not need a white leader who was possessed of some grand idealistic vision. The country had suffered enough from ideologues in the past. What was needed – and what De Klerk supplied – was the courage to acknowledge two fundamental points: that the black people of South Africa had a right to live and vote in the country and that the only man who could speak on behalf of the majority of them was Nelson Mandela. His predecessors had blinded themselves to these truths and their stupidity exacted a terrible reckoning in the lives of millions of South Africans. It would be a grave mistake to believe that De Klerk was motivated by altruism or by feelings of shame or guilt about the past. He was not. The last white president knew that time was simply running out. What has earned him the respect of the world is the courage that he employed in forcing through reforms and dragging the majority of the Afrikaners with him towards the ultimate reality of black majority rule. For a man who knew only too well the hatred that the security forces felt for the ANC, it took remarkable self-possession to release Mandela from jail and unban the black liberation movements. De Klerk came from a family steeped in the traditions of Afrikaner nationalism. As a government minister he had enthusiastically defended the worst injustices of apartheid. 'We would never accept integration,' he was quoted as saying in 1975.

What is now clear is that the events of the eighties, P.W. Botha's stumbling and crudely handled attempts at reform that ended in even greater repression, convinced De Klerk that only radical change would dig whites out of the deep pit created by four decades of apartheid rule. Although Botha had initiated the process of dialogue with Mandela while the latter was still a prisoner, he lacked the will and courage to release the world's most famous political detainee. What is also clear, however, is that De Klerk still believed in the protection of group rights when he began the negotiations with Mandela. The Nationalists' early constitutional proposals revolved around complicated plans for power-sharing and a dual presidency well into the future. The fact that South Africa was destined to be ruled by the majority had not yet been fully accepted. There was a sense that Mandela had been released from prison so that De Klerk could co-opt the ANC into a system of eternal coalition. It is true that the state President faced powerful challenges from the right and from within the security forces. Senior police and army generals repeatedly assured him of their loyalty, but his own intelligence sources told of mutinous noises in the ranks. Confronting the powerful security establishment was a dangerous job and one De Klerk seemed notoriously reluctant to undertake, until Judge Richard Goldstone forced him into action. Many thousands of black lives were lost as a result of the activities of rogue elements in the security forces, yet De Klerk repeatedly refused to tackle the problem. The reluctance to act may well have been motivated by a fear of rebellion among the army and police, but it poisoned the relationship with Mandela at a time when the two men most needed to find each other. De Klerk bristled with indignation whenever he was accused of failing to deal with township violence. I recall a presidential cocktail party in Cape Town where a journalist from a Swiss newspaper repeatedly asked De Klerk about the Third Force. Why was he doing nothing when newspapers were continually unearthing evidence of security force wrongdoing? De Klerk sipped his whisky patiently, sucked on his ever present cigarette and patiently rebutted the charges. But his questioner was relentless. There was evidence and De Klerk was doing nothing. Eventually the President lost his patience and stormed away from the group. One of the other journalists claimed he heard De Klerk say to his press officer as he headed for the door, 'Just get me away from that pig now.' It was a rare flash of temper from a man who had made his political career out of presenting a cool, collected image. Nevertheless I am convinced that history will judge his failure to stem the excesses and corruptions of the security forces in a more benign light than most foreign correspondents have found themselves able to do. What matters is that he brought *most* of the soldiers and policemen with him.

His detractors in the ANC pointed out that, unlike Mandela, De Klerk did not have any personal friends among the other race groups. His social milieu was exclusively white and he suffered severe embarrassment over persistent rumours that he and his wife, Marike, had forced their son Willem to end his relationship with a coloured model. Marike de Klerk was in fact once quoted as describing coloureds as 'nonpeople'. The opening up of the National Party to all races was not pushed with any degree of vigour until the last twelve months before the election. Although he had begun to talk to real black leaders De Klerk was still – in 1990 – thinking of himself as a white leader. The negotiations and the looming inevitability of an election changed that. In the early months of 1994 F.W. de Klerk and the once whiter-than-white Nationalists had to take to the road and canvass for political support among those they had once oppressed.

We are standing outside Potchefstroom Town Hall. It is a dull town even by the mind-numbing standards of the Western Transvaal. This was the town where the Conservative Party scored their famous by-election victory over the National Party. The victor that night was a tubby, bespectacled racist named Andries Beyers. Tonight he is on hand to welcome President De Klerk. Andries Beyers is one of the vast legions of South African pragmatists, political hucksters who have realized that the days of white rule are really over. Mr Beyers is no longer a racist. He no longer believes in a white homeland. In fact he is busy shaking any black hand he can find. The National Party is full of them: men and women who have seen the future and placed their money on F.W. de Klerk. The President went to university in Potchefstroom but he is more likely to remember it as the town whose by-election prompted him to call the referendum on reform in March 1992. The referendum saw whites voting by an overwhelming majority to endorse the negotiations process and freed De Klerk from any serious political threat from the right.

Tonight in Potchefstroom the hall is full. Most of those who have come are white National Party supporters, but there is a fair sprinkling of coloureds and a few blacks. Before De Klerk gets up to speak there is an excruciatingly embarrassing attempt to sing 'Nkosi Sikelel' iAfrika'. De Klerk mumbles to himself while a few brave black voices attempt to fill the void created by the absent white voices. This is not real politics. This is window-dressing. The party that sent police to shoot at people for singing 'Nkosi Sikelele' is now grasping for the words of the anthem in the belief that it will win them votes.

But when he gets up to speak De Klerk delivers a powerful performance. He is a streetfighter, punching left and right, stoking up the coloured fears of ANC domination, blasting the right-wing for its threats and criticizing Buthelezi for his obstructionism. Across the country the Nats are playing the same game. The message is stated in varying degrees of crudity but the bottom line is the same: vote ANC and you will lose what you've got. They are wild, undependable, they are ruled by the Communists. The National Party, the party with no past, is offering a much safer alternative. He is Frederik Willem de Klerk, the former lawyer, the man with nearly two decades of experience in government. We are the party who abolished apartheid, say the Nats, quietly neglecting to mention that they were the ones who invented it.

The following day I follow De Klerk through the small farm towns of the Western Transvaal. The voting pitch is aimed almost totally at blacks and coloureds. In the coloured areas the emphasis is heavily on ANC bashing. The black crowds get something a little different: lots of references to jobs and housing. When National Party representatives talk to black farmworkers they liken the ANC and the Nationalists to farm animals. It is agonizingly patronizing and embarrassing. The Nats seem to think that rural blacks are simple folk who appreciate their bovine fables. Not Petrus, a labourer whom I meet at a taxi rank in Potchefstroom. 'It's kind of funny, really. We will listen to him but most of us will be voting for Mandela,' he says. There are reports from around the platteland of farmers rounding up their workers to attend National Party rallies. Free food is on offer and a half-day off from work. This guarantees a healthy sprinkling of black faces in the crowd and fosters the illusion among party strategists that they might really be making inroads into the ANC's support base. As for F.W. de Klerk, he generally avoids attacking Mandela in black areas. He is shrewd enough to know that even blacks who might be sympathetic to the Nationalists regard Mandela as a heroic figure. There are huge audiences in the coloured areas. A coloured woman tells me she is voting for the Nationalists because she doesn't want to be over-run by blacks. 'Even after everything the Nats did to you?' I ask. 'It doesn't matter and anyhow De Klerk has said he is sorry,' comes the reply. The ANC does not help its cause by hounding De Klerk out of townships. The sight of unruly, stone-throwing mobs burning National Party posters fuels coloured anxieties about the ANC.

The Nationalists' campaign finishes with a big rally in Cape Town's Civic Centre. De Klerk is given a hero's welcome by the largely coloured crowd. The Cape has a coloured majority and De Klerk needs those votes if he is to stave off an ANC landslide and the Nationalists are to win control of the regional government. In the same city that witnessed the destruction of coloured areas to facilitate the dream of apartheid, F.W. de Klerk is the man of the hour.

On the night before the election – 25 April – I was attending a party in the British Ambassador's residence in Pretoria. Sir

Anthony Reeve, an astute if somewhat reserved man, had invited the British electoral observer team to drinks and supper. I was discussing the right-wing threat, the recent bombings, etc., with one of the security officers travelling with the party. 'I think they have a fair kick left in them yet,' he said, as he tucked into a plate of curry and salad. A few moments after that one of the embassy's political counsellors rushed in to announce that a booming noise had been heard coming from the centre of Pretoria. 'The cops in Arcadia say there's been an explosion,' he declared to the room at large. After a few minutes of frantic telephone calls to the police, my office and home, I jumped into the car and headed in the direction of the explosion. The news was sparse: three right-wingers had driven up to a black drinking club and hurled a bomb inside. There were some people dead and a lot of damage. The killers had escaped. From a distance I saw blue lights flashing, crowds of people gathering. Once inside the police cordon, I was able to move around freely. The crowds were kept back and it was possible to look at the damage. The drinking club had been largely constructed of corrugated iron that had been ripped and buckled by the force of the explosion. As far as I could gather most of the survivors had left the scene quickly after the attack. As I walked back across the roadway I noticed two bodies lying side by side. They were both dressed in blue overalls that had been ripped by the blast and were covered in blood. A white policeman came along and placed blankets over the dead men. Camera crews switched on their lights and for a few seconds the gory scene was illuminated. And then there was darkness again and the crowds, unable to see the bodies any longer, began to drift away. Later that night a white man appeared at the scene and began to act suspiciously, according to the police. A young Afrikaans-speaking constable called on the man to halt, which he refused to do. The policeman opened fire and killed the white man. As far as I know he was the last South African to die as a result of political violence under white rule.

The morning of the election has arrived. I am up before first light and the radio is broadcasting information on traffic and the best routes to polling stations. Apart from the right-wing bomb there has been no serious incident of political violence overnight. In fact police report one of the quietest nights for months. Paulina, who has worked as a cook and housekeeper for the BBC for more than ten years, comes into the kitchen smiling. 'The day is here. I can't believe it is happening,' she says. This first day is for the old and the sick. I ask Paulina if she minds waiting another day to vote. 'Not at all. After all these years, another day won't matter,' she replies. Tomorrow Paulina and her friends will go in a group to the local polling station. 'It will be like a party,' she explains.

On the way into the office I notice there is almost no traffic on the roads. The government and the ANC – at this stage the two seem to be almost synonymous – have decreed that the voting days should be public holidays. There is a small protest from business but the population at large seems delighted. Milton is waiting at the office and he looks happier than I have ever seen him before. 'I can't really believe this. Is it happening, Fergs, man? Is this really happening?' he asks. I am having trouble believing it myself but by the time we reach Soweto the evidence is already gathering outside polling stations.

It is cold this morning and Soweto is blanketed by the fog of coal fires. In the half-light we can see shadows becoming people. They are old folk from the Meadowlands district and they are wrapped in blankets; the men are wearing balaclavas, the women have scarves wrapped tightly around their heads. Because neither I nor Milton can really believe that these black South Africans are going to vote for the first time in their lives, we stop the car and ask an old man where he is going. He must be in his seventies. His hair is completely grey and he moves with the aid of a walking frame. 'I am going to the vote. It is up in the church. Sorry now, I cannot speak because I do not need to be late for this,' he says, continuing on his slow progress. We offer him a lift but he declines. He tells us he is meeting with some friends at the next corner. They are going to go together.

Further along the road we come to the first polling station, the Church of the Immaculate Conception. About six people are sitting on a bench next to the entrance of the church. Milton recognizes several of the voters. There are shouts of 'Hey, Milly' and 'Come here, Nkosi' as we approach the group. In this part of Soweto, in most parts of Soweto it seems, Milton is a homeboy, widely liked and always welcome. The returning officer is a priest who comes out and tells us that there is a problem. The ballot papers and boxes have arrived but there is no sign of the election monitors. 'We are supposed to start in fifteen minutes, but there is nobody to oversee the vote,' he says. The priest is thin and tall and wears thick glasses that give him a look of sternness entirely appropriate to his job as shepherd of this first flock of voters. He goes to a church office and begins to phone around frantically in search of the monitors. We listen to the radio news and there are similar difficulties around the country. But here in Soweto nobody is really bothered about the delay. People tell us repeatedly that a few more hours after a lifetime without votes makes no difference.

The first person in the queue at the Anglican Church of the Resurrection is Anastasia Ncgobo, aged sixty-eight. She is a big, bustling township woman who has lived through the very worst of Soweto's violent past. 'Man, I could not sleep last night. I was tossing and turning, so I got up and stayed up, because this is a thing that only happens once and who was I to be able to sleep when we are going to vote,' she announces. 'I am here remembering all the people who suffered for this day, all of the children who was killed and Mr Mandela going to prison and the young boys who went into exile . . . oh, it's too much, man, too much suffering has happened for this day.' She stops talking for a second and considers what she has said. Then she speaks again. 'But in the end we know it was worth it. To be here and going to vote. I never thought I would see it in my lifetime. It is the greatest day of our lives, really it is.' The other old folk who are sitting beside her murmur their approval.

The crowd at the church is getting bigger all the time. Soon the line of old people and the sick stretches around the block. The sun has come and is burning away the chill. Everybody is happy and relaxed. There are no complaints when a group of youths push a man in a wheelchair to the top of the queue. I look along a line of faces. The people here look tired and worn out, and they will probably have to wait all day because the observers still haven't arrived. But there is something else in those stoic expressions. What name can I give to the look that beams out at me on this April morning in the township of Soweto? It is the face of freedom. I know that will sound sentimental to you, but that is what I see right in front of me. I am here watching the past disappearing under the slow shuffling feet of several hundred pensioners. Milton comes up to me and I notice the tears in his eyes. And then the feelings well up in my chest and the warm drops of happiness begin to sparkle in my eyes and seep slowly down my cheeks. We look at each other and say nothing. I am thinking I am happy beyond words to see this, to be here with my friend on the day his people walk to freedom. But in my joy there is room for some melancholy. I think of the poor ruined people who have died along the way to this glorious moment: the victims of the township wars, the people killed by bombs and land-mines, those necklaced and hacked to death, the children driven into exile and the others brought up in a system that taught them to fear their fellow man. So much sad, bloody history has gone into this luminous moment in this small church in Soweto. And I am thinking too of John Harrison, who wanted so much to be here. My friend had spoken so often about this day. He had *yearned for it, wondering how he could do justice to the immensity of it all, planning his story months in advance. But today his house is empty and his widow far away in London, pondering the early news and the countless memories it evokes.*

The day passes into a night of warm laughter and cheering. At the Johannesburg Civic Centre, a concrete and glass monstrosity on a height overlooking the city centre, I watch as soldiers from the SADF lower the old flag, the flag of apartheid, and raise the new emblem. The red, green, white, blue, black and gold flag climbs slowly under a full moon and a star-blazing sky, while 'Nkosi Sikelel' i Afrika' is played and the people around me erupt into the most beautiful cheering I have ever heard. It is the sound of happiness forged into one voice. This is the most uncomplicated moment in South African history. The crowd is a mixture of black and white, and freedom allows them the simple right to be together, uncompromised by their colour and undemanding of each other, one people in one nation on this night of magic and laughter in the City of Gold. People are dancing in front of me. A white woman grabs a black man and kisses him. He falls to his knees, laughing and shaking his head, and then he gets up and kisses the woman's hand. The land that had been lost to humanity has come home. South Africa is born again.

The following day, 27 April, millions of South Africans turned out to vote. Among them was Milton Nkosi, who, at the age of twenty-eight, entered a polling booth for the first time in his life and placed his mark on a ballot paper. He did it minutes after his father, Henry, who was also a beginner in the art of voting. Milton's mother had voted the evening before because she suffered from a serious hip injury and was regarded as infirm. When he came out of the polling station in his home district of Orlando West, Soweto, Milton was smiling from ear to ear. 'Well, what was it like?' I asked. 'Oh, like no big deal,' he said. Then he looked at me and burst out laughing. 'What do you think it was like? It was bloody brilliant, that's what it was like. It was brilliant, man, to walk up there and take the pen and cast my vote.' About an hour after Milton had exercised his franchise a convoy of big cars pulled up outside the schoolroom where voting was underway. 'Jesus, it's De Klerk,' Milton shouted from the middle of a group that had surrounded the cars. The state President had come to Soweto. He smiled and was given a polite welcome by the crowd as he made his way into the polling station. 'He's welcome to come here if he wants. I'm not voting for him but he's got the right to visit,' one man commented. When he came out again De Klerk agreed to an interview. He told me the day was the culmination of everything he had worked for. He was happy. Very, very happy. People in England should come and see what a good country South Africa was. They should realize what the South Africans had achieved. 'What has happened here is remarkable,' he said. The outgoing President had cast his vote in Pretoria.

Nelson Mandela voted many miles away in Natal, at a small school outside Durban. He was followed by a large retinue of journalists who recorded the moment for posterity. 'It is the beginning of a new era,' he said to loud cheering from his supporters. Mangosuthu Buthelezi cast his vote in Ulundi and, although he complained about the poor organization of the vote in Natal, he did not ultimately manage to frustrate the process. Terre'Blanche and his henchmen stayed at home, sulking on their farms, but the overwhelming majority of Afrikaners did turn out to vote. The man who fractured the right-wing, General Constand Viljoen, spent election day trying to ensure that the Freedom Front maximized its share of the poll. It is worth remembering that just a few months earlier both he and Buthelezi had been warning of civil war.

I cannot speak for other observers but I know that I felt a unique sense of privilege at having been present to watch the triumph of democracy in South Africa. Forget the problems about the lack of voting materials, the arguments over the fiddling of the vote in Natal, the appalling delays in counting. At the end of the day the South African election was not about the details or even the percentages of victory and defeat. It was about something much greater: the triumph of the human spirit. It was as if the South African people, black and white and brown, had taken a collective deep breath and blown away the blinding cobwebs of the past. In the final analysis it was they who had reclaimed the beloved country, they who had broken the bondage of fear.

Postscript: The Unchained Land

So many journeys travelled on a single trip.

André Brink, *The Wall of the Plague*

It is nearly midnight in the city of Johannesburg and the streets are full of dancing, cheering people. Down in Soweto there are parties going on at every street corner. The army is out on patrol and every time an armoured vehicle appears the crowds cheer and clap. It is nearly midnight in the Republic of South Africa and the country is in the grip of an unfamiliar ecstasy. From the top floor of the Carlton Hotel I can see hundreds of people swarming around the streets of the central business district. They are running up towards the Rand Supreme Court bearing posters of Mandela. Others have taken up position just outside the front door of the hotel and are chanting 'ANC, ANC, ANC', a mighty roar that echoes around downtown. There are many whites among the celebrating crowd. Nobody is afraid here. When I venture out on to the streets people grab me by the hand and I am pulled into the middle of a happy, dancing group. A white shopkeeper who lives near to my home, a man I had previously thought to be a dour conservative, walks up and says hello. 'Isn't this bloody marvellous? For the first time in my life I don't feel ashamed of being white,' he says. Nearly all of my white friends speak of their sense of relief. Tony Wende, a young sound engineer and a writer, tells me of his pride in being South African. He wants to know if I really understand what it means for him, someone who detested the white state profoundly, to say what he is saying. 'I had an American passport but tomorrow I am going to go out and get my South African passport,' says Tony.

Earlier that evening I had been standing in the ballroom of the Carlton when Nelson Mandela entered and formally claimed victory on behalf of the ANC. Africa's oldest liberation movement was the last to come to power. The hall was a happy maelstrom. Mandela danced on stage and hugged his friends and senior colleagues one by one. Earlier F.W. de Klerk had calmly and with great dignity conceded victory to the ANC. As he did he promised to work together with Mandela. There seemed to be tears in De Klerk's eyes as he spoke the last words of the last white president in the last seconds of white power on the continent of Africa. I watched the speech with Carl Niehaus, the ANC's chief spokesman, who had spent seven years in jail because of his armed opposition to the white state. 'It was a really gracious speech, a good speech,' said Carl. Perhaps De Klerk had never truly envisioned the moment, perhaps that explained the definite tinges of emotion in the voice of a man who had made his political career out of putting pragmatism before passion in his public life.

But he too should feel happy on this night of nights in South Africa. He has saved his people from the wilderness of apartheid. De Klerk has shown more courage than any white leader in history. To do it he gambled and placed his trust in the good intentions of Nelson Mandela and now he has, in his own terms, won. The election might have delivered a 62 per cent share of the vote to the ANC and 20.4 per cent to the Nationalists but this is a solid showing for a party that still represents the minority population. De Klerk has the satisfaction of knowing that the Cape is in National Party hands thanks to the support of the coloured community. Down in Natal, Buthelezi has managed a narrow victory. There is outrage on the part of the local ANC. Harry Gwala and his comrades believe there has been wholesale rigging of the vote and intimidation. But Mandela will hear none of it. There is talk of a court action against Inkatha by the ANC in Natal, but this is quashed on the orders of ANC head office. This is an election in which each of the main players must have something to show. For

Mandela it is enough to know that he has won at national level. He will be president and the ANC, while short of the two thirds majority, will be the biggest party in the National Assembly. The ANC has won control of all but two of the nine assemblies. Everybody knows there has been a deliberate decision on the part of the main leaders to accept a flawed result. One of De Klerk's senior aides tells me: 'The point is that the election happened. The percentages are a reasonable reflection of the people's feelings. Everybody knows that they may be wrong by a couple of percentage points but people are just so relieved to have gotten through the past few weeks that I can't imagine anybody causing serious trouble over this.' The Independent Electoral Commission has made heavy weather of counting the votes and in a few areas the army had to helicopter in extra supplies of voting materials. There were no independent monitors at large numbers of polling stations in Natal. Phantom ballot boxes appeared in Inkatha strongholds stuffed with votes for Buthelezi. He wins the election in Natal.

Inkatha wins just over 10 per cent of the national vote but its profile is almost exclusively Zulu. After all his earlier war talk Buthelezi agrees to join the first Government of National Unity as Minister of Home Affairs. His one-time ally in the Freedom Front, General Constand Viljoen, manages to win just 2.17 per cent of the vote. It is clear that most Afrikaners have in fact voted for De Klerk. Nevertheless it is enough of the vote to allow Viljoen to continue pursuing the notion of a white homeland through democratic means. The peaceful election is the last nail in the coffin of the right-wing extremists. Power has changed hands in South Africa and there is nothing they can do to turn back the clock.

It is obvious that Mandela has decided to put the national interest first and forget about the percentage points that may have been denied his organization because of the fiddling and crookery in Natal. In his speeches he does what nobody else seems willing to do. He praises the handling of the election by the commission. 'The calm and tolerant atmosphere during the election depicts the South

Africa we can be. We might have our differences but we are one people with a common destiny,' he says. Overnight we all feel the difference in South Africa. I do not know quite how to describe it beyond telling you that everybody I know feels much lighter about their lives.

The South Africa that Nelson Mandela has inherited has been given a tremendous psychological boost, yet it remains a country with deep and dangerous fault lines. The years of minority rule might have created a solid infrastructure and the most developed economy in Africa, but they have also been enormously wasteful in terms of misdirected spending. It is worth reminding oneself again of the statistics. Six million people unemployed; ten million with no access to running water and twenty-three million without electricity; fewer than 50 per cent of black children under the age of fourteen attending school and nine million destitute. All of them look to the new government to provide, in the words of the ANC's election slogan, 'peace, jobs, and freedom'.

When Mandela spoke of *the struggle* he looked beyond the years of revolutionary politics, the years of black rebellion and white resistance. Beyond those years lay the great spaces of the future, in which the population was set to double by the turn of the century and the competition over scarce resources – the Third World's greatest problem – set to escalate to potentially frightening levels. By the time of Mandela's election as president the economy had suffered severely from the effects of sanctions and the cost of maintaining the apartheid superstate. Economic growth had been declining persistently since the late 1960s while Gross Domestic Product fell by nearly 2 per cent between 1990 and 1993. Many large industries had laid off thousands of workers. One of the most worrying statistics concerned the economy's ability to absorb newcomers on to the labour market. By the year of the election only 6 per cent of those preparing to come into the jobs market could be accommodated.

All that being admitted South Africa is undoubtedly better placed than any other country on the continent to stage an economic revival. It still has large mineral deposits and, as mentioned earlier, the infrastructural base is essentially sound. The roads are good, the telephones work, there are banks and airports and universities and the agricultural sector, although suffering the effects of drought and debt, continues to produce plentiful supplies of food for South Africa and her neighbours. With political stability and the peaceful election, foreign-investor confidence should return. This is vital, as private-sector investment, both domestic and foreign, is seen as being the key to enabling the new government to deliver on its promises.

Mandela and his ministers are telling big business that a peaceful, wealth-creating South Africa is dependent on their support. He is talking about a social contract between government, the trade unions and the private sector. In return for investment the ANC hopes to deliver peace and stability. After a long period of dithering the ANC has produced an economic policy that is decidedly centrist and has shied away from any serious intention to nationalize the mining and banking sectors and seize white-owned farms. When the white Finance Minister, Derek Keyes, resigned for family reasons soon after Mandela became president, another white business figure was selected to replace him. Mandela's goal was clearly nation-building. The new ANC-led government has committed itself to a programme of reconstruction and development. The promises made do not seem unrealistic as long as the new government maintains fiscal discipline and does not follow the 'borrow and spend' policies that have ruined so much of Africa. There is to be a major national housing programme, a healthcare policy that looks after all the children of the nation, and a drive to get children back to school. This last question, as I outlined in an earlier chapter, remains one of the most depressing facets of post-apartheid life in South Africa. A nation where children roam the streets, where the schools are empty and vandalized, is setting itself on a course for disaster.

At the time of writing – January 1995 – the government of national unity began to experience its first serious disagreements. F. W. De Klerk launched a blistering attack on the ANC and hinted that the Nationalists might be preparing to pull out of the cabinet. The issue which prompted this threat was the same one that had caused repeated bitterness between himself and Mandela over the previous four years: the security forces. Mandela had been made aware of a secret amnesty granted in the final months of white rule to policemen implicated in acts of terror against the ANC and its allies. His reaction was furious. At a cabinet meeting he openly called De Klerk's integrity into question while announcing that the amnesty was null and void. The policemen would have to apply for indemnity and this would only be considered after they had made a full disclosure of their crimes. At the root of this disagreement – yet again – was Mandela's sense that De Klerk had been less than honest with him. The memories of the township wars and the dark role played by elements of the police and military were still fresh in the minds of the ANC leadership. Mandela clung to the basic precept that without confession there could be no redemption.

De Klerk bridled at the thought that Mandela could overturn arrangements made by the previous administration. His pride was already wounded by the junior role his party was being given in the day-to-day running of the country. The ANC, it seemed, was simply tolerating the Nationalists at the cabinet table. It had no intention of treating them as anything like equals. The decision to forge ahead with the setting up of a Truth Commission formally to acknowledge and record the evils of the past was symbolic of the ANC's determination to ensure that forgiving did not mean forgetting. The Nationalists could only watch as their control over the security forces and the civil service was slowly eroded. The resignation of the Commissioner of the Police, Johan Van Der Merwe, early in the life of the new administration opened the way for the badly needed restructuring of the force. The new ANC ministers found varying degrees of co-operation in their civil service departments. It was, however, made clear to those judged to be obstructive that they would have no future under an ANC-led administration. The slow takeover of the machinery of government seemed set to accelerate as the country approached the first anniversary of the elections.

The ANC's early months in power were by no means trouble free. A rash of industrial disputes underlined yet again the determination of the unions to flex their political muscle irrespective of the demands of nation-building. Similarly the former guerrillas of Umkhonto We Sizwe were to test the patience of the ANC leadership with a succession of strikes and protest marches. To his immense credit Mandela refused to bow to the demands of the former guerrillas and they were given the choice of returning to their assembly points or of being dismissed. The relationship between the ANC and the unions is a more difficult problem. The mass mobilizing power of COSATU and its affiliates is vital to the ANC's plans to gain an increased majority at the next elections. A head-on confrontation with the unions is therefore not regarded as being an option.

This may produce a situation where the Mandela government will prove unwilling to confront unrealistic wage demands. With Asian labour markets able to produce at much lower prices South Africa cannot afford to entertain a situation where wages rise while productivity remains static.

The choice facing the ANC between union support and sound economic practice is a harsh one, with the potential for serious industrial unrest. One of the few people who appeared capable of bridging the growing divide between the demands of government and trade unions was Joe Slovo. As a former leader of the ANC's military wing and a senior communist, Slovo had impeccable radical credentials. As a potential intermediary between the government and the more disaffected members of its constituency, he was invaluable. His death from cancer in early January represented a tragic loss to the country.

I had met and interviewed Slovo on several occasions and found him to be a man of remarkable common sense. He had come a long way from the Stalinism and blind support of Soviet tyranny that had marked the earlier part of his life in exile. For years white South Africa had regarded him as public enemy number one. He was at the very top of the security forces list of ANC targets. Yet Joe Slovo had made his own remarkable journey. Here was a man who had directed a guerrilla war against Pretoria, whose wife had been murdered by agents of the white state, and who had yet managed to persuade himself and the ANC that power-sharing with whites was the only way forward. In doing so he still managed to retain the support of the township radicals. Apart from the assassinated ANC leader Chris Hani and Mandela himself, it is hard to imagine any other figure in the movement being able to convince the militants of the need for such a compromise. History will record Slovo's contribution as pivotal. His death robbed the country of a man of vision and integrity.

That latter characteristic seemed in short supply as the ANC became enmeshed in a series of scandals involving senior figures. The charismatic anti-apartheid campaigner Alan Boesak was forced to withdraw as South Africa's ambassador designate to the United Nations in Geneva when it was alleged that he had misused funds donated to the struggle by Scandinavian aid agencies. As if that were not bad enough, Winnie Mandela bounced back into the headlines with accusations that she had misappropriated funds donated to the ANC by Benazir Bhutto. Several senior members of the ANC's women's league resigned in protest at what was described as Mrs Mandela's dictatorial leadership.

Winnie Mandela's controversial actions eventually prompted Nelson Mandela to dismiss her from the South African government.

The question I am repeatedly asked is what will happen to South Africa once Mandela and his generation of ANC leaders dies. Of the immediate future I do not have any great apprehensions. The trouble is more likely to come much later – not after Mandela's death but after the next generation of leaders has moved on. It will happen if men like Thabo Mbeki and Cyril Ramaphosa become old without delivering a better country for the young. It is then that the millions who have never been educated, who have lived their youth on the streets, may try to claim their inheritance through violence, the ballot box having failed to deliver jobs and houses and hope. The first glorious steps have been taken away from apartheid, away from the politics of the streets. The people of South Africa have every right and reason to feel relieved and happy. But unless the young are encouraged back into their classrooms and until such time as they can see the prospect of a future that will make them truly equal with whites, South Africa will remain prone to outbreaks of political violence and rising crime. The ANC and their Nationalist coalition partners must be wary of becoming a self-serving elite. It has happened throughout Africa with disastrous consequences for democracy. The arrogance that the ANC displayed in its attitude to the candidacy of Winnie Mandela and the torture of prisoners in its camps gives serious cause for concern. Is it the seed of a future carelessness and indifference to what is right and what is wrong? I hope not, but I worry that it is. There is also a tendency among some senior figures towards self-enrichment – what is known in Africa as the 'Wa Benzi' ('People of the Mercedes–Benz') syndrome. The resentment felt by ordinary people who see their leaders grow fat while they go hungry should not be underestimated. What will save the ANC and its allies from going the way of the rest of Africa will, I believe, be the people of South Africa, whose willingness to demonstrate, to protest and to loudly denounce bad government has delivered the country the miracle of a democratic election. Although fractious and argumentative, South Africans are people of remarkable common sense. They are fortunate to live in a beautiful land that is not possessed by ancient hatreds.

My journey is nearly over, ending where the new South Africa begins. It is still dark outside and I have barely slept at all in the past forty-eight hours. But although sick from lack of sleep I do not need any encouragement to get out of bed. The clock tells me that it is four a.m. In less than fifteen minutes I am in the car, driving to Pretoria in the dark. I pass the cars of other journalists along the way. There are coachloads of policemen and civil servants. Everybody is going to Pretoria. At the university, where we have been told to assemble, there are searchlights and sniffer dogs. There is an endless wait in the cold for accreditation. But we are on the road again as the sun comes up behind the hills that surround the city. There are miles of razor wire, and paratroopers are stationed every few yards along the road. When we reach the Union Buildings, seat of white power since the turn of the century, the group of journalists is broken up into those who will be standing among the crowds and those who will be placed in the amphitheatre where Nelson Mandela will be sworn in as President of South Africa. I go with the latter group. As the day warms up and the sun finds its way into every crevice and corner of Herbert Baker's beautiful building, there is a steady stream of world leaders arriving to fill the seats in front of the bullet-proof stage. I look up and notice sharpshooters positioned along the rooftop overlooking the stage. The largest cheers of the day are reserved for Yasser Arafat and Fidel Castro. The ANC members in the audience stand and chant 'Fidel, Fidel' when the Cuban dictator arrives. He was a friend in times of desperation and this is not forgotten. Sitting directly in front of me is General Constand Viljoen, who led the South Africans against Castro's forces in Angola. I wonder what he thinks as he watches his former arch-enemy take his seat to rapturous applause.

But of course what matters is that Viljoen is here along with the heads of the army, the navy and the airforce. When Mandela arrives the three heads of the armed services walk to his car and salute their new Commander-in-Chief. With that small gesture they mark the passing of power to the representative of the majority. 'I, Nelson Rolihlahla Mandela . . .' he begins and then syllable by syllable he gathers the presidency of a united South Africa into his breast. It is over within a few minutes. And then we hear a droning noise in the distance that becomes a roar as the jets and helicopters of the South African Airforce fly overhead. The jet-streams carry the colours of the new South African flag. This, I think to myself, is the moment, the transition completed. Three centuries of wrong are drowned in the sheer joy of this morning. It is clear that the crowd feels this too. They cheer and cheer and cheer as the airforce completes the fly-past. Cannons are booming a salute for Nelson Mandela, who then walks down to greet the crowd. There on the lawns of the Union Buildings, against all the odds of history, he takes the hand of F.W. de Klerk and raises it with his own into the air. This is the end and the beginning, this is the victory of decency and common sense, it is the victory of all South Africans.

Afterword

After writing the first edition of this book I returned to Ireland for a long summer holiday. I needed to put time and space between Africa and myself and think about the future. The crucial distance between the reporter and his subject had evaporated and I badly needed to be away from the haunting presence of the past. The story had changed me and I felt older and a lot less certain about where I was going than at any time in my life. When I showed my wife the first proofs of this book she read them with tears in her eyes. 'I know we lived through this but I never want to go through it again – do you understand me?' she said. Anne, who had come through years of worrying about my safety and enduring the presence of fear, had reached the end of the road. And so in Ireland, surrounded by family and friends, we made a conscious effort to close out South Africa. We retreated to our cottage in Ardmore on the south-east coast and tuned in to the soft rhythms of village life. I consciously avoided people who wanted to talk about South Africa and spent long hours fishing and walking the remote cliffs. The BBC appointed me to the post of Asia Correspondent in the autumn and there remained only the task of returning to Johannesburg to pack up house and move on. We flew back at the beginning of the southern summer and were met at the airport by Milton, as energetic as ever. The BBC Bureau was now under the direction of my successor George Alagiah and was busy reporting the evolving democratic order. Many of those who had shared the elations and the dangers of the past few years had moved on. The country and the story had

changed. I felt out of place, a carry-over from an unrecogniz-
able time.

We spent a week packing up the house, removing all
evidence of our life there, until we were left with an empty,
echoing shell. The physical traces of our presence were erased
easily, disappearing into a steel container for the month-
long journey to Hong Kong. With the process of packing
complete, we drove out to the farm of our old friends
Barbara and Jim Bailey in the foothills of the Magaliesberg
mountains, about an hour from Johannesburg. The farm had
been a place of refuge for us during the mad days of the
township wars. Almost every Sunday we would go there and
walk the fields, sending clouds of guinea fowl rising into the
air as we approached their hiding places in the long grass.
Afterwards we would drink wine or homemade lemonade
and listen to the chorus of evening insects and cattle on the
distant hills. The Baileys were 'liberals' in the finest sense of
the word. They projected their respect for humanity and
their belief in equality through deeds rather than words. Jim
was the founder of the legendary *Drum* magazine, which had
given a generation of black journalists and writers their first
mass-circulation outlet. Barbara had founded several schools
on her property as well as a game farm which was designed
to give township children an experience of wildlife denied to
their parents. That evening we took one last walk on African
soil. The dirt road that runs alongside the Baileys' farm was
heavy with dust that would remain until the rains arrived in a
couple of weeks and brought relief to the thirsty farms of the
highveld. As we walked back along the path, the sun sinking
in brilliant shades of crimson behind the Magaliesbergs, we
heard a long keening sound in the distance. It stopped for a
second and then started again, this time with more force.
'They're wild dogs. They've come from the bush for food,'
said Barbara. We listened closely and heard the howling of

several animals over the next few minutes. The sound gradually drifted away until we were left again with the low muttering of the cicadas and the shouts of the farm labourer's children playing at the stream below us. Barbara looked at me and smiled. 'That was Africa, Fergal. It was saying goodbye to you. It is time to go,' she said. I would like to have stayed for the rains, to have watched them fall on farm and city, on every street where we ran breathless and afraid, on all the millions whose sorrows and triumphs we witnessed, and on the distant corner of the bush where John Harrison's ashes were scattered. But I knew that staying was impossible. I had to leave. The following morning I drove to the office and said goodbye to my colleagues. Milton was not there when I arrived so I penned a short note. In it I thanked him for having been with me through the previous four years. I told him to take care and never forget the extraordinary moments we had known together.

There was a great deal more left unsaid, things that as best friends we did not need to say. I had just finished writing and placed the note in his postbox when Milton walked into the room. 'Yoho, my man, did you think you could escape without seeing me?' he asked, the inevitable broad smile lighting up the room. I opened my mouth to speak but could find no words. Clumsily and hurriedly I threw my arms around him and mumbled two words: 'Goodbye, brother.' I pulled away and he did not follow. I was leaving and we both knew that the world we had inhabited together was gone. The days of the township wars, the great demonstrations were part of the historical archive now, and we were all moving on. What was there left to us? What could I answer when I asked to add up the good and the bad and then compare? There was loss and grieving and fear to be sure, but there was so much more that was good and true. There was the bond of friendship and of memory, and greatest of all there was the land we had explored and known together. As I packed the car to go to the airport, a fax arrived at my home from Milton. He quoted my favourite words from André Brink: 'The land that has happened inside us, that nobody can take away, not even ourselves . . .'

March 1995

READ MORE IN PENGUIN

In every corner of the world, on every subject under the sun, Penguin represents quality and variety – the very best in publishing today.

For complete information about books available from Penguin – including Puffins, Penguin Classics and Arkana – and how to order them, write to us at the appropriate address below. Please note that for copyright reasons the selection of books varies from country to country.

In the United Kingdom: Please write to *Dept. JC, Penguin Books Ltd, FREEPOST, West Drayton, Middlesex UB7 OBR.*

If you have any difficulty in obtaining a title, please send your order with the correct money, plus ten per cent for postage and packaging, to *PO Box No. 11, West Drayton, Middlesex UB7 OBR*

In the United States: Please write to *Consumer Sales, Penguin USA, P.O. Box 999, Dept. 17109, Bergenfield, New Jersey 07621-0120.* VISA and MasterCard holders call 1-800-253-6476 to order all Penguin titles

In Canada: Please write to *Penguin Books Canada Ltd, 10 Alcorn Avenue, Suite 300, Toronto, Ontario M4V 3B2*

In Australia: Please write to *Penguin Books Australia Ltd, P.O. Box 257, Ringwood, Victoria 3134*

In New Zealand: Please write to *Penguin Books (NZ) Ltd, Private Bag 102902, North Shore Mail Centre, Auckland 10*

In India: Please write to *Penguin Books India Pvt Ltd, 706 Eros Apartments, 56 Nehru Place, New Delhi 110 019*

In the Netherlands: Please write to *Penguin Books Netherlands bv, Postbus 3507, NL-1001 AH Amsterdam*

In Germany: Please write to *Penguin Books Deutschland GmbH, Metzlerstrasse 26, 60594 Frankfurt am Main*

In Spain: Please write to *Penguin Books S. A., Bravo Murillo 19, 1° B, 28015 Madrid*

In Italy: Please write to *Penguin Italia s.r.l., Via Felice Casati 20, I–20124 Milano*

In France: Please write to *Penguin France S. A., 17 rue Lejeune, F–31000 Toulouse*

In Japan: Please write to *Penguin Books Japan, Ishikiribashi Building, 2–5–4, Suido, Bunkyo-ku, Tokyo 112*

In Greece: Please write to *Penguin Hellas Ltd, Dimocritou 3, GR–106 71 Athens*

In South Africa: Please write to *Longman Penguin Southern Africa (Pty) Ltd, Private Bag X08, Bertsham 2013*